LOCATION
AND ENVIRONMENT
OF ELDERLY
POPULATION

SCRIPTA SERIES IN GEOGRAPHY

Series Editors

Richard E. Lonsdale • Antony R. Orme • Theodore Shabad
James O. Wheeler

LOCATION
AND ENVIRONMENT
OF ELDERLY
POPULATION

Stephen M. Golant
University of Chicago

1979

V. H. WINSTON & SONS
Washington, D.C.

A HALSTED PRESS BOOK

JOHN WILEY & SONS

New York   Toronto   London   Sydney

V. H. Winston & Sons, a Division of Scripta Technica, Inc.,
Publishers
1511 K Street, N.W., Washington, D.C. 20005

Distributed solely by Halsted Press, a Division of John Wiley
& Sons, Inc.

Library of Congress Cataloging in Publication Data

Golant, Stephen M.
   Location and environment of elderly population.

   (Scripta series in geography)
   Bibliography: p.
   Includes index.
   1. Aged—United States—Dwellings. 2. Gerontology—
United States. 3. Anthropo-geography—United States.
I. Title. II. Series.
HD7287.92.U54G64   301.5'4   79-13621
ISBN 0-470-26788-7

Composition by Marie A. Maddalena, Scripta Technica, Inc.

To Rose and Eddy,

my parents

LIST OF CONTRIBUTORS

Stephen S. Birdsall, Associate Professor, Department of Geography, University of North Carolina at Chapel Hill

James R. Bohland, Associate Professor, Department of Geography, University of Oklahoma

Lexa Davis is a doctoral student in the Department of Geography at the University of Oklahoma

Michael J. Dear, Assistant Professor, Department of Geography, McMaster University

Stephen M. Golant, Associate Professor, Department of Geography, University of Chicago

D. Richard Lycan, Professor, Department of Geography, Portland State University

Rosemary McCaslin is a lecturer in the School of Social Service Administration at the University of Chicago

Douglas McKelvey is a Research Associate in Policy Development at the National Transportation Policy Study Commission

John Mercer, Assistant Professor, Department of Geography, University of British Columbia

Eric Moore, Professor, Department of Geography, Queen's University

Mark Publicover is a doctoral student in the Department of Geography at Queen's University

Graham Rowles, Assistant Professor, Department of Geology and Geography, West Virginia University

Gundars Rudzitis, Assistant Professor, Department of Geography, University of Texas at Austin

Rolf R. Schmitt is a Research Associate in Policy Development at the National Transportation Policy Study Commission

James Weiss was Director of the Center for Population Research and Census at Portland State University (deceased)

Robert F. Wiseman, Associate Professor, Department of Geography, University of Kansas

Jennifer Wolch Assistant Professor, Department of Urban and Regional Planning, University of Southern California

Maurice Yeates, Professor, Department of Geography, Queen's University

CONTENTS

DISCARDED

vii

PART III. PLANNING METHODOLOGIES AND STRATEGIES

INTRODUCTION

Chapter 1

RATIONALE FOR GEOGRAPHIC PERSPECTIVES ON AGING AND THE AGED

Stephen M. Golant

The early 1970s was an intellectually exciting time in which to begin study of the processes and the problems of adult aging and human development. In the late 60s, a three-volume work was produced that summarized the scientific findings and issues of gerontology—a loosely defined grouping of academic disciplines unified in their scientific focus on aging and old age.[1] Although this compendium indicated the considerable progress made in the previous decade, it also uncovered various areas of inquiry in which research was needed. Many issues and problems were available for the academic researcher to address, irrespective of his discipline loyalties. For others, these volumes were a testimony to the utility of interdisciplinary research approaches and they thereby opened up opportunities for seminars and research projects that included teams of academics from the social and physical sciences, as well as from the humanities. In the area of applied research, it was not difficult for the research and policy recommendations of the 1971 White House Conference on Aging (and its numerous preliminary state and local workshops) to capture the imagination of younger Ph.D.s in a host of scientific disciplines.[2] What better opportunity existed to carry out socially relevant research investigations, with their potential public policy implications, under a fiscally responsive federal government umbrella?

For the geographer, the potential of applying his own conceptual and operational perspectives to the issues and problems of aging and the aged appeared particularly promising, because there were obvious gaps in the literature relevant to his discipline's focus. Particularly significant, researchers studying the

1

aging process were reevaluating many of their earlier theories and models in their consideration of the importance of situational and environmental influences.[3] However, their theoretical and empirical concerns were largely influenced (expectedly so) by the intellectual orientations of a few selected social sciences; in particular, sociology, psychology, economics, and political science. Although geography as a discipline was not represented, it could be argued that several questions addressed by these social scientists would be more effectively studied by geographers. Moreover, when such apparently geographical analyses did exist, often they were relegated to tangential sections of investigations and reports and were found lacking in their scientific and research quality.

Nonetheless, the geographically relevant writings of these social scientists stimulated the research interests of several geographers. Certain discussions in a popular article written by the psychologist Birren in *Psychology Today* are exemplary:

> Paradoxically, it is in the most deteriorated areas of cities that aged persons may live independent lives, piecing together for themselves the combinations of needed services. That's why such care should be taken in the redevelopment of these areas. The replacement of deteriorated areas with high-rise housing may put shopping areas out of reach at the same time that it drives rents too high for the aged poor. It is often almost impossible to get to new shopping centers on foot.
>
> Older persons become discouraged by a succession of obstacles that would not inhibit the young: high bus steps, the need to cross wide, busy streets to catch a bus, fast-changing traffic lights, high curbs and inadequate building labels. The aged may do without banks, doctors, repair services, dentists, shops, lawyers and parks because of the energy it takes to get to them.[4]

The research on aging by psychologist Lawton and his colleagues at the Philadelphia Geriatric Center, who were influenced by the emerging field of environmental psychology, had considerable impact. One of their research issues, which could hardly fail to interest the geographer whose own discipline had historically sustained an interest in "environmentalism," concerned the validity of the "environmental docility" hypothesis:

> the more competent the organism—in terms of health, intelligence, ego strength, social role performance, or cultural evolution—the less will be the proportion of variance in behavior attributable to physical objects or conditions around him.[5]

In the 1970s too, the intellectual climate of geography as an academic discipline appeared receptive to the initiation of research on the topic of aging and old age. By the 1960s, geographers were stressing the importance of studying the social and behavioral processes underlying society's spatial organization and the relationships observed between people and their economic, social, cultural, and political landscapes. Research by geographers such as Lowenthal, Kates, Burton, Morrill, Dacey, Wolpert, Brown, Moore, and Pred emphasized the scientific utility of process-oriented perspectives on a wide ranging set of geographic inquiries.[6] In this period, writings by nongeographers served as a particularly important catalyst for this shift in intellectual and research orientation. Thus the precedent for disciplinary cross-fertilization was well established. Concomitantly, writings by Buttimer in 1968 and 1969 awakened many North American geographers to the French origins of an American "social geography" and, in so doing, provided an epistemological basis for focusing on socially defined population groups as a point of departure in geographic investigations.[7] The late sixties also witnessed an increased concern by geographers about their "social responsibility," and this resulted in a host of studies on such topics on poverty, health care, racial injustice, crime, social deprivation, pollution, and civil disorder.[8]

The first published statement in North America of the contribution that geographers could make to aging research had earlier appeared in 1966 in the "Geographical Record" section of the scientific journal, *Geographical Review*. It brought to the attention of American geographers the French research investigations of Rochfort and several demographic studies of the aged in the United States. Reported by Zelinsky, geography's contribution was largely confined to describing more rigorously the residential location patterns of elderly people and the origins and destinations of their migration flows.[9] In 1972, the first North American geographic research monograph on the subject of the aged also emphasized the spatial organization theme, investigating the residential location patterns and transportation behavior of the elderly population, treating these as a manifestation of the social and psychological processes of aging.[10] A significant measure of the changing scope of the geographer's interest in gerontology was marked by the "Geographical Record" note in the *Geographical Review* in 1974. Consistent with the increased interest by geographers in social problems and issues, Peet and Rowles stressed the role of geographers in finding solutions to the problems of older people.[11] Emphasizing geography's renewed interest in studying the mutual relationships between man and his environment, the authors questioned how the "spatial organization of the environment facilitated or prevented the elderly from enjoying the kind of lifestyle they deemed appropriate."[12]

Since 1974, the interest by geographers in gerontological research has slowly but steadily increased. Therefore, it appeared appropriate to convene a special session at the 1978 Annual Meeting of the Association of American Geographers (in New Orleans) to report on the progress of research to date. The theme of the session, "Locational and Environmental Research on the Elderly Population," was purposely selected to emphasize the broad scope of geographic inquiry. This session served as a stimulus to bring together in one volume, for the first time, original papers written by geographers on themes involving the aging or the aged population.[13] The original five papers were rewritten especially for this volume and were joined by nine other papers written by geographers both in academic and nonacademic positions. This chapter will elaborate on why the session and, in turn, this volume identified "location" and "environment" as its themes and will argue for the relevance of and need for geographic inquiry into the subject of aging and old age.

GEOGRAPHIC INQUIRY AND GERONTOLOGY

How does one marry an interest in geography and gerontology? This question is primarily asked by gerontologists whose information about the content and themes of geography as a social science is unintentionally incomplete or inaccurate. In part this results from the fact that compared with most other academic disciplines, geography's membership is small and only a handful of researchers are actively engaged in gerontological related inquiries. More importantly, geographers themselves disagree on the nature of their discipline, address an extremely diverse range of research topics, and consequently communicate an inconsistent image of their discipline's content and scope.[14] Geographers are less likely to ask this question; they have long ago learned to accept the topical and methodological diversity of their discipline. In large part, this reflects a history of geographic thought in which geographers not only have tolerated the diffusion of concepts and methodologies from other disciplines into their own but indeed have welcomed them. The questions most frequently posed by geographers, on the other hand, concern the scientific legitimacy of directing time and energy to one particular social grouping, the aged, and the validity of studying the processes that underlie aging as a sufficiently important and independent source of explanation for geographic patterns, relationships, and processes. As a general response to these questions, it is appropriate initially to identify three reasons why a disciplinary approach to gerontology is advantageous both to the relevant scientific discipline and to the science of aging and the aged.

First, the specialized conceptual foundations and operational perspectives of a particular discipline will yield a body of information that can be profitably incorporated into a hybrid scientific inquiry, such as gerontology. As the editors of a compendium of papers concerned with the social aspects of aging expressed it:

> Each discipline approaches the study of aging and the aged in terms of its own constructs and subject matter, contributing its unique strengths to an understanding of the topic. This multidisciplinary focus, we believe, substantially enriches the intellectual resources available for understanding the social dimensions of aging.[15]

A second rationale for a disciplinary approach to gerontology depends on the argument that the scientific discipline itself will be enriched by considering and selectively assimilating a body of knowledge, the development of which has not been confined by the usual disciplinary boundaries. It is then expected that the study of the biological, psychological, and social aspects of aging will yield conclusions that may profitably be integrated within the scientific discipline and will lead to the improved formulation and articulation of that discipline's theories, models, relationships, or descriptions.

The third reason reiterates the importance of the exchange of knowledge between gerontology and other scientific disciplines, but distinguishes the purpose for which this exchange takes place. At all levels of government, professional planners and administrators in numerous agencies are engaged in decision making on matters of social planning and policy formulation that are influencing the quality of life of older people. In this forum a particular urgency exists to incorporate diverse substantive knowledge and operational expertise about aging and old age that are found in the different disciplines.

The three rationales for a disciplinary approach to gerontology having been outlined, it is now appropriate to discuss each of these as they specifically apply to geography *qua* discipline.

THE CONTRIBUTION OF GEOGRAPHIC INQUIRY TO GERONTOLOGY

Human Geography as a Field of Inquiry

The question of geography's relevance to gerontology is a legitimate one, if only because geography as a social science is so often poorly understood, possessing a distorted image in the minds of scholars in other disciplines; indeed, it is sometimes ignored as a social science.[16] Thus, to insure a common frame of reference, it is useful to outline, however briefly, the major topics of inquiry that are undertaken in contemporary human geography—a recognized subfield of geography. Human geography can be conceptualized as addressing two broad and interdependent themes: (1) the spatial organization of people and their institutions,[17] and (2) the study of environments as occupied by people.[18]

The following topics illustrate the first of these themes: (a) the contemporary or historical description of society's spatial organization which refers, first, to the locational patterns and spatial structure of the population's and institutions' attributes and activities and the physical or man-made structures in which these are housed (these attributes and activities may be of a demographic, social, economic, psychological, political, or cultural nature), and, second, to the locational patterns and spatial structure of the population's or institutions' transportation, migration (mobility), and communications movements or flows, and their physical channels; (b) the description or explanation of the processes or factors underlying society's spatial organization; (c) the population's and institutions' attributes, activities, physical structures, and patterns of spatial interaction that distinguish places (e.g., countries, regions, landscapes, communities, neighborhoods, or buildings) from each other—geography as study of chorological differentiation.

These topics illustrate the second theme: (a) the contemporary and historical description of a population's adjustments or adaptations to its occupied environment; (b) the evaluation of how social, economic, psychological, political, cultural, physical, and natural structures and processes systemically contribute to or underlie these adjustments and adaptations; (c) the holistic understanding of the mutual ways in which a population manipulates and is manipulated by the environment it occupies and uses; (d) the description of the environmental cognitions (representations, images, beliefs, intentions, values, and attitudes), environmental perceptions, and felt environmental experiences of individuals and populations; (e) the evaluation of the social, psychological, cultural, and historical processes underlying these cognitions, perceptions, and experiences.

The Study of Environments Occupied By People

The need to conceptualize and measure the environments occupied by people is now well accepted by social and behavioral scientists seeking explanations and understanding of the aging process. The environment is identified as an integral component in one of the more rigorous conceptual and methodological approaches to the study of aging, namely, the analysis of how age, period, and cohort effects influence patterns of aging and contribute to an understanding of the problems of old age.[19] Within this framework, the investigation may focus on the "effects of environmental opportunities and constraints on performance over the life-span generally, and in late life specifically" or, alternatively, on the "hypothesis that the environments in which members of a cohort matured were different in some consequential ways."[20] In both instances, there is an explicit recognition of the importance of environmental variation and change and their interaction effects with individuals and populations.

However, the meaning and measurement of environment and the implied experiental level of person-environment transactions are often unclear.[21] In its most general meaning, "environment" refers to "the forces external to individuals which tend to shape or influence their responses."[22] In practice, the conceptualization and measurement of the environment usually depends on the substantive area in which the researcher has competence, which, in turn, reflects his membership in a particular discipline. Thus, for the sociologist, "environment" variously refers to family structure, parental behavior, or the social network of significant others, or, in a comparative sense, to a society's degree of modernization and modernity. For the social psychologist, it can refer to the individual's interpersonal relationships; and for the political scientist, to a society's governmental and political institutions. For the anthropologist, it often refers to the cultural values of a society; and to the architect, to the form and functional qualities of the built micro-environment. What unfortunately emerges from such discipline-focused approaches is an artificially fragmented environment, the parts of which belie their membership in an interdependent system.

In another sense, the environments studied by gerontologists can be characterized as restricted in that the populations of elderly have been studied in a set of places and institutional contexts that do not accurately represent the total reality of their residential situation. Thus, the elderly studied have usually occupied inner cities, deteriorated or run-down neighborhoods, redeveloped areas, new public housing projects, retirement residences, and old age institutions. Relatively few environmental analyses exist of the disproportionately large population of healthy elderly people living in middle-class, middle-income neighborhoods and communities located in stable and viable areas of central cities and in older suburbs, small cities, and towns.[23]

To be sure, among the social and behavioral scientists actively studying aging and aged, a few have employed holistic, integrated conceptualizations of the environment. Noteworthy in this regard is Lawton, who has carried out careful and thoughtful research on the subject.[24] For example, Lawton conceives of the "environment" as an ecological system having five components: the individual, the physical environment, the personal environment, the suprapersonal environment, and the social environment (see Chapter 5).[25] However, other than the research of a few, fragmented and restricted studies of the environment's influences on human aging have been more the rule than the exception.

To obviate these approaches, a representative cross-section of the places and spaces occupied by elderly people that captures the everyday situations in which its members are experiencing and behaving must be studied. Such an approach recognizes the obvious—that the "individual never functions in a single environment, but in many overlapping contexts."[26] In this regard, it is legitimate to contend that the discipline of geography is particularly well adapted to study the environments of man and environment-behavior relationships, without suffering from the weaknesses of previous approaches. A report of the Association of American Geographer's Task Force on Environmental Quality has discussed the characteristics of geography which gives it a comparative advantage over other disciplines seeking to investigate man-environment relationships.[27]

First, geography has had a long tradition as a synthesizing discipline of "insights and materials." When dealing with the study of complex "interactions between man and environment" (or the man-nature interface), "geographers quite properly assume that any subject matter may be germane and must be taken into account more or less systematically." Consequently, the environmental components and relationships singularly addressed by any of the social and behavioral sciences may be integrated into the geographer's inquiry.

Second, "the profession's past experience with simplistic explanations—notably environmental determinism—make most geographers reluctant to accept single-factor propositions about cause-and-effect relations." Thus, the geographer brings to environment-behavior studies a "synthesizing, holistic approach."

Third, methodologically, geographers are particularly well trained to carry out analyses requiring "diverse kinds of information." Geographers are "exposed to and trained in a variety of data-gathering techniques, from field observations and laboratory analyses to interviews and questionnaires, from historical, archival, and library sources to attitudinal surveys, from cartographic and statistical analyses to descriptive and holistic syntheses."

Fourth, the geographer's concern with locational variation and spatial relationships make him particularly sensitive to how environments differ from each other and the factors likely to be most responsible.

Fifth, "geographers have examined landscapes and artifacts seen to varying degrees as both 'natural' and 'cultural'; they avoid sharp dichotomies between these realms." They are "constantly reminded that the physical environment is felt and responded to through screens of perception and cognition."[28] The 1960s witnessed much new research by geographers who adopted behavioral (i.e., cognitive, perceptual, and experiential) approaches to both man-environment relationships and locational analysis.[29]

Sixth, geographers recognize that "environmental issues and problems vary widely in areal scope and consequently in the degree to which local, regional, and global approaches are germane."[30] The geographer's focus on the environment is not restricted to any spatial scale; rather, the situational context of a study may vary from the room or the building to the region or the world and will often simultaneously comprise a nested hierarchy of such environmental units (see Chapters 2, 5, and 6 for an illustration of this range).[31] This flexibility is important because much research cannot be carried out in one neatly compartmentalized areal unit. For example, in studying the effects of the public housing project on its occupants' well-being, the researcher must simultaneously consider the interdependent influences of the dwelling, the building, the neighborhood, and the community to obtain an integrated portrayal of the impact of the immediate residential environment.

Finally, with regard to geography's epistemology, questions that are framed in both scientific and humanistic philosophical frameworks, embracing such modes of thought as positivism, phenomenology, and existentialism, are equally acceptable. In turn, the purpose of the geographer's investigation may be to seek scientific laws and theory (nomothetic approach), as well as to "discover historical, particularistic (idiographic) knowledge and understanding of the objects of study."[32]

THE CONTRIBUTION OF GERONTOLOGICAL INQUIRY TO GEOGRAPHY

A consideration of age and aging as a social category will enable the geographer to carefully scrutinize a particular set of social and behavioral processes (associated with aging) and the ways in which these elucidate his own discipline's description and understanding of society's spatial organization, on the one hand, and the mutual relationships that exist between its people and the environments they occupy, use, and experience, on the other.

Chronological age is frequently used as an indicator of an individual's position in lifetime (elderly people are often designated by the age boundary, 60 or 65 years and older). This decision is usually dictated by methodological constraints, when more sophisticated age measures are, for various reasons, impractical.[33] Yet, it is agreed that aging is a multidimensional process, a product of biological, psychological, and social phenomena, and that chronological age is, at best, a rough indicator of the rate at which the individual is aging with respect to each of these processes.[34] Consequently, the aging of an individual is very much a subjective experience, which may bear no relationship to calendar time. The ambiguity of chronological age is best illustrated by observing the varying significance and interpretations given to it by different cultures.[35]

Of the various aspects or conceptualizations of age and aging, the "social age" of an individual is the most pervasive, referring, as it does, to "the individual's position in an age-grade or age-status system."[36] Age as a social characteristic provides a society with a basis for defining preferred or expected behavior; for allocating and differentiating social roles; for regulating the relationships between its members; for ascribing status; for distributing valued resources, rights, responsibilities, power, and prestige; for regulating participation in social institutions; for facilitating an individual's biological and psychological capacities; for regulating the timing and ordering of life events; and for influencing an individual's self-perceptions.[37]

Three other important aspects of aging are also frequently distinguished—the biological, psychological, and functional ages of the individual. Biological age refers to "an estimate of the individual's present position with respect to his potential life-span . . . [it] encompasses measurements of the functional capacities of the vital life-limiting organ systems . . . leading to the prediction as to whether the individual is older or younger than other persons of the same chronological age and hence whether the individual has a longer or shorter life expectancy than other persons of his average age." Psychological age refers to "the adaptive capacities of individuals, that is, how well they adapt to changing environmental demands in comparison with the average [person] . . . Psychological age is influenced by the state of the key organ systems like the brain and the cardiovascular system . . . [but also] involves memory, learning, intelligence skills, feeling, motivation, and emotions." Functional age is an "individual's level of capacities relative to others of his age for functioning in a given society"[38] (see Chapter 14).

Although aging is discussed most frequently in reference to the individual, other social scientists, particularly demographers, refer to the aging of populations or the aging of a society,[39] which defines a chronologically older population growing at a faster rate than the younger population. Aging, in this sense, is usually measured by the upward change in the population's median age or by the increasing proportion of its members aged 65 or older. The rate at which a population ages is a function of mortality, migration rates, and, most importantly, fertility rates (see Chapter 2).

Inevitably, the geographer studying the aged and the aging population must justify his social category group focus. To this end, it is relevant to argue that historically the social sciences, including geography, have provided many precedents for singling out certain social groups for detailed study. Accordingly, racial, ethnic, religious, and social status categories have served as a basis for social and behavioral science inquiries, and few would disagree that age is also a theoretically relevant dimension by which to differentiate members of a population from each other.

The danger of this perspective is to fall into the reductionistic trap of incorrectly attributing too much importance to a particular social categorization when describing or explaining patterns and relationships. For example, there is an inherent weakness in research designs that arbitrarily isolate older people as a population universe and subsequently draw inferences that, themselves, are predetermined by the subgroup selection. Even greater difficulties exist for the researcher who is insensitive to how differently his findings may be interpreted if cohort and period effects are adequately taken into account. To avoid such difficulties when interpreting age-related findings, the researcher must carefully review the assumptions that underlie his conceptualization of the aged population or of the aging process. In doing so, he must recognize that the considerable social and behavioral diversity of older people is testimony to the importance of other than age-related attributes. Moreover, to find that age is not significantly influencing a particular relationship should itself be an important "finding."

GEOGRAPHIC PERSPECTIVE ON AGING:
PLANNING AND PUBLIC POLICY CONTRIBUTIONS

Thus far, it has been argued that the geographer's focus on aging and the aged can be justified on grounds that both gerontology and geography, as scientific disciplines, will accrue benefits. However, there exists another and, in some ways, a simpler and more pragmatic rationale for geographers to focus on such subject matter. At the present time, the U.S. federal government has a large fiscal commitment to the elderly population. Twenty-four percent, or $112 billion, of the federal budget for fiscal year 1978 (5% of the Gross National Product) went for benefits and programs to older people.[40] A large and complex bureaucracy has resulted, dispersed throughout many agencies and departments, at all levels of government, charged with planning, justifying, coordination, administering, and evaluating the burgeoning number of existing and developing programs and benefits.

Whatever one's professional or personal sentiments about this particularistic approach to the provision of social welfare, whereby the elderly population is singled out as a special interest group, it now exists.[41] Furthermore, at least in the short-term, there is no evidence that, in terms of fiscal funding or organizational structure, the goals of these programs will change in any radical way.

It therefore behooves the responsible social scientist either to provide relevant arguments that an alternative universalistic approach to program development would yield higher social benefit to cost ratios, or to offer innovative recommendations that would improve the efficiency, in the form of greater benefits or lower costs of existing programs.

From this perspective, it is meaningful to ask in what ways the conceptual and methodological training of the geographer can be applied? What insight can the geographer provide that will improve the status of elderly programs and benefits or, alternatively, demonstrate that age is not the most useful criterion for program entitlement or eligibility?

Consistent with the spatial organization and man-environment themes of human geography, there would appear to be two productive research areas for the geographer to pursue. Broadly conceived, the first of these would consist of investigations focusing on the location of facilities—housing, services, benefits—that address the elderly population's needs and consider such questions as the following:'

-To what extent does the present location of facilities bear a just or equitable relationship to the locational demand for these facilities?

—In what ways can the spatial allocation of facilities be improved so as to be more spatially accessible to older people, that is, to involve lower transportation costs or fewer problems for either elderly clients or the facilities responsible for delivering services?

—What economies of scale are realized by the delivery of services to large residential concentrations of elderly people?

A second category of research investigations would focus on the environments and places occupied by elderly people and consider such questions as the following:

—For relatively small planning or administrative areas, such as census tracts or small communities, what types of data should be available to plan, administer, coordinate and evaluate the present and future needs of the elderly population? How should these data be classified and stored?

—Of those components of the residential environment that are having the most significant impact on the activity behavior of elderly people and on their psychological well-being, which are more amenable than others to manipulation and change?

SCOPE AND ORGANIZATION OF BOOK

In the gerontological literature, it is common to come across book titles and symposia themes such as "The Social Psychology of Aging," "The Sociology of Aging," and "The Political Consequences of Aging." The title of this book, with its emphasis on location and environment, reflects the fundamental focus of a geography of aging and the aged. Geography as the study of spatial organization (location) and geography as the study of man-environment relationships (environment) have been two persistent themes that have historically characterized geographic thought. Parts I and II, respectively, of this book include research investigations and syntheses addressing each of these two themes while illustrating the potential of a geography-gerontology interface. Part III consists of chapters that address issues relevant to both geographic themes, but have in common their focus on planning methodologies and strategies intended to assist professionals engaged in planning tasks or in public policy deliberations affecting the quality of life of the elderly population.

In a book of this type, it is of course impossible to cover all topics and issues that would be considered appropriate and relevant for geographic inquiry. One is limited by space and, in a small discipline in which research interests are so diversified, by interested academic bodies. Still, the selection of papers should serve to demonstrate the breadth of geographic inquiry—in terms of topics, methodology, and philosophical mode of inquiry. Just as importantly, it should underline the need and the potential for future geographic research on aging and old age.

The book is addressed to both geographers and gerontologists—a dual focus that unfortunately reduces the depth of coverage on certain topics. For geographers, it will have succeeded if it uncovers the excitement and rewards awaiting the researcher who addresses multidisciplinary issues having both theoretical and public policy implications. For gerontologists, it will have succeeded if it serves to legitimize geography as a social science capable of contributing to gerontological inquiry and thought.

NOTES AND REFERENCES

[1] M. W. Riley and F. Foner, eds., *Aging and Society: Vol. 1, An Inventory of Research Findings* (New York: Russell Sage Foundation, 1968); M. W. Riley, J. Riley, and M. Johnson, eds., *Aging and Professions*, Vol. 2 (New York: Russell Sage Foundation, 1969); M. W. Riley, M. Johnson, and F. Foner, *Aging and Society: Vol. 3, A Sociology of Age Stratification* (New York: Russell Sage Foundation, 1972).

[2] See Joseph S. Revis, *Transportation* (Washington, D.C.: White House Conference on Aging, 1971); Ira S. Robbins, *Housing the Elderly* (Washington, D.C.: White House Conference on Aging, 1971); U.S. Senate, Special Committee on Aging, *1971 White House Conference on Aging, A Report to the Delegates from the Conference Sections and Special Concerns Sessions, November 28–December 2* (Washington, D.C.: Government Printing Office, 1971).

[3] See *The Gerontologist*, Vol. 8 (1968), which was devoted to the themes of ecology and aging; *Housing and Environment for the Elderly* (proceedings from a conference on behavioral research utilization and environmental policy, San Juan, 1971); *Environmental Research and Aging: Report From an Interdisciplinary Research Development Conference*, May, 1973, St. Louis (Washington, D.C.: Gerontological Society, 1973); L. A. Pastalan and D. H. Carsen, eds., *Spatial Behavior of Older People* (Ann Arbor, Mich.: University of Michigan, 1970); "Research and Development Goals in Social Gerontology," *The Gerontologist*, special edition, Vol. 9 (1969).

[4] James E. Birren, "The Abuse of the Urban Aged," *Psychology Today*, Vol. 3 (March, 1970), pp. 37–38, 76.

[5] M. Powell Lawton and Bonnie Simon, "The Ecology of Social Relationships in Housing for the Elderly," *The Gerontologist*, Vol. 8 (Summer, 1968), p. 108.

[6] For overviews, see R. G. Golledge, L. A. Brown, and Frank Williamson, "Behavioural Approaches in Geography: An Overview," *Australian Geography*, Vol. 12 (March 19, 1972), pp. 59–79; Roger M. Downs and James T. Meyer, "Geography and the Mind," *American Behavioral Scientist*, Vol. 22 (Sept./Oct., 1978), pp. 59–77; John D. Eyles and David M. Smith, "Social Geography," *American Behavioral Scientist*, Vol. 22 (Sept./Oct., 1978), pp. 41–58; Thomas F. Saarinen, "Environmental Perception," in Ian R. Manners and Marvin W. Mikesell, eds., *Perspectives on Environment* (Washington, D.C.: Association of American Geographers, 1974), pp. 252–289; D. Lowenthal and J. J. Bowden, eds., *Geographies of the Mind: Essays in Historical Geosophy in Honor of John Kirkland Wright* (New York: Oxford University Press, 1976).

[7] Anne Buttimer, "Social Geography," *International Encyclopedia of the Social Sciences*, Vol. 6 (1968), pp. 134–142; Anne Buttimer, "Social Space in Interdisciplinary Perspective," *Geographical Review*, Vol. 59 (July 19, 1969), pp. 417–426.

[8] Eyles and Smith, op. cit., note 6, pp. 49–50.

[9] See W. Zelinsky, "Human Geography," *Geographical Review*, Vol. 56 (July, 1966), pp. 445–447, and the references cited therein.

[10] Stephen Golant, *The Residential Location and Spatial Behavior of the Elderly*, Department of Geography Research Paper No. 143 (Chicago: The University of Chicago, 1972).

[11] Richard Peet and Graham Rowles, "Social Geography," *Geographical Review*, Vol. 64 (April, 1974), pp. 287–289.

[12] Ibid., p. 288.

[13] Robert C. West and Clarissa Kimber, eds., *AAG Program Abstracts, 1978* (Washington, D.C.: Association of American Geographers, 1978), pp. 70–71. The special session was organized and convened by the author.

[14] For two scientific reports on the discipline of geography, see *Geography: The Behavioral and Social Sciences Survey* (Englewood Cliffs, N.J.: Prentice Hall, 1970); National Academy of Sciences-National Research Council, *The Science of Geography* (Washington, D.C.: National Academy of Sciences-National Research Council, 1965).

[15] Robert H. Binstock and Ethel Shanas, *Handbook of Aging and the Social Sciences* (New York: Van Nostrand Reinhold, 1976).

[16] The latest example is the omission of geography in a recent review of disciplinary approaches to gerontological inquiry. See George L. Maddox and James Wiley, "Scope, Concepts and Methods in the Study of Aging," in Robert H. Binstock and Ethel Shanas, eds., *Handbook of Aging and the Social Sciences* (New York: Van Nostrand Reinhold, 1976), pp. 3–34.

[17] See R. Abler, J. S. Adams, and P. R. Gould, *Spatial Organization: The Geographer's World View* (Englewood Cliffs, N.J.: Prentice-Hall, 1971).

[18] See Ian R. Manners and Marvin W. Mikesell, eds., *Perspectives on Environment* (Washington, D.C.: Association of American Geographers, 1974).

[19] For an overview, see Maddox and Wiley, op. cit., note 16.

[20] Ibid., pp. 16–17.

[21] For a discussion of the various possible levels of spatial awareness, see C. Norberg-Schulz, *Existence, Space, and Architecture* (New York: Praeger Publishers, 1971).

[22] Maddox and Wiley, op. cit., note 16, p. 22.

[23] For overviews of the research on environments by gerontologists, see Frances M. Carp, "Housing and Living Environments of Older People," in Robert H. Binstock and Ethel Shanas, eds., *Handbook of Aging and the Social Sciences* (New York: Van Nostrand Reinhold, 1976), pp. 244–271; M. Powell Lawton, "The Impact of the Environment on Aging and Behavior," in James K. Birren and K. Warren Schaie, eds., *Handbook of the Psychology of Aging* (New York: Van Nostrand Reinhold, 1977), pp. 276–301; M. P. Lawton and L. Nahemow, "Ecology and the Aging Process," in C. Eisdorfer and M. P. Lawton, eds., *Psychology of Adult Development and Aging* (Washington, D.C.: American Psychological Association, 1973), pp. 619–674; Paul G. Windley, "Evaluative Research: Housing and Living Arrangements for the Elderly," in U.S. Department of Health, Education and Welfare, Office of Human Development, *Evaluative Research on Social Programs for the Elderly* (Washington, D.C.: Government Printing Office, 1977), pp. 118–136.

[24] See note 23.

[25] M. Powell Lawton, "Planner's Notebook: Planning Environments for Older People," *Journal of the American Institute of Planners*, Vol. 32 (Mar., 1970), pp. 124–129.

[26] Marian Radke Yarrow, "Appraising Environment," in R. H. Williams, C. Tibbits, W. Donahue, eds., *Processes of Aging*, Vol. 1 (New York: Atherton Press, 1963), p. 205.

[27] David Lowenthal et al., "Report of the AAG Task Force on Environmental Quality," *The Professional Geographer*, Vol. 25 (Feb., 1973), pp. 39–46.

[28] Ibid., pp. 42–43.

[29] See note 6.

[30] Lowenthal, op. cit., note 27, p. 41.

[31] See, in particular, T. F. Saarinen, *Environmental Planning, Perception and Behavior* (Boston: Houghton Mifflin, 1976).

[32] Philip W. Porter, "Geography as Human Ecology," *American Behavioral Scientist*, Vol. 22 (Sept./Oct., 1978), p. 20.

[33] See the discussion in Bernice L. Neugarten and Gunhild O. Hagestad, "Age and the Life Course," in Robert H. Binstock and Ethel Shanas, eds., *Handbook of Aging and the Social Sciences* (New York: Van Nostrand Reinhold, 1976), pp. 35–57.

[34] James E. Birren and V. Jayne Renner, "Research on the Psychology of Aging: Principles and Experimentation," in James E. Birren and K. Warner Schaie, eds., *Handbook of the Psychology of Aging* (New York: Van Nostrand Reinhold, 1976), pp. 3–38.

[35] D. Cowgill and L. Holmes, eds., *Aging and Modernization* (New York: Appleton-Century-Crofts, 1972).

[36] Neugarten and Hagestad, op. cit., note 33, p. 36.

[37] Ibid.

[38] These definitions are quoted from Birren and Renner, op. cit., note 34, pp. 4–5.

[39] Donald O. Cowgill, "The Aging of Populations and Societies," *The Annals of the American Academy of Political and Social Science*, Vol. 415 (Sept., 1974), pp. 1–18.

[40] The benefits received from Old Age Insurance, Survivors and Disability Insurance (of the Social Security Act), Medicare, Medicaid, Supplemental Security Income, and Black Lung Benefits accounted for $94 billion; civil service, railroad, and military retirement programs accounted for $14 billion; and $4 billion will go to the elderly in the form of housing subsidies, food stamps, and social or employment services. These figures were presented in a speech by HEW Secretary Joseph Califano and reported in *Aging*, No. 285–286 (July–Aug., 1978), pp. 1–4.

[41] For a critique of this approach, see Amitai Etzioni, "Old People and Public Policy," *Social Policy*, Vol. 7 (Nov./Dec., 1976), pp. 21–29.

PART I

RESIDENTIAL LOCATION AND MIGRATION PATTERNS OF THE U.S. ELDERLY POPULATION

INTRODUCTION TO PART I

Accurate descriptions and explanations of the residential location and migration patterns of older people are fundamental aspects of scientific inquiry. The spatial organization of residences and movements can be viewed as one manifestation of the ways in which older people have adjusted to a host of social, behavioral, and environmental factors. Generalizations concerning these patterns also elucidate how and why places occupied by older people differ from each other. Other studies depend on such findings in their investigations of the ways in which older people's interactions with their environments are influencing their behavior and quality of life (see Part II). From a planning or policy perspective, residential locational analyses are necessary to evaluate older people's actual and latent demands for various services and benefits that address their needs. In turn, these analyses provide a basis for identifying the different ways, and the varying success, with which individual places have accommodated their older occupants (see Part III).

Chapter 2 (Part I) begins by briefly reviewing the unprecedented growth in the number of older people in the United States during the 20th century and examines the relative significance of birth, death, and immigration rates. Whereas many demographic analyses end at this stage, Wiseman's analytical discussion begins here. He shows how the growth of the older population did not occur uniformly across the United States and identifies those demographic factors most responsible for the residential patterning that emerged. He emphasizes how the growth of elderly concentrations in certain locations is due more to their low propensity to change residences than to their recent relocation adjustments.

Consequently, the size of their residential concentrations is often a reflection of the migration behavior of younger populations who are either disproportionately leaving or entering certain locations. Next, in one of the few analyses of its type, the author describes the interstate flow patterns of elderly people, showing that only a few states account for the large majority of in-migrants and out-migrants. His mapping of the spatial pattern of these migration flows, identifying those regions in which elderly migrants are most likely to originate and terminate their moves, is particularly noteworthy. He finds, for example, that the single largest migration stream begins in New York and ends in Florida—a flow nearly three times as large as any other. Wiseman concludes with a discussion of the factors most likely responsible for these migration flows and speculates that migration will be a more influential factor underlying the future location patterns of older people.

Chapter 3 also considers the residential location and migration patterns of older people and their determinants. However, whereas Wiseman's locational analysis focuses on the regions (and their nested hierarchy of states and counties) in which older people live, Golant classifies places according to their membership in three U.S. Census categories of population settlement distinguished by their urban-rural characteristics—central cities, suburbs, and nonmetropolitan areas. His analysis differs, too, in that greater emphasis is placed on more recent elderly population residential shifts and on how these compare with the relocation behavior of the total population.

He finds that the populations in central cities continue to become older, being occupied by increasingly higher concentrations of elderly people. However, the more dramatic population shifts since the 1950s have resulted in a rapidly growing suburban elderly population such that, by 1975, older people were equally distributed between central cities and suburbs of Standard Metropolitan Statistical Areas (SMSAs). This growth has been largely due to the aging-in-place of the earlier waves of younger migrants to suburban locations. He also finds that some of the largest concentrations of elderly are still located in nonmetropolitan areas, but that recently these places have actually become slightly "younger" owing to their more rapid growth of younger populations.

Golant reports that the majority of older people, when they do move, relocate within their same central city, suburban, or nonmetropolitan place of residence. Like Wiseman, he then examines the origins and destinations of older people who changed residential categories between 1970 and 1975. He finds that the most preferred destinations of older movers were the suburbs, followed by nonmetropolitan areas, with central cities a distant third. As a consequence of these gross migration flows, central cities experienced a net migration loss of about one-half million older people. Although suburbs experienced net migration gains, the largest net gains of older people were experienced by nonmetropolitan areas.

In Chapter 4, Rudzitis observes that recent reports of the large net out-migration of older whites from central cities and the net in-migration of older blacks into central cities have not been accompanied by research into the explanations of these moves. To address this deficiency, he first considers several models of migration developed by economists, sociologists, demographers, and geographers for their insights into the migration behavior of older people. He then reports on an analysis that considers 12 explanatory variables of 1960-1970 central city net migration rates of white and nonwhite elderly populations. He finds that older people, particularly whites, are attracted to newer, stable cities having higher concentrations of older persons, small percentages of black residents, and lower crime rates. These are also cities that have warmer climates and lower expenditures for public services. The model is relatively successful in predicting the central city migration rates of whites, but not of blacks, leading the author to recommend research in this area.

Chapter 2

REGIONAL PATTERNS OF ELDERLY CONCENTRATION AND MIGRATION

Robert F. Wiseman

America is aging. The proportion of its population now over 65 years of age (11%) has almost tripled since 1900 and could grow to almost 20% in the next century. The emergence of this stratum of elderly is historically unprecedented. Demographically, falling birth rates and rising life expectancy rates have produced societal aging only in a handful of countries in the most advanced stages of industrialization.[1]

Accompanying this growth of elderly population has been a steady increase in both theoretical and applied research—and with it a burgeoning growth of academic literature—that has focused on issues related to the aging of individuals and population and the problems of old age. This chapter focuses on a less studied set of questions:[2] how this growth has been manifested in the changing regional location patterns of elderly Americans and what have been the most relevant demographic processes responsible. The migration patterns of the elderly are given special attention, not only because they have been little researched, but also because they are viewed as having an increasingly important influence on the redistribution of the U.S. elderly population.

BURGEONING ELDERLY POPULATION

The proportion of the U.S. population aged 65 and older has risen from 4.1% in 1900 to 10.8% in 1977.[3] In 1900, there were 3.1 million persons aged 65 and older and 23.4 million elderly persons in 1977.[4] As dramatic as this increase has

21

1910

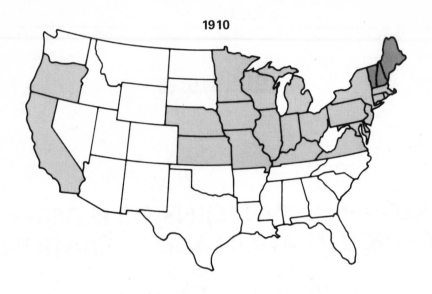

1930

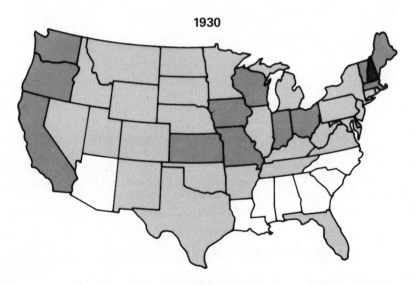

Fig. 1. Percentage of state population aged 65 and older, 1910–1970.

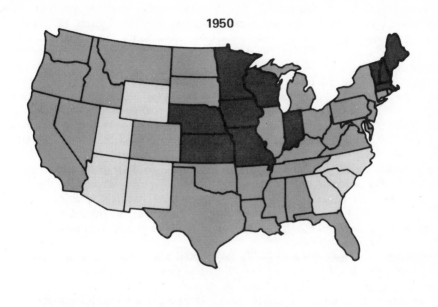

1950

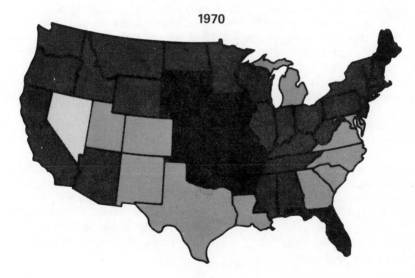

1970

1.5−3.9   4.0−6.4   6.5−8.9   9.0−11.4   11.5−14.6

been, population projections into the next century reveal further substantial growth of the elderly population. By the year 2000, estimates are that the population aged 65 and older will number almost 32 million, about 12% of the total population. However, by the year 2040, conservative predictions indicate there will be almost 55 million elderly people, representing 18% of the American citizenry.[5,6]

These trends are the result of three demographic factors: fertility, mortality, and immigration. Fertility, as measured by birthrates, has been an important factor in determining both the numbers and the proportion of elderly people. The high birthrates that characterized early decades in this century were responsible for rapid increases in the numbers of people who make up the elderly segment of society today. Particularly notable was the post-World War II baby boom, which today is holding down the proportion of older people in society, but which will swell the ranks of elderly persons in the early decades of the 21st century. Because of recent sharp declines in birthrates (the present cohort fertility rate is 1.8 children per woman), it is expected that, beyond the midpoint of the next century, the rate of growth and the proportion of elderly persons will begin to diminish.

Mortality rates have been declining since 1900. This decline, however, has not been experienced uniformly across all age groups. It has been much more significant at the lower portion of the age continuum and is particularly apparent in the reduction of infant mortality rates.[7] Despite general health improvements and increases in life expectancy during early decades of this century, recent advances in average life expectancy have been quite modest. In part, this is due to the fact that the major causes of death within the elderly cohort—heart disease, cancer, and stroke—still remain largely uncontrolled. Furthermore, it is generally thought that only small increases in life expectancy would result from the control of these diseases.[8] Thus, the overall impact of lower mortality rates on the elderly population has been to initially limit the proportion of older people by swelling the ranks of younger cohorts. It is expected that the role of mortality will remain modest in the relatively near future.

The effects of population immigration to the United States has been similar to the influences of fertility and mortality. Prior to World War I, large numbers of people immigrated to this country. The majority of these people contributed to growth in young and middle-aged birth cohorts, which today constitute a considerable proportion of the elderly population. Immigration declined significantly after World War I and therefore might be expected to play a much less important role in expanding the future elderly population. However, the illegal immigration of Mexicans, if unabated, could once again make this a significant factor in the future.

THE CHANGING SPATIAL DISTRIBUTION OF ELDERLY POPULATION

In general, the distribution of elderly persons closely parallels that of the population at large; in other words, the largest numbers of elderly persons are found in the most populous states.[9] In 1977, almost 25% resided in only three states—New York, California, and Florida. Another 25% resided in five additional states—Pennsylvania, Illinois, Ohio, Michigan, and Texas.

An examination of the changing state pattern of elderly concentration since the turn of the century indicates a population that has become less uniformly distributed throughout the country and that the spatial distribution of elderly concentrations is surprisingly dynamic. The diffusing "buildup" of the elderly population within the country can be seen in the successive darkening of the maps shown in Figure 1. In 1910, the residential location pattern of older people was fairly uniform throughout the nation, with low levels of concentration reported in most states. Only the New England states reported somewhat higher concentration, as did, to a lesser extent, Eastern, Midwestern, and Pacific states. By 1930, the pattern was becoming more complex, reflecting a widening range in the proportions of state populations which are aged 65 and older. Again, New England states, as well as some states in the Midwest and on the Pacific coast, had the largest concentrations, while many Southern states reported very low concentrations. In general, this pattern persisted until 1950. Between 1950 and 1970, Florida and Arkansas joined New England, Pacific, and Midwestern states in reporting the largest concentrations of older people. In fact, Arkansas, which ranked as only the 29th state in elderly concentration in 1950 with 7.8%, rose to second position in 1970 with 12.4%. Similarly, Florida, in 21st position with 8.6% in 1950, led the nation with 14.6% in 1970. Southeast coastal and Southwestern states continued to report relatively low concentrations, whereas Northeastern, Pacific, and Midwestern states reported concentrations near the national average.

Over time, then, it can be shown that, although the national percentage of elderly persons increased at a fairly constant rate, the spatial distribution of that increase was not experienced uniformly; in fact, the range of state concentration levels was increasing until 1976, when the lowest state concentration was 2.4% in Alaska and the highest was 16.4% in Florida. Concentrations of older persons in the Midwest have increased markedly during recent decades and careful examination shows that this concentration had slowly shifted westward over time.[10] A few New England states have retained notable concentrations of elderly persons throughout these decades, just as certain Southern and Southwestern states have consistently reported very low proportions of elderly persons (Table 1).

DEMOGRAPHIC TRENDS UNDERLYING STATE CONCENTRATIONS

The high concentrations of elderly that emerged in New England and the Midwest between 1950 and 1970 have been reinforced not by the in-migration of elderly persons but by the out-migration of younger populations participating in rural-to-urban migration streams, thereby leaving behind the elderly population. The essentially rural nature of increased concentrations is more readily apparent at a county level of aggregation (Fig. 2). It can be seen that counties that

Table 1. U.S. Population Aged 65 and Older, 1976

State	Total	Age 65+	Elderly as percent of state total
Florida	8,420,800	1,383,300	16.4
Arkansas	2,109,300	277,400	13.2
Iowa	2,869,800	366,700	12.8
Missouri	4,788,500	608,200	12.7
Nebraska	1,552,900	195,700	12.6
South Dakota	686,000	86,400	12.6
Kansas	2,310,000	288,600	12.5
Rhode Island	926,600	115,800	12.5
Oklahoma	2,766,400	339,500	12.3
Maine	1,069,900	127,700	11.9
Pennsylvania	11,862,100	1,404,100	11.8
West Virginia	1,820,700	214,400	11.8
Massachusetts	5,809,100	681,700	11.7
North Dakota	643,300	74,500	11.6
New York	18,083,700	2,067,600	11.4
Oregon	2,328,700	266,100	11.4
Wisconsin	4,608,800	522,600	11.3
Minnesota	3,964,700	455,400	11.2
Vermont	476,300	53,300	11.2
New Hampshire	822,300	91,000	11.1
Mississippi	2,354,400	259,300	11.0
Kentucky	3,427,900	372,700	10.9
New Jersey	7,336,300	786,700	10.7
Tennessee	4,214,300	452,800	10.7
Alabama	3,664,900	388,200	10.6
Connecticut	3,117,100	330,400	10.6
Arizona	2,770,400	235,200	10.4
Illinois	11,229,200	1,171,000	10.4
District of Columbia	701,800	72,400	10.3
Washington	3,611,800	373,500	10.3
Indiana	5,301,600	540,400	10.2
Montana	752,700	76,500	10.2
Ohio	10,689,800	1,088,800	10.2
California	21,519,700	2,120,700	9.9
Idaho	830,600	81,400	9.8
Texas	12,487,700	1,193,000	9.6
North Carolina	5,469,000	572,800	9.4
Louisiana	3,841,000	354,600	9.2
Michigan	9,104,100	833,600	9.2
Georgia	4,970,200	443,400	8.9
Delaware	582,100	514,000	8.8
Virginia	5,032,300	440,500	8.8
Wyoming	390,400	34,300	8.8
Colorado	2,582,100	217,700	8.4
Maryland	4,144,500	349,900	8.4
South Carolina	2,848,300	239,800	8.4
New Mexico	1,168,100	94,000	8.0
Nevada	609,900	46,700	7.7
Utah	1,228,000	94,300	7.7
Hawaii	886,600	59,800	6.7
Alaska	382,000	9,000	2.4

Source: U.S. Department of Health, Education, and Welfare, Office of Human Development Services, *The Elderly Population: Estimates by County*, 1976.

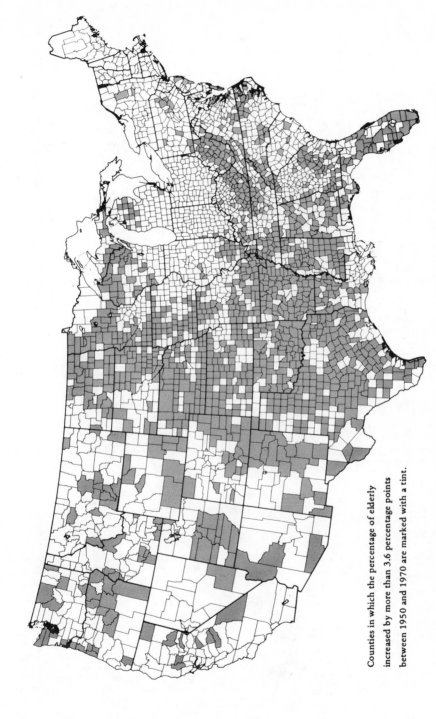

Counties in which the percentage of elderly increased by more than 3.6 percentage points between 1950 and 1970 are marked with a tint.

Fig. 2. Counties experiencing a large increase in percentage of elderly people, 1950–1970 (used with permission of *Geographical Review*, Vol. 68 (1978).

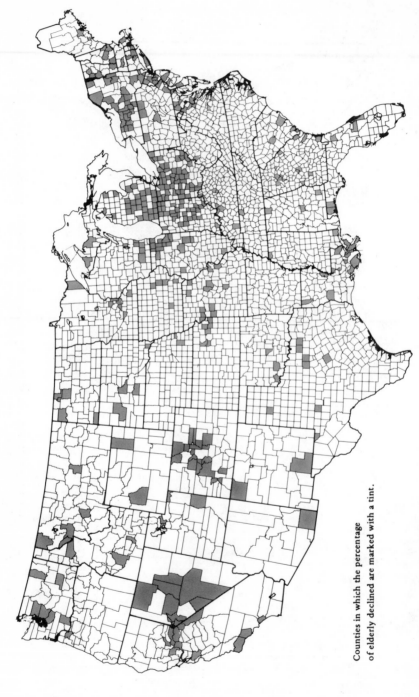

Counties in which the percentage
of elderly declined are marked with a tint.

Fig. 3. Counties experiencing a decline in percentage of elderly people, 1950–1970 (used with permission of *Geographical Review*, Vol. 68 (1978).

experienced an increase greater than the national average in elderly concentration between 1950 and 1970 are mostly found in rural areas. Two notable exceptions include, first, the concentrations that have developed in Florida and also Arkansas due to the large in-migration of older people, and second, counties located within the center of older and larger SMSAs Areas (see Chapter 3).

However, despite the fact that climate is an important factor in elderly migration, it is also clear that not all "Sun Belt" states are developing high concentrations of older people. In part this results from another significant demographic fact, namely, that just as elderly concentrations can be increased by the out-migration of younger populations, so too in-migration of younger populations can retard the development of elderly concentrations. In general, states and counties (as in the Pacific and Southwestern regions) with expanding economies and rapidly growing populations—resulting from the in-migration of population in response to economic opportunity—report relatively low concentrations of older people. For example, Arizona has attracted considerable numbers of retired persons to such places as Sun City; however, the concentration of elderly persons within this state barely exceeds the national average because of the concurrent influx of younger people. These trends between 1950 and 1970 can be observed in greater detail at the county level (Fig. 3). Three types of counties make up this distribution: (1) counties that have experienced large in-migration of younger populations because of growing economies and increased employment opportunities; (2) suburban counties in large SMSAs that received large numbers of younger movers; and (3) rural counties scattered throughout the eastern Midwest and Northeast. This latter group of counties, especially those in Illinois, Michigan, Ohio, and New York, are rural counties that earlier reported large concentrations of older persons. One explanation is that the population structure had "aged" to the point at which losses due to death became the most significant demographic factor.

Several processes, then, often acting in concert, account for the changing patterns of elderly concentration. Given the generally low migration rate reported for older people, it can be concluded that one of the most important demographic processes is "aging in place."[11] Residential inertia over a long time period results in the aging of a place's population, and if younger populations are not proportionately replenished through new births or in-migration, a high concentration of older people will result. In addition, as in several rural states, if large amounts of rural out-migration of younger populations are experienced, there will be still higher concentrations of elderly people. Finally, just as aging in place contributes to the development of elderly concentrations, the later phase of the same process, "dying in place," is often reponsible for a reduction in elderly concentrations.

INTERSTATE MIGRATION PATTERNS OF ELDERLY PERSONS

Over any 5-year period, the proportion of elderly who migrate to a different state is relatively small, though in absolute terms, there are large numbers of

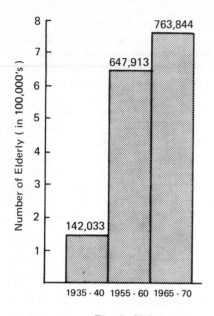
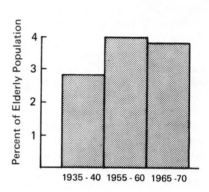

Fig. 4. U.S. interstate migrants aged 60 and older.

older people making such moves (Fig. 4). Age-specific mobility rates have not been reported consistently by the U.S. Census since the turn of the century, although 5-year mobility rates are reported in the census of 1940, 1960, and 1970, and a rate for 1950 is reported on a 1-year basis. Thus the changing interstate mobility rates of elderly people can be ascertained for only a limited period. Figure 4 shows that the proportion of elderly persons relocating during a 5-year period increased considerably between 1940 and 1960, whereas a modest decrease was reported during the period between 1960 and 1970. There has been considerable growth in absolute numbers of elderly persons engaged in interstate migration during this period. Earlier, this was due to a larger percentage of elderly persons who made interstate moves, but more recently, it is due only to the overall growth of the U.S. elderly population.

Studies that describe the spatial pattern of elderly interstate migration have been surprisingly limited. The few studies that do exist focus upon in-migration, out-migration, and net migration rates at regional, state, county, and central city scales,[12] and consequently lack specificity as to the origins and destinations of elderly migrants (see Chapter 3). A geographical description of the migration behavior of older people was obtained by analyzing the 1970 U.S. Census Public Use Sample of Basic Records for States (1/100), based on a 15% sample survey. From these data, for the period 1965–1970, a state-to-state origin-destination matrix was constructed for 11,214 interstate migrants aged 60 and older.

From this matrix states can be ranked according to the size of their out-migrating elderly populations (Table 2). New York dominates the list, having nearly twice as many elderly out-migrants as the next largest states—California and Illinois. Most out-migration flows of the elderly are restricted to a few states with the largest elderly populations; 50% of all older persons who engage in interstate migration move from only nine states—primarily in the Northeast and Midwest. Most states have fairly similar out-migration rates (out-migrants as percentage of state's 1970 total elderly population)—the average state out-migration rate is 4.4%—except states with small elderly populations, such as Alaska and Nevada. It may come as a surprise that California and Florida experience out-migration of large numbers of elderly persons, perhaps suggesting that at least some elderly migrants move to Florida and California only to leave at a later date.

In fact, as the ranking of states according to the size of their elderly in-migrants indicates (Table 2), Florida receives more elderly in-migrants than any other state—representing the destination for nearly one-quarter of the nation's interstate elderly migrants. It has more than twice the number of elderly in-migrants as California—ranked second. Arizona, a distant third, is closely rivaled by New Jersey, Washington, Texas, and Oregon. Comparison of states in terms of their in-migration rates (in-migrants as percentage of state's 1970 total elderly population) shows that in-migration flows are greatly impacting only a few states. Through in-migration, both Florida and Arizona increased their elderly populations by nearly 20% during the 5-year study period, whereas the average increase for all states was only 5%.

Thus interstate elderly migration patterns are characterized by a limited number of origins and destinations, especially the latter.[13] Most states experience a fairly similar proportion of elderly out-migrants, but, because of the wide variation in the size of their total elderly populations, a few states are the origins and destinations for most elderly migrants.

The spatial pattern of these flows is depicted in Figure 5 illustrating the largest volumes of interstate movements. The largest single migration stream originates in New York and ends in Florida—a flow nearly three times as large as any other. The next largest flows also terminate in Florida, but they originate primarily in the Midwest (Illinois, Michigan, and Ohio) and New Jersey. All flows into Florida, with the exception of those from California, originate in the Midwest and Northwest. The major origins of the California migration stream are the Midwestern states and New York. Although both Florida and California attract large numbers of elderly migrants from the Midwest, the origins of their other migrants are quite dissimilar. Very few elderly migrants from New England and mid-Atlantic states relocate to California; nearly all migrate to Florida. California also receives elderly migrants from other Pacific states, as well as Arizona and Texas, whereas Florida attracts very few migrants from states west of the Mississippi River. The nation's third largest elderly in-migration state, Arizona, has a flow pattern of in-migration similar to that of California in that it receives large numbers of elderly migrants from the Midwest.

The migration pattern of the elderly offers other generalizations. A high

Table 2. Interstate Migration of Persons Aged 60 and Older By State, 1965–1970

State	Out-migration			State	In-migration		
	Number (in 100s)	Percent of elderly migrants	Percent of state elderly population		Number (in 100s)	Percent of elderly migrants	Percent of state elderly population
1. New York	1,552	13.8	5.5	1. Florida	2,636	23.5	20.0
2. California	885	7.9	3.1	2. California	1,070	9.5	4.3
3. Illinois	882	7.9	5.9	3. Arizona	479	4.3	19.9
4. Ohio	543	4.8	4.1	4. New Jersey	460	4.1	4.3
5. Pennsylvania	537	4.8	3.2	5. Washington	412	3.7	4.5
6. Michigan	530	4.7	5.3	6. Texas	399	3.6	2.7
7. New Jersey	500	4.5	5.1	7. Oregon	340	3.0	6.3
8. Florida	464	4.1	3.6	8. New York	328	2.9	1.1
9. Texas	312	2.8	2.0	9. Ohio	323	2.9	2.1
10. Indiana	297	2.6	4.2	10. Illinois	288	2.6	1.9
11. Massachusetts	290	2.6	3.5	11. Pennsylvania	286	2.6	1.7
12. Missouri	268	2.4	3.5	12. Missouri	253	2.3	3.1
13. Virginia	215	1.9	4.0	13. Michigan	220	2.0	2.0
14. Minnesota	211	1.9	3.8	14. Maryland	215	1.9	5.3
15. Washington	194	1.7	3.9	15. Virginia	213	1.9	3.9
16. Connecticut	192	1.7	4.6	16. Indiana	186	1.7	2.7
17. Wisconsin	184	1.6	3.0	17. Arkansas	179	1.6	5.3
18. Arizona	169	1.5	7.4	18. North Carolina	172	1.5	2.5
19. Iowa	166	1.5	3.3	19. Tennessee	162	1.4	3.0
20. Washington, D.C.	166	1.5	19.6	20. Georgia	158	1.4	2.8

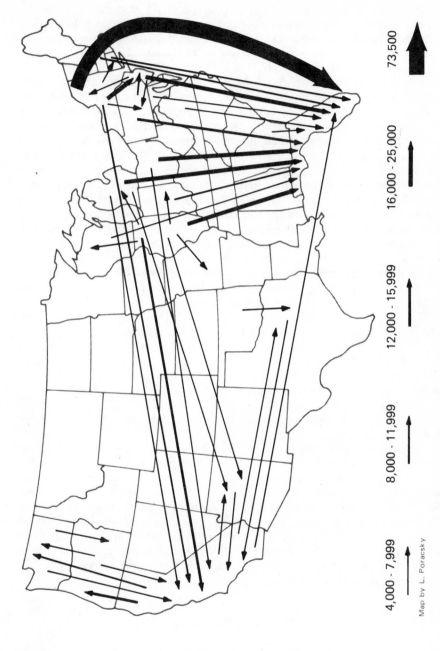

Fig. 5. Interstate migration pattern of persons aged 60 and older, 1965–1970.

73,500

16,000 - 25,000

12,000 - 15,999

8,000 - 11,999

4,000 - 7,999

Map by L. Poracsky

proportion of elderly interstate migrants transverse very long distances, suggesting that their migration patterns may differ from that of the general population.[14] Furthermore, there is a considerable lack of reciprocity among interacting pairs of states; in other words, very few states of origin are also major destination states. And there is a spatial bias in the pattern of elderly migration. In the eastern half of the nation, nearly all large flows originate in northern states and terminate in one southern state, Florida. The majority of the remaining flows are biased in a westerly direction, because most terminate in either California or Arizona. These three states are clearly the major national destinations for elderly migrants. However, regional centers of some importance also exist in Texas, New Jersey, Washington, and Oregon, as well as the Ozarks area of Missouri and Arkansas.

Of the many factors responsible for this migration pattern, the attractions of climate and recreational amenities appear the most important. In a study that examined the determinants of state migration rates, Cebula found that economic variables (tax levels and per capita income) were not strongly associated with elderly migration.[15] The most important factors were temperature differentials and availability of recreational facilities. Further evidence comes from studies that have examined the characteristics of migrants themselves, often in comparison to other groups.[16] When compared with nonmoving elderly, migrants are found to have higher incomes, better health, and are not likely to be members of minority groups. Couples predominate and are most likely to have moved from a suburban residential environment.[17] Thus, in general, the popular stereotype of retired affluent couples moving to recreational areas is supported.

A second type of migration movement sheds light on the spatial pattern of elderly migration. Of elderly interstate migrants, approximately 20% are returning to their state of birth. Northeastern states count high proportions of returning migrants among their elderly in-migrants far in excess of the 20% that might be expected; for example, Pennsylvania, 55.1%; New York, 43.2%; and Massachusetts, 45.1%.[18] In addition, several Midwestern states have large volumes of return elderly migrants.

A third type of interstate migration is motivated by the need for assistance or accessibility to relatives. Several facts indicate the importance of such migration shifts. Disproportionately large numbers of widows are found among migrants leaving retirement centers such as Florida.[19] Migrants are more often found residing in the homes of children than are nonmoving elderly and are more than three times as likely to reside in children's homes than locally moving elderly.[20] In addition, one of the frequently stated reasons for relocating is a desire to be near children.[21] It would appear that elderly persons, either experiencing or anticipating a loss of capacity and independence, move to the community of a close relative where they can avail themselves of assistance.

FUTURE RESEARCH

Government population forecasts of the future elderly population are usually limited to growth and size considerations. The usefulness of these forecasts is restricted because of their failure to consider how the future elderly population will be locationally distributed. Analyses of the present distributional patterns coupled with an understanding of the processes that produce this pattern should represent an important component of forecasting efforts.

It is likely that elderly migration will be more influential in determining the spatial pattern of tomorrow's elderly than it is today. In part, this is due to the highly concentrated spatial pattern of gross migration flows. It is also due to the larger number of elderly people who are relocating, despite low rates of interstate migration. There are signs, moreover, indicating that factors will be operating to increase the rate of elderly migration in the future. As a group, the elderly are expected to be relatively more affluent and, therefore, more able to afford the financial costs of migration. They will have had more frequent travel and vacation experiences, have higher levels of educational attainment, and consequently will have greater awareness of relocation opportunities. Further-more, their social networks will be more diffused regionally as a result of earlier migrations of their peers and family members. So, for example, the areas receiving large numbers of elderly migrants today will be foci of still larger elderly concentrations in the future.

Clearly, future research should be devoted to both improved understanding of the locational concentrations and shifts of the elderly population, and of the demographic and social processes most responsible. From such inquiries will emerge the baseline information necessary for making informed decisions concerning what impact elderly population growth or decline will have on the demand for housing and social welfare services (see Chapters 11 and 14).

NOTES AND REFERENCES

[1] Frederick R. Eisele, ed., "Political Consequences of Aging," *The Annals of the American Academy of Political and Social Sciences*, Vol. 415 (Sept., 1974), p. ix.

[2] A notable exception occurs at the intraurban scale of analysis where several studies have been conducted. For example, Bruce Smith and John Hiltner, "Intra-urban Location of the Elderly," *Journal of Gerontology*, Vol. 30 (1975), pp. 473–478; and Stephen M. Golant, *The Residential Location and Spatial Behavior of the Elderly: A Canadian Example*, Research Paper No. 143 (Chicago: Department of Geography, University of Chicago, 1972).

[3] U.S. Bureau of the Census, *Current Population Reports, Special Studies, Some Demographic Aspects of Aging in the United States*, Series P-23, No. 43 (Washington, D.C.: Government Printing Office, 1973), p. 5.

[4] Herman B. Brotman, *Part I Developments in Aging: 1977, A Report of the Special Committee on Aging, United States Senate*, Report No. 95-771 (Washington, D.C.: Government Printing Office, 1978), p. xxiii.

[5] Ibid.

[6] These forecasts do not presume a significant increase in the life-span. Although, the proportion of people aged 65 and older is not expected to increase substantially during this time period, there will be a dramatic increase of those people considered "old-old," aged 75 and older. This is important in that the "old-old" group generally makes up that segment of the elderly which most requires special attention and assistance.

[7] Ansley J. Coale, "How a Population Ages or Grows Younger," in Ronald Freedman, ed., *Population: The Vital Revolution* (Garden City, N.Y.: Anchor Books, 1964), pp. 47–58.

[8] Ibid., pp. 49–50.

[9] Brotman, op. cit., note 4.

[10] Thomas O. Graff and Robert F. Wiseman, "Changing Concentrations of Older Americans," *Geographical Review*, Vol. 68 (1978), pp. 379–393.

[11] See Stephen M. Golant, "Residential Concentrations of the Future Elderly," *The Gerontologist*, Vol. 15 (1975), pp. 16–23 for a previous discussion of this process.

[12] See Stephen M. Golant, Gundars Rudzitis, and Sol Daiches, "The Migration of Elderly From U.S. Central Cities," *Growth and Change*, Vol. 9, No. 4 (Oct., 1978), pp. 30–35.

[13] See also Stephen M. Golant, "Spatial Context of Residential Moves By Elderly Persons," *International Journal of Aging and Human Development*, Vol. 8, No. 3 (1977–1978), pp. 279–289.

[14] Cynthia B. Flynn, "A Comparison of Interstate Migration Patterns for the Elderly and the General United States Populations," a paper presented at the 31st Annual Scientific Meeting of the Gerontological Society, Dallas, Texas, Nov. 16–20, 1978.

[15] Richard J. Cebula, "The Quality of Life and Migration of the Elderly," *Review of Regional Studies*, Vol. 4 (1974), pp. 62–68. See also Larry M. Svart, "Environmental Preference Migration: A Review," *Geographical Review*, Vol. 66 (1976), pp. 314–330.

[16] Golant, op. cit., note 11; see also Calvin Goldscheider, "Differential Residential Mobility of the Older Population," *Journal of Gerontology*, Vol. 21 (1966), pp. 103–108.

[17] Jeanne C. Biggar, "Demographic, Socioeconomic, and Housing Differentials Among Elderly Mover Types: 1965–1970," a paper presented at the 31st Annual Scientific Meeting of the Gerontological Society, Dallas, Texas, Nov. 16–20, 1978.

[18] Charles F. Longino and Cynthia B. Flynn, "Going Home: Aged Return Migration," a paper presented at the 31st Annual Scientific Meeting of the Gerontological Society, Dallas, Texas, Nov. 16–20, 1978.

[19] Ibid.

[20] Biggar, op. cit., note 17.

[21] Goldscheider, op. cit., note 11; and Antony Lenzer, "Mobility Patterns Among the Aged," *The Gerontologist*, Vol. 5 (1965), pp. 12–15.

Chapter 3

CENTRAL CITY, SUBURBAN, AND NONMETROPOLITAN AREA MIGRATION PATTERNS OF THE ELDERLY

Stephen M. Golant

Major trends of population movement—such as from rural to urban areas, from central cities to suburbs, and most recently from larger urban agglomerations back to smaller cities and towns—have resulted in migration being a major demographic component underlying the changing population settlement pattern of the United States. Although comparable residential moves by the elderly population have played a less important role in this group's changing location pattern, they are for several reasons of interest to social scientists and policy makers. First, these residential shifts provide one measure of changing housing and locational preferences in response to changing life styles and levels of personal competence; second, they reveal the relationship between net migration flows and the overall growth or decline of elderly people in different locations; and third, they represent one diagnostic indicator of potential adjustment problems experienced by a location's recent elderly in-migrants and also by the social, economic, and political institutions which must accommodate their service needs.

We begin this chapter by examining the residential growth and distribution patterns of older people (aged 65 and over) in metropolitan and nonmetropolitan areas and by relating these patterns to comparable settlement trends of the total population.[1] This initial analysis serves as a useful background for the major focus, namely, an investigation of the patterns and implications of recent migration flows of elderly people between and within metropolitan and nonmetropolitan areas of the United States.

Table 3. Size, Distribution, Growth, and Concentration of Noninstitutionalized Total Population and Population Aged 65 and Older in Central Cities, Suburbs, and Nonmetropolitan Areas, 1970 and 1975

Residential category	1970[a]		1975[a]		Percent change 1970–1975
	Number (in thou.)	Percent[b]	Number (in thou.)	Percent[b]	
Total population					
Total United States	199,819	100.0	208,683	100.0	4.4
Metropolitan areas	137,058	68.6 (100.0)	141,993	68.0 (100.0)	3.6
Central cities	62,876	31.5 (45.9)	60,902	29.2 (42.9)	–3.1
Suburbs[c]	74,182	37.1 (54.1)	81,091	38.9 (57.1)	9.3
Nonmetropolitan areas	62,761	31.4	66,690	32.0	6.3
Population aged 65 and older					
Total United States	18,899	100.0	21,127	100.0	11.8
Metropolitan areas	11,539	61.1 (100.0)	13,428	63.6 (100.0)	16.4
Central cities	6,251	33.1 (54.2)	6,737	31.9 (50.2)	7.8
Suburbs[c]	5,288	28.0 (45.8)	6,691	31.7 (49.8)	26.5
Nonmetropolitan areas	7,359	38.9	7,699	36.4	4.6
Percent of total population aged 65 and older					
Total United States	9.5		10.1		
Metropolitan areas	8.4		9.5		
Central cities	9.9		11.1		
Suburbs[c]	7.1		8.3		
Nonmetropolitan areas	11.7		11.5		

[a]1975 data are April-centered averages from the *Current Population Survey*; 1970 data are also from the *Current Population Survey* and have been adjusted by excluding inmates of institutions and members of the Armed Forces residing in barracks for comparability with 1975 data. Boundaries of Metropolitan Areas and Central Cities are as defined by the 1970 Census.

[b]Percentages in brackets indicate the intrametropolitan distribution of the population.

[c]Suburbs refer to population and territory outside central cities but in Metropolitan Areas.

Sources: U.S. Bureau of Census, "Mobility of the Population In The United States: March 1970 to March 1975," *Current Population Reports* Series P-20, No. 285 (1975); U.S. Bureau of the Census, "Population Profile of the United States: 1975," *Current Population Reports* Series P-20, No. 292 (1976); U.S. Bureau of the Census, "Social and Economic Characteristics of the Population in Metropolitan and Nonmetropolitan Areas: 1970 and 1960," *Current Population Reports* Series P-23, No. 37 (1971).

THE CHANGING RESIDENTIAL LOCATION PATTERN
OF THE ELDERLY[2]

In central cities,[3] the population aged 65 and over has been increasing since the 1950s at more than twice the rate of the total population.[4] This growth rate differential was particularly large during the 1970–1975 period when central cities, as a group, experienced an absolute decline in total population (−3.1%), but a 7.8% increase in the population over 65 (Table 3). During this period, the percentage of the central city elderly population increased from 9.9% to 11.1% and central cities continued to be the home of large residential concentrations of elderly people.

The aging of the central city population is probably the most frequent observation made by social scientists and planners who report on the location of older people in the United States. Although correct and important, such a characterization may lead to a deceptive, if not erroneous, conclusion concerning the changing location patterns of the elderly. The explanation for this is as follows. During the same 1970–1975 period the growth rate of the suburban elderly population (26.5%) was far greater than that of the elderly in central cities (7.8%). The more rapid growth of the elderly population in suburban areas was reflected in the changing intrametropolitan locational distribution of the elderly. By 1975, although 32% of the total U.S. elderly population was still located in central cities, the same percentage was also located in the suburbs and thus the metropolitan elderly population was equally distributed between central cities and suburbs. The aging of the U.S. suburban population has gone relatively unnoticed, because in the past the absolute number of elderly people in the suburbs has been relatively small. Nevertheless, since 1950 the suburban elderly population has been increasing faster than the total suburban population. Between 1970 and 1975, the suburban elderly population increased at almost three times the rate of the total suburban population, and by 1975 over 8% of the suburban population was 65 and older. The relatively higher rate of growth of the elderly population, both in suburban areas and central cities, combined with the slower suburban growth rates of the total population and the absolute decline of the total central city population, have resulted in U.S. metropolitan areas becoming "older."

Between 1950 and 1970, the elderly population also grew much faster in nonmetropolitan areas; the total nonmetropolitan population experienced either little or negative growth during the same period.[5] In 1970 some of the largest concentrations of older people (11.7%) were found in small towns, urban places, and rural nonfarm places. Another national trend began, however, that had the effect of reversing this pattern. The drain of total out-migrants from nonmetropolitan to metropolitan United States had largely ceased by the 1970s, and nonmetropolitan counties began gaining about 350,000 total migrants per year from metropolitan areas.[6] Thus, for the first time in recent history, a nonmetropolitan total population growth rate (6.3%) actually exceeded the metropolitan area population growth rate (3.6%).[7] Over this 1970–1975 period, the growth rate of the total population in nonmetropolitan areas exceeded the growth of the nonmetropolitan elderly population. Consequently, nonmetropolitan areas actually became "younger," and the percentage of the population 65 and older decreased (from 11.7% to 11.5%) for the first time in several decades.

The proportion of the U.S. elderly population living in nonmetropolitan areas has also declined. The growth of elderly people in nonmetropolitan areas has increased steadily since the 1950s, but at a slower rate than the growth of the metropolitan elderly population; between 1970 and 1975, the growth rates were 4.6% and 16.4%, respectively. Consequently, by 1975 only 36% of the population 65 and older lived outside of metropolitan areas.

In considering the last 25 years, we can make the following generalizations concerning the changing locational distribution of the elderly population compared with that of the total population. (1) Like the total population, the elderly population has become increasingly centralized in metropolitan areas, though they are still more likely to occupy nonmetropolitan areas than the total population. (2) Within metropolitan areas, the elderly population has become decentralized due to its greater occupancy of suburban residential locations. Although distribution differences are small, the elderly are still more likely than the total population to occupy central cities.

DEMOGRAPHIC PROCESSES UNDERLYING THESE TRENDS

The above residential growth and distribution patterns of older people reflect the aging-in-place and the residential inertia of middle-aged and older populations. For several reasons,[8] older people make less frequent location adjustments than younger people. Despite significant changes in family status, the inappropriateness of a dwelling, or the declining physical and social status of neighborhoods or communities, many older people move only when severe health or financial difficulties make it impossible to maintain independent households.[9] Even though residential relocation is one mechanism by which older persons are redistributed (along with population losses due to death), it is generally a less important component of the growth or decline of a location's older population[10] (for exception, see Chapter 2).

This is in direct contrast to the redistribution patterns of the total population, in which the frequency of residential adjustments is higher and migration has greater significance as a demographic component. These migration patterns indirectly influence the residential patterns of subsequent generations of elderly people, because the residential locations of elderly people are often indicative of destinations they selected earlier in their lives. Long in his analysis of the lifetime mobility expectations of the U.S. population confirmed that by the time an individual reaches old age, his residential adjustments are behind him, and the probability is low that additional moves will be made.[11] Usually no more than one move is made, and it is likely to be a short distance, often within the same county.[12]

Since the 1920s there has been a steady increase in the proportion of the total metropolitan population living in the suburbs. This is largely accounted for by suburban net migration gains resulting from the exodus of population from central cities. A large percentage of this suburban population passed through a family-rearing stage of life, so further growth was guaranteed by high fertility rates (particularly in the 1945–1959 period). It is the aging-in-place of these earlier migrating cohorts which largely explains the steadily increasing concentration of older people in U.S. suburbs. In turn, the declining growth of an older population in central cities reflects the smaller size of the population cohort that did not participate in the move to the suburbs.

The initially large growth of the elderly population in nonmetropolitan areas was due to the aging of the population left behind as a result of the rural-urban migrations of the 1940s and 1950s. The selective out-migration of younger people substantially reduced the size of the cohort that would have become old in nonmetropolitan areas. As a result, growth rates of elderly people in nonmetropolitan areas have been declining over the last 20 years.

THE RECENT MIGRATION PATTERNS OF OLDER PEOPLE

Data and Procedures

The source of the data for the following analysis is the Bureau of the Census survey report, "Mobility of the Population of the United States: March 1970 to March 1975."[13] A sample of approximately 47,000 households in the conterminous United States were interviewed in March of 1975 and the sample was weighted and inflated to represent the total civilian noninstitutional population by age, race, and sex.[14]

Respondents were asked whether they lived in the same house for the past 5 years. A person giving a positive response was classified as a *nonmover*. A person giving a negative response was classified as a *recent mover*, and then asked information regarding the geographic location of his previous residence. If the mover relocated within the same metropolitan area, his previous place of residence was identified as either central city or suburbs. If he did not relocate within the same metropolitan area, his previous residence was coded as either central city or suburbs in *another metropolitan area*, or as a *nonmetropolitan area*. For the purposes of this analysis, the previous and the present place of residence of all movers were classified into one of three *residential categories*: central cities, suburbs, and nonmetropolitan areas (nonSMSAs).

It is important to emphasize that a population which moves within the same residential category may not necessarily be relocating within the same place. For example, persons identified as moving within the central city residential category include persons who may have moved from the central city of one metropolitan area to the central city of another metropolitan area. The boundaries of all three residential categories were defined according to the 1970 Census Bureau place definitions. The 65-and-over age group was one into which movers and nonmovers were categorized. While chronological age may be a less than optimum measure of a person's stage in life, it is assumed to be roughly synonymous with the timing of certain critical events that accompany the physiological, psychological, and sociological processes of aging.

Several possibly biasing features of these data, some previously noted by Lenzer,[15] also exist: (1) Persons who moved between 1970 and 1975 but who died before the 1975 census enumeration are not counted. (2) The mobility status of persons is compared at two points in time—March 1970 and March 1975. There is no accounting of two or more moves which might have taken place between these two dates. Thus the census reporting will tend to underestimate the amount of residential mobility of a population. (3) About 7.3% of the total population and 6.4% of the elderly population are excluded from the analysis because in 1970 they were either living outside the United States or did not report their place of residence. (4) The survey does not include the institutional population of the United States, nor members of the armed forces living on post in group quarters or barracks. Consequently, the data do not include the residential relocations of older people from one institution to another or from a private home to an institution, moves particularly characteristic of people over age 75.

The Findings

Gross migration flows.[16] The older people most likely to have moved were living in central cities of metropolitan areas (Table 4). These people were also the least likely to remain in the same residential category once they had relocated. In contrast, older people living in nonmetropolitan areas were the least mobile and the least likely to change residential categories following relocation. This pattern was similar to the total population, but two observations are noteworthy: First, the least mobile total population group was living in the suburbs, not in nonmetropolitan areas. Second, older movers in general were more likely than the total moving population to remain in the same residential category after they relocated. However, this was not true for the total moving population living in the suburbs. This group was less likely to change residential categories than the older moving population.

About 1.3 million older people (30% of the older moving population, and 6.5% of the total older population) changed residential categories. Over half of these movers (53%) originated from central cities, and of these, the majority (35%) chose suburban locations. The remainder (18%) relocated to nonmetropolitan areas (Table 5). The other principal migration flow (20% of all residential category shifts) was from suburban locations to nonmetropolitan locations. As a consequence, almost one-half million older people (38% of all shifts) left metropolitan areas for nonmetropolitan locations. Moves from suburban to central city locations represented only 12% of all residential category shifts by the elderly. A small flow of elderly migrants moved from nonmetropolitan to metropolitan areas (15% of all shifts), and primarily to their suburban areas.

It is informative to focus on the relative frequency with which central city and suburban moving older populations selected certain destinations. Fifty-nine

Table 4. Residential Mobility of Total and Older Population, 1970–1975

Residential category in 1970	Initial "at risk" population in in 1970[a]	Moving population 1970–1975[a]		Population relocating in same residential category, 1970–1975	
		Number (in thou.)	Percent	Number (in thou.)	Percent in moving population
Population aged 5 and older					
Central cities	58,448	30,118	51.5	17,113	56.8
Suburbs	64,000	25,564	39.9	18,255	71.4
NonSMSAs	57,040	24,155	42.3	19,029	78.8
Total	79,488	79,837	44.5	54,397	68.1
Population aged 65 and older					
Central cities	6,727	1,659	24.7	979	59.0
Suburbs	5,924	1,216	20.5	802	66.0
NonSMSAs	7,120	1,375	19.3	1,177	85.6
Total	19,771	4,250	21.5	2,958	69.6

[a]Numbers and percentages only include persons who reported place of residence in 1970 and who moved within the United States between 1970 and 1975.

Source: U.S. Bureau of the Census, "Mobility of the Population in the United States: March 1970 to March 1975," *Current Population Reports* Series P-20, No. 285 (1975).

percent of the older people who moved from central city residences remained in a central city location (54% in the same central city (place), 5% in a different central city); 27% moved to a suburban location (16% in the same metropolitan area, 11% in another metropolitan area); and 14% moved to a nonmetropolitan area. Sixty-six percent of older suburban movers remained in a suburban location (51% in the same metropolitan area, 16% in another metropolitan area); 13% moved to a central city location (6% in the same metropolitan area, 7% in another central city); and 21% moved to a nonmetropolitan location.

How do these latter migration patterns compare with the total population of movers in central city and suburban locations? First, a higher proportion of the total population of movers previously living in central city locations subsequently moved to suburban locations (32%), and a smaller proportion relocated to nonmetropolitan areas (11%). Second, the total suburban population of movers were more likely to remain in suburban locations after they relocated (71%). However, if they did leave suburban locations, they were more likely than older movers to select central cities and less likely to select nonmetropolitan areas.

Net migration flows. While 680,000 older people moved from central cities between 1970 and 1975, only 226,000 moved into them. The result was a central city net loss of 454,000 older people (Table 6). The exchange of older

Table 5. Size and Distribution of Gross Population Mobility
Flows, 1970–1975

Residential category in 1970	Residential category in 1975 (in thou.)			
	Central cities	Suburbs	NonSMSAs	Totals
Population aged 5 and older				
Central cities	*17,113*	9,765 (38%)	3,240 (13%)	13,005 (51%)
Suburbs	3,828 (15%)	*18,255*	3,481 (14%)	7,309 (29%)
NonSMSAs	2,159 (9%)	2,967 (12%)	*19,029*	5,126 (20%)
Total	5,987 (24%)	12,732 (50%)	6,721 (26%)	25,440 (100%)
Population aged 65 and older				
Central cities	*979*	446 (35%)	234 (18%)	680 (53%)
Suburbs	156 (12%)	*802*	258 (20%)	414 (32%)
NonSMSAs	70 (5%)	128 (10%)	*1,177*	198 (15%)
Total	226 (18%)	574 (44%)	492 (38%)	1,292 (100%)

Notes:

Italic figures are movers who remained in same residential category during relocation.

Totals and percentage distributions do not include italic figures.

Suburbs refer to population and territory outside of central cities in SMSAs.

Figures only include persons who reported place of residence in 1970 and who moved within the United States between 1970 and 1975.

Source: U.S. Bureau of the Census, "Mobility of the Population in the United States: March 1970 to March 1975," *Current Population Reports* Series P-20, No. 285 (1975).

people between central cities and suburbs located in the same metropolitan area accounted for the largest proportion of this net loss. As a result of these intrametropolitan moves, central cities experienced a net loss of 189,000 older people. They had a net loss of another 101,000 older people who relocated to suburbs in different metropolitan areas. Thus central cities experienced a net loss of 290,000 older people to suburban locations. The remaining net loss experienced by central cities, 164,000 older people, was from population exchanges with nonmetropolitan areas. Combined with the net gain of 130,000 older people that nonmetropolitan areas received from suburban locations, metropolitan areas had a net loss of 294,000 older people to nonmetropolitan areas.[17] Suburbs, in turn, had a net gain of 160,000 older people once their net loss to nonmetropolitan areas had been deducted.

Net migration rates. Net migration rates were calculated using the 1970 residential category's at-risk population as the base (Table 4). Focusing first on elderly net migration, the largest net out-migration rate was found in central cities (−67.5), primarily as a result of losses to the suburbs (−43.1), but also to nonmetropolitan areas (−24.4) (Table 6). The largest net in-migration rate was

Table 6. Net Migrants and Migration Rates, 1970–1975

Residential category in 1970	Residential category in 1975 (in thou.)			
	Central cities	Suburbs	NonSMSAs	Totals
Population aged 5 and older				
Central cities	—	−5,936(−101.6)	−1,081(−18.5)	−7,018(−120.1)
Suburbs	+5,936(+92.8)	—'	− 514(−8.0)	+5,423(+84.7)
NonSMSAs	+1,081(+19.0)	+514(+9.0)	—	+1,595(+28.0)
Population aged 65 and older				
Central cities	—	−290(−43.1)	−164(−24.4)	−454(−67.5)
Suburbs	+290(+48.9)	—	−130(21.9)	+160(+27.0)
NonSMSAs	+164(+23.0)	+130(+18.3)	—	+294(+41.3)

Note: Base for migration rates equals per thousand at risk population in 1970 residential category. Net migrants and migration rate figures refer to gains, losses, or rates experienced by 1970 residential category as a result of its population exchanges with other 1975 residential category(ies).

Source: U.S. Bureau of the Census, "Mobility of the Population in the United States: March 1970 to March 1975," *Current Population Reports* Series P-20, No. 285 (1975).

experienced by nonmetropolitan areas (+41.3), almost equally a result of net gains from central cities (+23.0) and from suburbs (+18.3). The net elderly in-migration rate for the suburbs was relatively small (+27.0), because the high central city to suburbs net in-migration rate (+48.9) was offset by the suburbs to nonmetropolitan area negative net out-migration rate (−21.9).

Table 6 reveals the contrast between the net migration rates of the total population and those of the elderly population in each of the three residential categories. Total net migration rates were higher in the central cities and the suburbs and lower in nonmetropolitan areas which (as noted) had a relatively large elderly net in-migration rate.

Effectiveness of migration flows. Another useful measure for comparing the elderly and the total population migration patterns is the *migration effectiveness index.* It indicates the efficiency of an area's population turnover (the sum of an area's in-migrants and out-migrants) in effecting a net migration change. Statistically, the index for any residential category equals the absolute value of

$$100 \times \frac{\text{in-migrants minus out-migrants}}{\text{in-migrants plus out-migrants}}$$

The index ranges from 0, when the number of in-migrants is equal to the number of out-migrants, to 100 when the size of the in-migrants is large relative to the size of the out-migrants (or vice versa).[18]

Table 7. Migration Effectiveness Indexes, 1970–1975

Residential category in 1970	Residential category in 1975			
	Central cities	Suburbs	NonSMSAs	Totals
Population aged 5 and older				
Central cities	—	43.7	20.0	36.9
Suburbs	—	—	8.0	27.1
NonSMSAs	—	—	—	13.5
Population aged 65 and over				
Central cities	—	48.2	53.9	50.1
Suburbs	—	—	33.7	16.2
NonSMSAs	—	—	—	42.6

Source: U.S. Bureau of the Census, "Mobility of the Population in the United States: March 1970 to March 1975," *Current Population Reports* Series P-20, No. 285 (1975).

The most effective migration flow for redistributing the older population was between central cities and nonmetropolitan areas (an index of 53.9), followed closely by the elderly migration flow between central cities and suburbs (an index of 48.2).[19] In all residential categories except the flow between suburbs and all other categories, the migration effectiveness indexes are larger for flows of older movers than for flows of the total population of movers. In this regard, the sharpest disparity in the indexes (43.6 as opposed to 13.3) involved population exchanges between metropolitan and nonmetropolitan areas (Table 7).

SUMMARY AND DISCUSSION OF FINDINGS

Migration Preferences of Elderly

The majority of elderly persons, when they do move, relocate within their same central city, suburban, or nonmetropolitan place of residence. This was particularly true of elderly persons living in nonmetropolitan areas who tended to remain in nonmetropolitan areas after they moved. In contrast, the mobile central city elderly were far more likely to move to places in a different residential category (i.e., the suburbs or nonmetropolitan areas). An earlier study also revealed the restricted spatial context of residential moves by most elderly and found that the preponderance of their moves were within the same county or state.[20] The significance of this finding is also appropriate here:

This raises the interesting question of whether (and if so, why) the boundaries of these areas are as cognitively significant to the older person as his perceived neighborhood boundaries. That is, place attachment or the notion of "home range" may just as aptly be applied to larger spatial entities than "neighborhoods," and encompass cities, counties, or states as psychologically meaningful geographic areas. Certainly there is a rationale to ascertain whether in addition to distance constraints, other factors associated with friends, relatives, historical or symbolic attachments, or the familiarity of existing surroundings act to restrict the spatial context of residential moves by elderly persons.

Most of our subsequent findings concerned the migration behavior of the relatively small percentage of older people (6.5%) and of older movers (30.0%) who changed residential categories between 1970 and 1975. The most preferred destinations of these older movers were the suburbs, followed by nonmetropolitan areas; central cities were a distant third. The order of these location preferences mirrored that of the total population of movers except in terms of degree. Elderly movers showed a greater interest in moving to nonmetropolitan areas; they were less likely to move to suburbs and particularly reluctant to choose central cities.

As a consequence of these gross migration flows, nonmetropolitan areas experienced the largest net migration gain and rate of elderly people followed by a smaller positive gain and lower rate in the suburbs. Central cities in turn experienced a large net migration loss of about one-half million older people and had a large net out-migration rate. In contrast, the net migration flows of the total population resulted in the suburbs experiencing the largest net gain and rate, followed by nonmetropolitan areas which experienced a positive but much smaller gain and rate. Central cities again experienced a large net migration loss and rate.

What do these findings suggest about the geographic preferences of older people?[21] Without additional information about the personal characteristics of these older movers and attributes of their residential destinations, the following discussion only speculates as to the factors which affected their decisions.

The urban location theory literature offers insights as to why central cities should be attractive to older movers (for review of relevant literature, see next Chapter 4). Important attributes would appear to be the convenience of public transportation and the easy access to a wide range of urban facilities—including those which specifically address the needs of older people. This should be particularly true given the fact that old age increases the likelihood of mobility impairments and the greater dependence on public transportation and walking.[22] Because a high proportion of older people have low incomes, household budgetary allocations to both housing and transportation are likely to be smaller. Thus the availability of smaller sized, less expensive rental accommodations and the likelihood that the money outlay for transportation costs is likely to be relatively low would also argue for the attractiveness of central city locations. It might be expected that older people, who often have small households, would be willing to give up their larger sized, usually owned accommodations in the suburbs or nonmetropolitan areas to obtain the advantages of improved and relatively inexpensive transportation accessibility.[23] Finally, the central city

Factors Making Central Cities Unattractive	Factors Making Suburbs or Nonmetropolitan Areas Attractive
The uncertainties associated with unexpected and rapid neighborhood change.	The identification of suburban or nonmetropolitan areas as residentially stable locations.
The large absolute and relative numbers of older people.	The large absolute and relative numbers of younger people.
Locational constraints associated with the journey-to-work relationship no longer in effect.	The proliferation of regional and neighborhood commercial and institutional centers and districts outside central cities of metropolitan areas making the central business district only one of the many activity centers to which accessibility is important.
Higher prices and lower quality of consumer goods.	Lower prices and higher quality of consumer goods.
The competition from ethnic and black population groups for the available supply of lower rent housing units.	An increase in the number of multifamily apartment units outside central cities in metropolitan areas, facilitating moves to smaller and less expensive housing quarters.
The conversion of rental units to condominiums and cooperatives.	The increased availability of public housing units, and various types of retirement housing designed for older persons.
The predominance of older, less attractive, harder to maintain, or less safe building structures.	The availability of smaller owned units for older persons seeking to remain owner-occupants.
A view of central cities as unsafe places to live because of higher crime rates and the hazards associated with high automobile traffic levels.	A view of suburban or nonmetropolitan areas as safer places to live because of perceived lower crime rates and low automobile traffic levels.
A view of the central city as too complex and difficult to use.	A view of suburban or nonmetropolitan areas as being smaller scale, less congested and complex, and easier to use.
Greater air pollution particularly critical for older persons with respiratory problems.	An assessment that air is cleaner.
A declining percentage of population perceived as "middle class".	A growing proportion of persons living alone, separated, divorced, or who were never married living outside central cities in metropolitan areas. Thus these locations are socially attractive to older persons, a high proportion of whom have comparable statuses.
A decrease in family accessibility in the central city due to the continuing out-migrations of younger white populations, including the family and relatives of older persons.	The pattern of earlier central city-suburban migrations increasing the probability that the older person's children or other relatives will be living outside central city locations.
The difficulties of driving automobiles in traffic congested locations.	The increased likelihood that members of more recent generations of older persons will be automobile drivers facilitating residential occupancy in locations requiring accessibility by car.
A less attractive regional location.	A more attractive regional location.

Fig. 6. Factors underlying the selection of destinations by elderly movers.

should be able to offer an attractive social situation because it contains high building and neighborhood concentrations of older people. This would be a positive factor for many elderly who enjoy social contact and relationships with persons in a similar stage of life.[24]

These factors undoubtedly help explain why a large proportion of elderly movers relocated within central cities and why a small flow of older people moved to central cities from suburbs and nonmetropolitan places. However, in accounting for the large net migration losses of elderly people from central cities, other factors must be operating which, on balance, make central cities relatively less attractive than suburbs and nonmetropolitan places.

Figure 6 identifies several factors which might contribute to the relative unattractiveness of central cities.[25] For each factor that serves to "push" older people from the central city (column 1), a companion factor (column 2) serves to "pull" them to the suburbs or nonmetropolitan areas.

Not distinguished in Figure 6, however, are the factors which might make nonmetropolitan areas more or less attractive than the suburbs as destinations for elderly movers. We can recall from Table 5 that 30% of the migration shifts by the elderly who changed residential categories involved population exchanges between the suburbs and nonmetropolitan areas. The result was a net gain of 130,000 elderly people in nonmetropolitan areas.

It is difficult to begin to speculate on why elderly migrants selected nonmetropolitan areas more frequently than the suburbs. However, we can hypothesize that certain groups of nonmetropolitan areas might be more attractive than others. In this regard, at least three groups of nonmetropolitan areas (not necessarily independent of each other) might be particularly attractive to older people: First, nonmetropolitan areas recently experiencing population and economic growth;[26] second, those containing or located near natural amenities (e.g., warm climate, open space, water, beaches), major recreation areas, or retirement developments;[27] and third, those located within the commuting fields of major metropolitan areas containing major activity centers and large suburban regional shopping and service centers.[28]

Migration and Population Growth Patterns

In absolute and relative terms, the size of the elderly moving population is small, and the size of the elderly moving population changing residential categories is even smaller. Consequently, with few exceptions the migration flows of elderly people are unlikely to influence substantially the future shifts in their metropolitan-nonmetropolitan locational distributions.[29] The present location pattern of the late middle-aged population—a high proportion of whom will survive and age in their existing residential locations—is likely to be a superior demographic indicator.

Nontheless, the accuracy of elderly population growth predictions for a location will be improved to the extent that the impact of their migration patterns can be ascertained. In this regard, our findings yield the following generalizations:

(1) The net migration pattern of elderly people is generally in the same direction and of the same magnitude as their overall locational growth patterns. The declining growth of the elderly population in central cities is consistent with their large net migration losses and rates. Both suburbs and nonmetropolitan areas experienced substantial net migration gains and rates which were consistent with their overall elderly population growth. However, given the much larger net migration gain and rate of elderly people in nonmetropolitan areas than in the suburbs, we might have expected nonmetropolitan areas to have had a higher growth rate of elderly people; in fact, the suburbs experienced the greatest growth of elderly people.

(2) The net migration flows of elderly people have tended to reinforce a decentralized residential distribution pattern of elderly people within metropolitan areas, but have tended to counter the increased centralization of older people in metropolitan areas.

The Ability of Places to Accommodate Recent Elderly Movers

Our data do not provide information concerning the attributes of suburban and nonmetropolitan areas occupied by recent elderly movers, nor do they indicate the present economic, health, or housing status of these former movers. We can only speculate about the success of these residential adjustments. If not now, then certainly in the long-term, the quality of life experienced by these recent elderly migrants will depend on their ability to obtain access to organized health and social welfare services.[30] As these people age in their present locations, there is an increasing probability that they will require such organized supports in order to maintain independent living arrangements and to cope successfully with everyday life. This raises the question of whether the places they have selected will be able to accommodate their developing needs.

Research, planning, and social policy have focused on the elderly who live in central (or "inner") cities. It is usually this specific subgroup that are implicitly referred to when speaking of the poor, isolated, alone, less healthy, and less educated older population. However, our data have emphasized that larger numbers of older people are now living in suburbs or moving from metropolitan areas to nonmetropolitan areas. Moreover, other evidence suggests that a significant proportion of older people who occupy regular housing in older suburbs, towns, and smaller cities of metropolitan areas are facing old age as the many elderly in inner cities without sufficient resources to cope successfully with the complexities of day-to-day living.[31] The problems and needs of these people may be less visible because they are dispersed over a wider geographic area, or because positive stereotypes are held concerning the quality of life in middle-class or working-class communities. Nevertheless, for these elderly persons, the problems of growing old will be just as significant and real. Some measure of how central city and suburban elderly differ in the aggregate with respect to several population and housing indicators is found in Table 8.

It is presently unclear whether older people who live in suburbs or nonmetropolitan areas—whether recently settled or long-time residents—are

Table 8. Central City-Suburban Differences in the Population and
Housing Characteristics of Household Heads, Aged 65 and Older
in the United States, 1970

Characteristic	Urbanized areas (percent)	
	Central cities	Suburban areas
Male heads	55.1	62.3
Black	13.0	3.1
Elementary education only	59.6	54.8
Married	40.9	52.4
Widowed	43.0	40.5
Living alone	43.7	35.2
Living with roomers, lodgers	3.1	2.0
White collar occupations	44.9	47.5
Blue collar occupations	36.0	34.5
Service occupations	18.2	16.4
Presently working	19.6	22.1
Owner-occupants	53.0	70.2
Same residence over 20 years	33.9	33.5
Same residence less than 1 year	9.5	8.2
Occupying one room	4.1	1.5
Occupying units built before 1939	63.0	45.8
Occupying units, mobile homes	0.7	3.4
Occupying 50+ unit buildings	11.1	4.3
Units valued under $10,000	28.7	14.4
Units rented under $60 per month	30.4	19.3
Units lacking plumbing facilities	4.4	3.3
Annual income under $5,000	62.7	51.9
No automobile	50.9	32.0

Source: 1970 U.S. Census unpublished 1/1000 Public Use Sample. Percentages calculated by author.

experiencing difficulties in reaching services that address their functional or behavioral impairments, and the extent to which this accessibility is necessary for their well-being. An obvious question is whether the services and facilities to satisfy their needs can be found in their immediate geographic locations, or whether they must be accessed in more distant locations—perhaps only in the central city. We need to establish whether these concerns are unfounded; perhaps suburban and nonmetropolitan communities are or will be developing service systems which will address the needs of all age groups—including the elderly. Perhaps, too, the older people who have chosen to live in less service-accessible locations will have less need for the organized social welfare environment because they will be able to depend on personal or family resources to a greater degree.

NOTES AND REFERENCES

[1] Based on U.S. Bureau of the Census geographical classifications, a metropolitan area is a Standard Metropolitan Statistical Area (SMSA) consisting of a county or group of contiguous counties that contain at least one city of 50,000 or more residents or two contiguous cities which a combined population of at least 50,000. Contiguous counties are included in an SMSA if they are socially and economically integrated with the central city. The only exception to this definition occurs in New England, where boundaries of towns and cities are used instead of counties. Nonmetropolitan areas (nonSMSAs) include all population and territory outside SMSAs.

[2] In this brief overview we report only on national demographic trends. These population growth and distribution patterns will vary according to regional location and the size of urban and rural places. We also do not report on how these patterns differ according to racial (black-white) differences; see also Brian, J. L. Berry and Donald C. Dahmann, "Population Redistribution In The United States in the 1970s," *Population and Development Review*, Vol. 3, No. 4 (Dec., 1977), pp. 443–471.

[3] The component geographic parts of an SMSA are referred to as the central city and balance (or fringe). The largest city in the SMSA is designated as the central city, though additional cities of the SMSA may be included as part of the central city if they are of sufficient size. The balance of the SMSA includes all remaining territory of the SMSA. While it is often referred to as the "suburbs," it contains a wide diversity of settlement types, including substantial territory and population which are rural (farm and nonfarm), small town, and small urban in character; L. F. Schnore, *Class and Race in Cities and Suburbs* (Chicago: Markham, 1972). We will use the term "suburbs" in our analysis.

[4] U.S. Bureau of the Census, *Census of Population, General Population Characteristics*, 4 Part 5A (1950); 1, Part 1 (1960); 1, Part 1 (1970) (Washington, D.C.: Government Printing Office); Bureau of the Census, "Population Profile of the United States: 1975," *Current Population Reports*, Series P-20, No. 292 (1976).

[5] U.S. Bureau of the Census, *Census of Population, General Population Characteristics*, op. cit., note 4.

[6] C. L. Beale, *The Revival of Population Growth in Nonmetropolitan America*, Economic Research Service, ERS-605 (Washington, D.C.: Department of Agriculture, 1975).

[7] Berry and Dahmann, op. cit., note 2.

[8] See S. M. Golant, *The Residential Location and Spatial Behavior of the Elderly*, Research Paper No. 143 (Department of Geography, University of Chicago, 1972); S. M. Golant, "Residential Concentrations of the Future Elderly," *The Gerontologist*, Vol. 15 (1975), pp. 16–23; S. M. Golant, "The Housing Tenure Adjustments of the Young and the Elderly," *Urban Affairs Quarterly*, Vol. 13 (1977), pp. 95–108; S. M. Golant, "Spatial Context of Residential Moves by Elderly Persons," *International Journal of Aging and Human Development*, Vol. 8 (1978), pp. 279–289.

[9] S. Newman, *Housing Adjustments of Older People: A Report of Findings from the First Phase* (Survey Research Center, Institute for Social Research, University of Michigan, 1975); M. P. Lawton, M. Kleban and D. Carlson, "The Inner-City Resident: To Move or Not To Move," *The Gerontologist*, Vol. 4 (1973), pp. 443–448.

[10] The important exception is at the state level where a few specific states have experienced large net migration gains of elderly people, while another small group of states experienced large net migration losses (see Golant, 1978, op. cit., note 8. With few exceptions (C. Jack Tucker, "Changing Patterns of Migration Between Metropolitan and Nonmetropolitan Areas in the United States: Recent Evidence," *Demography*, Vol. 13, No. 4 (Nov., 1976), pp. 435–443; Golant, 1972, 1975, 1978, op. cit., note 8; S. Golant, G. Rudzitis, and S. Daiches, "The Migration of the Elderly From U.S. Central Cities," *Growth and Change*, Vol. 9 (October, 1978), pp. 30–35; R. F. Wiseman and M. Virden, "Spatial and Social Dimensions of Intraurban Elderly Migration," *Economic Geography*, Vol. 53 (1977), pp. 1–13), the literature that has addressed the changing intra- and inter-metropolitan residential patterns of older people has failed to analyze the contribution made by net

migration as distinct from surviving cohorts aging-in-place (see Donald O. Cowgill, "Trends in the Ecology of the Aged in American Cities, 1940-1950," *Journal of Gerontology*, Vol. 12 (Jan., 1957), pp. 75-80; "Residential Segregation by Age in American Metropolitan Areas," *Journal of Gerontology*, Vol. 33 (1978), pp. 446-453; C. Goldscheider, "Intrametropolitan Redistribution of the Older Population," *Pacific Sociological Review*, Vol. 9 (1966), pp. 79-84; J. M. Kennedy and G. F. DeJong, "Aged in Cities: Residential Segregation in 10 U.S. Central Cities," *Journal of Gerontology*, Vol. 32 (1977), pp. 97-102; B. W. Smith and J. Hiltner, "Intraurban Location of the Elderly," *Journal of Gerontology*, Vol. 30, No. 4 (July, 1975), pp. 473-478; T. L. Smith and D. G. Marshall, *Our Aging Population in the United States and Wisconsin*, Population Series No. 5, Department of Rural Sociology, University of Wisconsin, 1963).

[11] L. H. Long, "New Estimates of Migration Expectancy in the United States," *Journal of the American Statistical Association*, Vol. 68 (1973), pp. 37-43.

[12] Cf. also Golant, 1978, op. cit., note 8.

[13] U.S. Bureau of the Census, "Mobility of the Population in the United States: March, 1970 to March, 1975," *Current Population Reports*, Series P-20, No. 285 (1975).

[14] Statements regarding the reliability of the sampling estimates can be found in U.S. Census, ibid.

[15] A. Lenzer, "Mobility Patterns Among the Aged," *Gerontologist*, Vol. 5 (1965), pp. 12-15.

[16] In this chapter we will refer to all population flows as "migration" flows, recognizing that the term is sometimes reserved for only long distance moves.

[17] For comparable findings regarding the net out-migration of the elderly from central cities, see Golant et al., 1978, op. cit., note 10. Research by Tucker (op. cit., note 10) also indicated that the propensity of older people to migrate to nonmetropolitan areas increased between 1960 and 1970.

[18] U.S. Department of Commerce, Bureau of Census, *The Methods and Materials of Demography* 2, prepared by H. S. Shryock, J. S. Siegel, and Associates (Washington, D.C.: Government Printing Office, 1971), p. 656.

[19] We do not have information from these data on how the characteristics of in-migrants differ from out-migrants; this information would provide additional insight into the effectiveness of these population exchanges.

[20] Golant, 1978, op. cit., note 8.

[21] In some cases, the term "preference" may not accurately depict the moves initiated by elderly people, if in fact they are not made voluntarily. Residential adjustments may reflect "little choice" responses to accommodations which have become unsuitable for various reasons. We would expect that moves by the elderly into the households of their children and moves of shorter distances would more likely be involuntary in the above sense.

[22] S. M. Golant, "Intraurban Transportation Needs and Problems of the Elderly," in M. P. Lawton, R. J. Newcomer, and T. O. Byerts, eds., *Community Planning for an Aging Society* (Stroudsberg: Dowden, Hutchinson, & Ross, 1976), pp. 282-308.

[23] Golant, 1977, op. cit., note 8.

[24] S. M. Golant, "Locational-Environmental Perspectives on Old-Age-Segregated Residential Areas in the United States," in R. J. Johnston and D. T. Herbert, eds., *Geography and the Urban Environment*, Vol. 3 (London: John Wiley & Sons, 1979).

[25] "Hypothetically," because very little research has been conducted to ascertain the motives underlying intrametropolitan and intermetropolitan moves by older people.

[26] With respect to regional location and population size, the nonmetropolitan areas experiencing the greatest growth have been located in the West, particularly in places of more than 25,000 people; in the South, particularly in places of less than 2,500 and more than 25,000 people; and in the Northeast in places of 2,500 to 25,000 people (Berry and Dahmann, op. cit., note 2).

[27] K. C. Land, "Social Indicator Models: An Overview," in K. C. Land and S. Spilerman, eds., *Social Indicator Models* (New York: Russell Sage Foundation, 1975).

[28] See D. O. Cowgill, "The Demography of Aging in the Midwest," in A. M. Rose and W. A. Peterson, eds., *Older People and Their Social World* (Philadelphis: Davis, 1965).

[29]The exceptions will be the relatively few places with large elderly net in- or out-migration rates. See also note 10.

[30]See Stephen M. Golant and Rosemary McCaslin, "A Functional Classification of Services for Older People," *Journal of Gerontological Social Work*, Vol. 1, No. 3 (Spring, 1979); see also, Chapter 14 in this book.

[31]M. Gutowski, *Housing Related Needs of the Suburban Elderly* (Washington, D.C.: The Urban Institute, 1978).

Chapter 4

DETERMINANTS OF THE CENTRAL CITY MIGRATION PATTERNS OF OLDER PERSONS[1]

Gundars Rudzitis

A recent study has established that U.S. central cities have experienced a net out-migration of older people, but found this pattern only applied to older whites,[2] whereas there was a net in-migration of older blacks to central cities. Since little research has been carried out on the central city migration patterns of older people, we have little understanding of the factors underlying these residential shifts (see, however, Chapter 3 for preliminary speculations). However, the migration literature contains numerous theoretical discussions of the internal migration patterns of the total U.S. population.[3] It is beneficial, therefore, to review these formulations for the insights they give into the locational preferences of the elderly population. We will then propose and evaluate an empirical model of the determinants of the central city net migration rates of the white and black elderly populations.

THEORETICAL FORMULATIONS

Spatial Equilibrium Models

The family of spatial equilibrium models are derived from the land rent theories of economists.[4] The household or individual is viewed as associating with various housing locations certain utility levels or benefits. It is assumed that the household seeks to maximize its utility given the financial constraints of its budget. Since the dominant travel trip of the household is its journey to work, the model states that households trade the costs of housing consumption against the costs of making a longer journey to work; i.e., for a given workplace and bundle of housing attributes, households try to minimize their total location costs and not simply the costs of their worktrip. In less complex versions of the model, certain simplifying assumptions are introduced: (1) There is a central place of employment; (2) total transportation costs will increase the farther away from the city center the family locates; (3) the land values (price per square foot of housing or land space) are highest in the city center and decline with increased distance from it; and (4) residential densities decline with increased distance from the city center. For any pattern of intraurban residential locations to be in equilibrium, each consumer of housing will be at his optimal location when the savings he realizes in housing costs (of space and other housing attributes) by locating farther from the city center are just offset by the increased transportation costs which result from his longer journey-to-work.

How do these models apply to the older population? Muth has argued that because most members of the older population no longer work, the journey-to-work constraint is not applicable.[5] If most of the places of employment are at or near the city center, then retirement relaxes the pull to reside near the center in order to minimize travel costs (in terms of money and time costs). With these models, one would expect that older persons would move away from the city center and disperse over a wider area. The implication is that older persons will migrate out of central cities to relocate in the suburban or fringe area of the metropolitan area or move to a different place.

Stage in Life Models

Stage in life cycle models generalize about how the demand for housing and locational attributes changes as the person or family experiences certain of the following critical social events: young adulthood, marriage, childbearing, childrearing, the departure of children from the household, retirement, and widowhood.[6] These models predict that households with adequate income or savings and which are not confronted by institutional constraints (such as racial discrimination) will move from small, centrally located quarters to increasingly larger, and more suburban located housing, often in neighborhoods with proximity to good schools. The occupancy of low density, suburbanized, decentralized housing will be most characteristic of households with the highest family status (i.e., when their family size reaches a maximum). When persons age and children leave the household, married couples may sell their home and either buy a smaller house or rent an apartment closer to the center of the metropolitan area. Finally, when a spouse dies, the sharing of a household with family or relatives may be considered. Thus, the life cycle model would predict that older people will relocate closer to the city center after childrearing is completed, but possibly later join their children's households in the suburbs following the death of a spouse.

Push-Pull Models

This approach dichotomizes the forces that promote or constrain migration into "push" and "pull" factors. The migrant is seen as a person who moves in response to various external forces, which may be social, cultural, or economic in nature. The push model relates gross out-migration to the local characteristics of an area. The push factors are generally negative conditions at the point of origin that contribute to persons leaving a place. Some examples of push factors are high unemployment rates, dissatisfaction with employment, low wages, poor working conditions, dying industries, dissatisfaction with life in the present community, racial factors, or lack of adequate social and public services.

The pull factors are represented by the greater opportunities of one area relative to another. The pull model relates gross in-migration to the local characteristics of an area. Examples include better employment opportunities, family contacts, better educational facilities, or better social and public services (see Chapter 3).

Behavioral Models

The behavioral models focus on the factors underlying the decision of whether and where to seek a new residence.[7] The importance of an individual's beliefs, attitudes, and perceptions is stressed in this formulation more than in the previous models.

Behavioral models assume that persons have certain values and expectations which influence how they evaluate the attributes of their dwelling and neighborhood. A place is considered to have a level of utility that expresses a person's net satisfaction or dissatisfaction with it.[8] The place utility concept is closely related to the application of push-pull effects in that in the aggregate such factors can yield a negative or positive evaluation of a place. The individual's moving decision is viewed as dependent upon whether his place utility falls below some threshold level, whereupon migration to another place with a higher anticipated utility is predicted to occur. Such potential movers must engage in the process of information gathering and evaluation that is necessary to choose a site.[9] Consequently, the decision of an older person to migrate would be seen as a decision-making process whereby that person must search out residential alternatives which satisfy certain criteria and then compare their place utilities.

Cost-Benefit Models

A not dissimilar approach employed by economists assumes the person or household makes a "rational" decision of whether to move or not by weighing the benefits and costs of migration.[10] Each potential migrant, it is assumed, considers the present value of his existing residential site (its net advantages over his expected life) in comparison with an alternative site, along with the costs of moving. By determining which alternative results in the largest benefit or the least cost, a decision to move or stay can be made.

The individual's estimation of these costs and benefits assumes a rational decision-maker with complete and accurate information and analytical skills. Despite these difficulties, Bogue argues that this is a fruitful approach because economic and employment considerations weigh very heavily in any decision to migrate.[11] However, we know that employment considerations are not of great importance for most of the older population. What, then, would a cost-benefit approach suggest for this segment of the population? If older persons move, they have less lifetime than younger persons to derive benefits from a residential adjustment. If the discounted benefits of older persons are less than those of younger persons, then it can be hypothesized that migration will decrease with age.

Location-Specific Amenities Approach

Recently, a few researchers have argued that migration takes place as a result of change in demand for location-specific amenities.[12] It is assumed that people demand location-specific goods and facilities in the same way they demand food, clothing, or automobiles. Consequently, if there is any change in demand for these location-specific goods, it can only be satisfied by moving to appropriate places. With regard to the older population, it can be argued that aging is accompanied by predictable changes in the demand for location-specific goods. With retirement and the pursuit of leisure-oriented activities, older persons may respond by migrating to places that contain desirable site attributes.

Of various possible site-specific natural, social, and cultural amenities, climate has most consistently been empirically verified as an important determinant of migration.[13]

AN EMPIRICAL MODEL OF ELDERLY CENTRAL CITY NET MIGRATION

Model Formulation

Linear least squares regression models were constructed in order to evaluate the determinants underlying the variation in central city net migration rates (the dependent variable) of the total older population and of white and nonwhite (primarily black) older populations, treated separately. Twelve explanatory (independent) variables were selected to measure various influences on the decision to migrate, and specifically to evaluate the relative attractiveness (or unattractiveness) of central cities.

The hypothesized relationships tested in the model can be discussed briefly (see Table 9). If older persons demonstrate a propensity to migrate to smaller cities, then population size should be a variable of some significance. The social and economic differences between older and younger cities is reflected by the variable, age of the housing stock (the percentage of housing that was built prior

Table 9. Linear Least Square Regression Analysis of Central City Net Migration of Total, White, and Black Elderly Population

Independent variables	Dependent variables		
	(1) Total net migration rate	(2) White net migration rate	(3) Black net migration rate
Constant	−1.682	−.9156	−6.458
Population. Central city population size, 1970 (in 100,000s)	.00007 (.0001)	−.00003 (.0001)	−.0008 (.0008)
Over 65. Percent population 65 and older, 1970	14.00** (1.90)	21.81** (2.75)	−6.233 (10.6)
Unemployed. Unemployment rate, 1970	2.251 (3.83)	1.382 (5.56)	89.99** (33.5)
Blacks. Percent population black, 1970	−.2239* (.123)	−.0728 (.179)	.5708 (1.08)
Crime. Per capita crime rate, 1970	−.0120* (.003)	−.0245** (.005)	−.0237 (.029)
Built by 1950. Percent housing stock 20 years or older	−6.604** (.514)	−7.934** (.745)	−7.597 (4.49)
Same as 1965. Percent population living in same house, 1965–1970	3.679** (.733)	4.329** (1.11)	14.55* (6.75)
Median income, 1970 (in 1,000s)	.0262 (.052)	.0128 (.075)	.6279 (.452)
Expenditures. Per capita government expenditures, 1970	−.00004 (.0005)	−.0021** (.0007)	.0079* (.004)
Jan temp. Mean January temperature	.0231** (.006)	.0164* (.009)	.0379 (.056)
July temp. Mean July temperature	.0158* (.007)	.0143 (.010)	−.0385 (.062)
Rain. Mean annual precipitation	−.0123** (.005)	−.0049 (.007)	−.0792* (.043)
R^2	.66	.62	.12
F	44.15	35.63	2.95

Notes: Numbers in parentheses are standard errors.
  *Statistically significant at 5% level.
  **Statistically significant at 1% level.

to 1950). An indication of the population and social stability of the central city is measured by the variable, percentage of persons residing in the same house between 1965 and 1970. If, as suggested, employment is not an important consideration for older migrants, then the level of unemployment in the central city should not be a significant factor in the decision to migrate. If older persons wish to reside in cities where there is a concentration of the older population, then the percentage of the city's population that is older than 65 should be important. However, if older white persons prefer to live in racially segregated neighborhoods, then the black composition of the central city should play a role in migration decisions. Because older people frequently express their fear of living in neighborhoods with crime, distinguishing central cities according to their crime rates should be important. With retirement there is often a sharp drop in older people's incomes. Consequently, older persons should be concerned with the cost of living in the central city. There are two surrogates for living costs in this model. The first is the median income of the area. Higher income areas generally are associated with higher living costs. In fact, the argument is often made that the higher cost of living in an area results in comparatively higher wages offered to attract persons to these places. The other surrogate is per capita local government expenditures. Higher expenditures imply a higher cost of living.

The other variables in the model measure the significance of climate (a measure of a place's amenity) as a determinant of central city migration rates. The climate variables used were 30-year temperature means for the months of January and July, thereby facilitating a measure of the effects of relatively warm winters and hot summers. Similarly, central cities were differentiated according to the mean amount of precipitation they received.

The Data

For 280 central cities,[14] 1960–1970 net migration rate estimates for the white and black population aged 55 and older in 1960 were calculated based on components of population change data prepared by Oak Ridge National Laboratory.[15] The Oak Ridge data are derived from 1970 first and second count U.S. population published volumes. The net migration estimates for central cities during the 1960–1970 period were derived by the census forward survival ratio method using constant 1960 place boundaries.

While net migration estimates provide one measure of a central city's attractiveness, its limitations as a variable should be recognized. In reality there are no "net migrants" but rather groups of older people who are entering and leaving central cities. In this regard measures of in-migration and out-migration rates would have been preferable, but data limitations prevented such an analysis. The data from which the independent variables were constructed were obtained from several published sources.[16]

Results

The calculated linear least squares regression coefficients for the three net migration models (total population, whites, and blacks) are shown in Table 9. The same set of independent variables were tested in all three models. Examining the total migration model first (equation 1), it can be seen that the size of the concentration of older persons in the central city positively affects the net migration rate. As the percentage of older persons increases, the net migration into the central city increases. However, population size of the central city has no significant independent effect. As expected, the unemployment rate in the central city is not significant. Older persons tend to migrate to younger cities, as shown by the negative sign on the "built by 1950" variable. Nevertheless, although the older population migrates to younger cities, these cities have a relatively stable population, as reflected by the positive sign on the "same as 1965" variable.

Other hypothesized relationships are also important. The net migration rate of older persons is lower in central cities containing larger concentrations of black population. Older persons avoid central cities with higher crime rates. The cost of living measures are statistically insignificant in equation 1. Net migration is not statistically related to the median income or local government expenditures of a central city. However, all the climate variables are statistically significant. Older persons migrate to places that have warmer temperatures and less precipitation.

The variables in equation 1 account for 66% of the total variance, which is high degree of explanatory power for such a cross-sectional analysis.

Equation 1 grouped together both white and nonwhite migration. Focusing on the white net migration model (equation 2), there are, as expected, many similarities with equation 1, because the majority of older migrants represented in equation 1 are white. Thus, many of the same general relationships hold. The percentage older than 65, the crime rate, the percentage of houses built prior to 1950, the percentage of persons living in the same house as in 1965, and the January temperature variables have the same signs and are all significant. In addition, the local government expenditure variable displays a significant negative relationship. That is, white migrants are relocating to central cities where expenditures for various services are lower, which may indicate an area with a lower cost of living. The variables that are no longer statistically significant include "percentage of blacks" and the "July temperature." Sixty-two percent of the variance is explained by the white migration equation.

On examining the black net migration model (equation 3), it is found that the same independent variables do not successfully explain the central city migration patterns of older blacks. In contrast to equations 1 and 2, equation 3 explains only 12% of the variance. Moreover, the majority of the variables are insignificant. However, for the first time the unemployment variable has a significant positive effect on net migration. In the aggregate, older blacks migrate to areas with higher unemployment rates. Surprisingly, these areas are also cities with relatively stable populations, as shown by the positive sign on the "same house as 1965" variable. However, in contrast to white migrants, older blacks migrate to cities where government expenditures increase, indicating perhaps a greater need for public services. The only climatic variable that is significant is the amount of precipitation. Older blacks tend to migrate to areas with relatively less rainfall.

Summary and Implications

The analysis reveals that various central city characteristics are important in explaining the net migration flows of the white population, but that population size was not among them. In general, older persons migrate to newer but relatively stable cities, as measured by the amount of mobility within the central city. These cities are also occupied by higher concentrations of older persons, with relatively smaller percentages of blacks and lower crime rates. These are cities that have warmer climates, hence highlighting the importance of amenity characteristics, and they are characterized by lower expenditures on public services.

The model explaining the net migration patterns of older blacks was relatively unsuccessful, indicating a different model formulation is required. Only 3 of the 12 variables in the regression equation were statistically significant. It is evident that a different set of factors are operating to influence the net migration patterns of older blacks as opposed to older whites.

NOTES AND REFERENCES

[1] I have benefited from discussions with Stephen Golant, Philip Graves, and Oded Hochman. I am also indebted to Melissa Eisenberg and Dean Libbee for their able research assistance.

[2] S. Golant, G. Rudzitis, and S. Daiches, "The Migration of the Older Population from Central Cities in the United States," *Growth and Change*, Vol. 9 (Oct., 1978), pp. 30–35.

[3] A good summary of this research is found in M. Greenwood, "Research on Internal Migration in the United States: A Survey," *Journal of Economic Literature*, Vol. 13 (June, 1975), pp. 397–433.

[4] W. Alonso, *Location and Land Use* (Cambridge, Mass.: Harvard University Press, 1964); R. Muth, *Cities and Housing* (Chicago: University of Chicago Press, 1969); E. Millis, *Studies in the Structure of the Urban Economy* (Baltimore: John Hopkins Press, 1972).

[5] R. Muth, *Urban Economic Problems* (New York: Harper & Row, 1975).

[6] P. Salins, "Household Location Patterns in American Metropolitan Areas," *Economic Geography*, Vol. 47 (June, 1971), pp. 234–248; N. Foote, J. Abu-Lughod, M. Foley and L. Winnick, *Housing Choices and Housing Constraints* (Toronto: McGraw-Hill, 1960); A. Speare, "Home Ownership, Life Cycle Stage and Residential Mobility," *Demography*, Vol. 7 (Aug., 1970), pp. 449–465.

[7] J. Wolpert, "Behavioral Aspects of the Decision to Migrate," *Papers and Proceedings of the Regional Science Association*, Vol. 15 (1965), pp. 159–169; E. G. Moore, *Residential Mobility in the City* (Washington, D.C.: Association of American Geographers, Resource Paper No. 13, 1972); L. A. Brown and E. G. Moore, "The Intra-Urban Migration Process: A Perspective," *Geografiska Annaler*, Vol. 52 (1970), pp. 1–13.

[8] Wolpert, op. cit., note 7.

[9] J. Margolis, "Internal Migration: Measurement and Models," in A. A. Brown and E. Neuberger, eds., *Internal Migration: A Comparative Perspective* (New York: Academic Press, 1977), pp. 135–147.

[10] L. A. Sjaastad, "The Costs and Returns of Human Migration," *Journal of Political Economy*, Vol. 70 (Oct., 1962), pp. 80–93.

[11] D. J. Bogue, "A Migrants' Eye View of the Costs and Benefits of Migration to a Metropolis," in A. A. Brown and E. Neuberger, eds., *Internal Migration: A Comparative Perspective* (New York: Academic Press, 1977), pp. 167–182.

[12] P. E. Graves and P. D. Linneman, "Household Migration: Theoretical and Empirical Results," *Journal of Urban Economics* (April, 1979); P. E. Graves, "Migration and Climate," unpublished paper, 1976; "A Life-Cycle Empirical Analysis of Migration and Climate by Race," *Journal of Urban Economics* (Jan., 1979); and "Income and Migration Reconsidered," *Journal of Human Resources* (1979); S. W. Polachek and F. W. Horvath, "A Life Cycle Approach to Migration: Analysis of the Perspecacious Peregrinator," unpublished paper, 1976.

[13] R. F. Cebula and R. D. Vedder, "A Note on Migration Economic Opportunity and the Quality of Life," *Journal of Regional Science*, Vol. 13 (Aug., 1973), pp. 205–211; P. E. Graves, "A Reexamination of Migration, Economic Opportunity and the Quality of Life," *Journal of Regional Science*, Vol. 16 (April, 1976), pp. 107–112; Ben-chieh Liu, "Differential Net Migration Rates and the Quality of Life," *Review of Economic and Statistics*, Vol. 57 (Aug., 1975), pp. 329–337; E. L. Ullman, "Amenities as a Factor in Regional Growth," *Geographical Review*, Vol. 44 (Jan., 1954), pp. 119–132.

[14] The data set originally included 309 central cities. However, data unavailability for certain variables for some of the smaller central cities reduced the final total to 280 cities.

[15] P. Ritchey and B. Bishop, *The Components of Change for the Adult Population of Cities by Age, Sex, and Color*, 9 Vols. (Washington, D.C.: Government Printing Office, 1974).

[16] U.S. Bureau of the Census, *U.S. Census of Population* (Washington, D.C.: Government Printing Office, 1973); U.S. Department of Commerce, *County and City Data Book*, 1972 (Washington, D.C.: Government Printing Office, 1973); U.S. Department of Commerce, *Climatological Data, National Summary* (Asheville, N.C.: National Oceanic and Atmospheric Administration, various years).

PART II

THE ENVIRONMENTAL CONTEXT OF ELDERLY PEOPLE

INTRODUCTION TO PART II

Various social and behavioral sciences have demonstrated increased interest in researching the significance of man's multidimensional environment as a source of variation in his behavior. The environmental transactions of an individual may elicit a range of responses along several dimensions. These environments, for example, facilitate or inhibit human activities or perceptions, may be a source of need gratification or need frustration, may be a source of enjoyment and satisfaction or stress and anxiety, may socially integrate or socially isolate, or may be a source of emotional enrichment or emotional impoverishment. Underlying gerontology's particular interest in the environment is an assumption that old age is accompanied by a greater vulnerability in the face of external forces. From this perspective, the contributions in Part II have in common their attempts to better define and understand the impact that environments, which are occupied, used, and experienced by older people, have on activity or behavior and what role is being played or can be played by public policy interventions.

The first chapter (Chapter 5) serves as a valuable introduction to the various research and planning issues that can be addressed by the geographer concerned with the interaction of the physical environment with older people. Yeates argues convincingly that the manipulation of the physical environment might be the most effective way in which to satisfy various needs of older people, including their successful functioning in different social roles. So, for example, self-care needs, loneliness, access to medical care, and the need for independence may be effectively addressed by appropriate environmental strategies. Yeates categorizes the physical environment into settings that can be arrayed along a continuum according to geographic scale (for example, room, dwelling, building, neighborhood, city, and metropolis) and suggests that certain roles and needs might be better served at certain levels than at others.

In the second contribution (Chapter 6), Rowles focuses on the older person who relocates to the potentially "alien microscale environment" of the old age institution. About 20% of the U.S. population will enter long-term care institutions during their lifetime and, for this reason alone, the impact of the institutional environment on human behavior deserves investigation. The author focuses on the adjustment problems confronted by the older person entering this radically different "last new home." Rowles' specific concern is with the potentially disruptive environmental experiences of the older person. For instance, the older person must orient himself to a totally new spatial environment, with new cues, routes, boundaries, and barriers. Moreover, the institutional environment, in contrast to the older person's previous home, is one in which affective bonds do not exist and in which stimuli that can trigger memories and fantasies are absent. In light of this experiential vacuum, Rowles identifies various strategies by which to alter or manipulate the institutional environment in order to make it more congruent to the cognitive and emotional needs of the older person.

The next chapter (Chapter 7) also concerns how people feel about the place in which they live. However, Bohland and Davis focus on the urban neighborhood and the way in which its attributes contribute to people's overall residential satisfaction. Their investigation differs also in that it is not restricted to older people; rather, it deals with the way age differences influence the nature of the environmental experience. The authors report on a survey research analysis that evaluated how four environmental dimensions—safety, neighborliness, physical appearance, and convenience—contributed to a population's overall level of satisfaction with the neighborhood. On the basis of their findings, Bohland and Davis argue that after retirement there is a change in the criteria by which residents evaluate their neighborhood and that the reasons underlying responses to the neighborhood environment may be very different. One of their conclusions echoes an argument made earlier by Yeates that improvement in the living environments of older people will often benefit all age groups.

In Chapter 8, the focus shifts from the experiential environment of the older person to the concrete environmental consequences of governmental intervention in the private housing market. Mercer discusses the housing supply strategies adopted by the Canadian government and, in particular, by the province of British Columbia. Traditionally, in Canada, as in the United States, most subsidized low-rent housing for older people has been generated through new housing construction. Mercer identifies which factors have been most important in influencing where new senior citizen housing has been located and why, inevitably, certain communities are underserved. He considers the newest approach to providing low-rent housing in British Columbia, which is to grant "direct housing allowances" to older people so that they can afford already existing housing units at below-market rents. In evaluating the locational consequences of this new program, the author concludes that older tenants have greater flexibility in choosing where they can live and thus have a greater opportunity to remain in their existing (higher-rent) units or neighborhoods.

Another component of the older person's environment that is amenable to manipulation by governmental intervention is a place's transportation system. The failure of transportation facilities to adequately address the travel needs of older people is a frequently identified problem. Elderly people who suffer the most when transportation facilities are inadequate are those without cars who are living in low-density suburban or rural areas where large distances must be transversed to reach most destinations. The final two chapters in Part II focus on the strengths and weaknesses of federal and local transportation policies and strategies in urban (Chapter 9 by Rolf Schmitt) and rural areas (Chapter 10 by Douglas McKelvey). The authors consider how successful these policies have been in alleviating the transportation difficulties of older people and of the service facilities that assume responsibility for their travel needs.

Chapter 5

THE NEED FOR ENVIRONMENTAL PERSPECTIVES ON ISSUES FACING OLDER PEOPLE

Maurice Yeates

A detailed concern for the way the environment and older people interact is important for three main reasons.[1] First, the potentially deleterious effects of the environment on behavior can increase as a person ages. One obvious example of this is the weather: Inclement conditions may be a greater impediment to outdoor travel for older people than for those who are more physically active. Second, the environment is potentially easier to manipulate than other factors, such as social or psychological factors that influence the living conditions of the elderly. To continue with the example of the weather, it is possible to overcome inclement conditions by the provision of door-to-door transportation and home locations close to amenities. Third, well-designed and planned environments, although particularly necessary and beneficial for the elderly, are also of utility to those in other age groups.

THE MEANING OF ENVIRONMENT

At the outset, it is important to understand that the word "environment" can be defined widely, although in this discussion it will refer to the "physical environment," one of the five components outlined in Lawton's conceptualization of the environment as it pertains to the elderly.[2] Briefly, the five components are the individual, the interpersonal, the suprapersonal, the behavioral, and the physical environments.

71

The individual environment embraces the personality, skills, and physical capability of a person. It includes, therefore, the personal context of the way in which an individual looks at and is involved with the "world." In order to cope with the world, the older person develops "a complex of modalities—action, orientation, feeling, and fantasy," each of which have been discussed at length by Rowles[3] (see Chapter 6).

The interpersonal environment is a result of the interaction between the older person and his family and friends. For example, this component of the environment is extremely important in the common case of the older woman living with her daughter and family.[4] The way the older person is allotted space in the house (which child gives up a bedroom?), partakes in the daily chores and tasks (the daughter may ask why she is the one who has to accept responsibilities of this kind), and is accorded a place in family discussions all influence the quality of the interpersonal environment.

The suprapersonal environment involves the social characteristics of a particular situation. The atmosphere of a setting might change and, along with it, the behavior pattern of the older person. Two examples may clarify the importance of this particular component. An elderly couple may have lived in a particular neighborhood for many years and have felt comfortable with it. However, changes occur because of an influx of a different social group, which results in a different type of behavior in the streets, the stores, and the local park. Consequently, the older couple begins to distrust the environment and starts to behave in a hyperdefensive and secretive way. The second example, related by Newcomer, is institutional.[5] It concerns the addition of people from a mental hospital to a nursing home for older people. As a result, the older people may start to regard themselves as less capable and expect less of themselves.

The fourth component of environment is defined broadly as "social" because it includes the norms and rules that govern how people behave. The standards of any society, whether it be in the home, school, local government, nursing home, university, or nation, are set, to a large extent, by the framework of social mores and rules within which that society operates. Nearly all levels of society have been greatly affected by the tremendous changes in behavioral norms and rules that have occurred during the past two decades. In fact, it could be argued that the elderly have been the most affected because they have had to readjust the most frequently.

Lawton's fifth component, the physical environment, is of greatest concern in the ensuring discussion, although changes in the physical environment can affect some of the other elements of environment as well. As conceived by Lawton, the physical environment includes:

> all natural features of geography and climate that directly influence man; concrete manmade structures and objects that limit and facilitate behavior; space and distances between man and objects; and the less concrete systems of stimuli and rewards that are subsumed in the term "resources."[6]

THE ROLES AND NEEDS OF THE ELDERLY

The central argument of this chapter is that the quality of the physical environment can influence the extent to which the needs of older people can be provided for and contribute to their successful role adjustment.

It is important to recognize that the term "elderly" is not all inclusive, because it refers to a diverse population, and the level of needs and the types of roles that can be played vary enormously according to their social, psychological, and health characteristics. To illustrate, Neugarten divides the elderly into two groups, the young-old and the old-old, on the basis of physical attributes and possible lifestyles.[7] The young-old, generally those between the ages of 55 and 75, are mobile, active, ready to experiment with different types of work and leisure, and often socially gregarious. This lifestyle reflects a freedom from the responsibilities of work and families, from the worries of rapidly failing health, and from financial concerns. In contrast, the old-old, generally those older than 75, are usually subject to severe health limitations and are restricted in their range of activities.

The Roles of the Elderly

North American society does not provide or recognize a role for the elderly beyond that of engaging in perpetual leisure. Although the busy reader may find that an idyllic prospect, it was George Bernard Shaw who commented that "a perpetual holiday is a working definition of hell." The leisure role would be quite acceptable if we knew how to adapt ourselves and interact with others in a leisure situation. Unfortunately, the elderly are usually in a position of coping with role loss, and the task of preparing for a leisure situation is invariably ignored.

The elderly are required to adjust to a number of role losses during a limited time-span. Three of the most obvious of these relate to death of a spouse, departure of adult children, and retirement from paid employment. Adjustment to role losses of these types requires: (1) an environment that promotes the value of nonwork learning experiences, and (2) recognition of a transitional preretirement phase of less formal work and lengthier periods of leisure.

Examples can be provided of obvious methods for preparing for role loss and inevitable lesiure. Women, in particular, now realize that they must seek and develop a role beyond that of mother in the home. All participants in the labor force, whether male or female, recognize that nonemployment pursuits should be developed early in life and maintained throughout the employment period. However, many elderly are not in a situation of recreation but re-creation, and few re-creational interests that were not initiated in earlier years are pursued later in life and continued into retirement.[8] The tragedy is that a wide variety of learning environments are provided for the young, but similar environments designed to promote re-creation are not as readily available for the elderly.

Beyond development of a will to cope with role loss, it is also evident that the change in roles should not be so abrupt and that older people should continue in a "work" environment for as long as they feel able. With the gradual extension of the life-span, it is apparent that, by the turn of the century, the average person of 60 will have the outlook, health, and vigor of a person of 50 today; someone of 70 will be like a person of 56; and a person of 90 will be like a person of 70.[9] There is, therefore, a gradual change in attitude toward retirement, in which the preretirement phase is regarded as a period of less formal work and lengthier periods of constructive leisure. Recent legislation raising the retirement age is a recognition of this concept.

For the elderly whose work role and income have been removed artificially by forced retirement and who are becoming inactive, a most important function in life is the ability to take care of oneself. In this regard, the interesting issue concerns the type of physical environment that is most able to support self-care for as long as possible.

Environment and the Self-Care Role

The importance of the interaction between the supportive nature of elements that can be built into the physical environment and the self-care role can be illustrated by two composite examples. They involve men, in their middle 90s, whose spouses were alive and reasonably active until their deaths 10 years ago. Both men had led extremely active but quite different lives, and they had been able to remain reasonably active in a work-leisure situation until their middle 70s. The great difference was, however, in the physical environment and the different supportive services that were available in the two environments.

George has always lived in a big metropolis, and when his wife died he retained ownership of the small two-bedroom house that he and his wife had occupied for the previous 15 years. Their son and his family resided a few miles away. Community shops, a branch library, and evening classes in a local school were easily accessible via public transportation. These elements of the physical environment were utilized by both George and his wife, and new friends were cultivated (particularly young people in their 20s). George is now quite fragile and bent. His pension income and savings have been almost totally eroded by inflation, but he manages to retain his self-care role and alertness.

Perhaps he is lucky, but he is also well supported by the urban environment in which he is located. A "meals-on-wheels" program delivers one good meal each day, friends drop by to chat for about half an hour each day, a woman who is paid by a local agency comes to clean the bathroom, bedroom, and lounge (the only rooms he occupies) once a week, and a nurse's assistant visits weekly for an hour to give him a bath and check his medical supplies and condition. His son visits on Sundays and spends a few minutes taking care of the small yard. The important point is that the cleaning, nursing, and meals-on-wheels services can only be provided in a reasonably high-density urban environment where many elderly can be serviced in one neighborhood. There are also employment opportunities of many kinds available for his son and family, as well as the community shops, library, and recreational educational facilities of which he took advantage until recently.

Hans was a farmer and an extremely active member of the farming community in his county. He and his wife had three children who are now living hundreds of miles away in small towns. Hans stayed active for a long time; by renting much of his land, he managed to stay on the property and limited his farm interests to a few animals. However, after the death of his wife he began to deteriorate physically, and there were no support services available in the rural community other than local friends, who usually lived at least half a mile away. So, the family decided that Hans should move into an elderly institutional facility in the town of one of his children (see Chapter 6).

This particular nursing home is quite attractive and reasonably expensive. The lawns, trees, and shrubbery are well kept. Hans has his own room with a color television, and he brought his favorite chest of drawers. The staff of the home is pleasant and cheerful, and the meals are well planned and nutritious. Programs in crafts and so forth are available for those who are interested and who require some kind of therapeutic treatment. In this environment Hans became institutionalized rather quickly, thought of the past far more than the present, and longed to be back in his known environment. Unfortunately, his known environment was not suitable for older people who needed some outside support to maintain their self-care role (see Chapters 14 and 15).

The discussion of the situations of Hans and George is not meant to imply that big city environments are better for old-old people than are rural environments. The two cases are meant, however, to illustrate (1) the importance of role readjustment through life and (2) the necessity for highly accessible services, both direct and indirect, to support the role changes that occur. Reasonably high-density urban environments provide a more economical situation for such services, although there is no real reason (other than cost) why such services cannot be provided in rural environments. Interestingly, George survives on an annual income of $3,500, out of which he pays a nominal amount for his meals and house-cleaning services, whereas the nursing home for Hans has a minimum annual cost of $10,000.

For those interested in the impact of the physical environment on the elderly, it is, therefore, vital to understand how it can facilitate role readjustment and self-care. Some environments are more suitable than others, as the extreme examples of the low-density rural vis-a-vis the high-density urban illustrate. Nevertheless, there is a whole range of physical environments, including high-rise, low-rise, suburban low density,[10] small town, and big city areas, that have potential utilities for the elderly. Saarinen presents one framework for such an analysis in his examination of environmental perception and behavior at different geographic scales, but this needs to be reformulated in a role-playing context.[11]

The Needs of the Elderly

Although any discussion that focuses only on the needs of the elderly is somewhat limited (because other population groups have similar needs that can be examined in a more general societal context),[12] there is no doubt that in the context of public policy, the short-run problem-solving approach is politically most appropriate. Public policy requires a clear identification of the issue, of the target population to which the issue applies, and of some policy that could be implemented with a program to ameliorate the issue (see Chapter 8). Thus, it is not surprising that most studies adopt an "identification of the need" approach. This does not, however, imply that old age is regarded as a social problem, because, if it is an issue, the excellent work by Fischer indicates that it is so because it is made to be that way.[13] The areas of concern can be quite clearly identified as health and medical care, finances, loneliness, housing, and transportation. The question that arises is how can the physical environment be used to cater to these needs.

Health and medical care. A most serious concern is spatial access to medical facilities, and in this regard certain locations and population groups are at a greater disadvantage than others (see Chapters 9 and 10). A typical illustration of the unequal access that exists is the blood pressure monitoring clinic that is available free on Thursdays to the elderly in a small town. For those who can afford automobiles and are able to drive, the services of the clinic are quite accessible, but the small town does not have a bus system, and if a person cannot drive a car, the only alternatives are taxis, walking, or as passengers in the auto of friends or relatives. For example, Rosa, who tries to attend the blood pressure clinic every Thursday, states categorically that the clinic is really an "activity" for those with cars who like something to do in the afternoon. For those who do not have cars, the clinic is difficult and, in her view, more costly to attend. As a consequence, she cannot understand why a greater array of services are not provided in the same place. Currently, for a variety of medical services she must attend the county hospital, which is 10 miles away.

Finances. The financial situation is an extremely important concern for the elderly because retirement means an immediate income reduction of about 40% to 50%. A reduction of this magnitude may be bearable if there has been sufficient opportunity to save, but for most people this opportunity has not really existed, and if it has, inflation has taxed the investments. Financial independence is vital because it is coupled with personal independence and dignity; it is difficult to be independent and retain one's dignity while depending on handouts from others. That is why most old people are deeply concerned about inflation, social insurance, and medical costs.

Although it may appear that changes in the physical environment have little to do with the financial situation of the elderly, there is one way in which the interaction between the two is of deep concern. A disproportionately large segment of the elderly are located within the inner city of urban areas, and a large number of this population are poor and have physical limitations of one kind or another. It is evident, however, that improving the quality of the immediate inner city environment, for example, its safety, its housing standards, its services (drop-in day care centers, drug and alcohol rehabilitation clinics), can help alleviate the conditions of poverty without reducing the independence of the people involved.

Loneliness. Although loneliness is not confined to the elderly, the older segment of the population is certainly more prone to this condition than are others, because with age comes increasing immobility, death of a spouse, deaths of friends, physical impairment such as reduction in hearing and sight, and lack of contact with the immediate family. The various conditions leading to loneliness require sensitive consideration.[14]

The whole question of the types of housing structures and arrangements that might help to promote interaction and independence is a vital concern to those interested in the effect of the physical environment. Porteous provides some useful insights into the kinds of questions that are being asked and that need answering.[15] For instance, at the geographic scale of the urban community, is it better for the elderly to be segregated in concentrations, or more integrated by scattering homes for the elderly into all sections of the city? The most conclusive evidence tends to suggest that levels of social interaction and well-being are greater when older people live among other older people.[16]

The potential importance of environmental features found in a residential structure for the elderly is provided by the following example. This development in the oldest and poorest section of a town, consists of 50 one-bedroom and efficiency apartments. It was built with a government loan on land, owned by the municipality, that was formerly occupied by a warehouse (see Chapter 8). It is two stories high and constructed around a courtyard, but several of the units have balconies overlooking the street. The interior contains a meeting room and communal dining area for people who live in the apartments and for other elderly in the neighborhood to use during the day.

In this situation, older persons can take advantage of the privacy of their apartments, yet interact with neighbors in the activities offered in the meeting area or the dining room where one meal (at minimal cost) is provided daily. The apartment building is well situated with respect to shopping facilities, and buses to the downtown area and suburban facilities stop either at the main door of the apartment or within a block.

The people indicate a high level of satisfaction and particularly appreciate the option to participate in the activities and trips, which are organized by a committee of the elderly involved with the help of a social worker "activator" when necessary. The older people also enjoy watching the street activity from their rooms or balconies (see Chapter 7).

It is difficult not to compare this particular project favorably with others, privately financed, in middle-income and upper-income parts of the same city. These have a similar number of apartments, but there are no common meeting areas other than the manicured lawns. They are not well served by public transportation and the people renting the units must drive to visit shopping facilities. Of course, it can be justifiably argued that the former is heavily subsidized, whereas the latter is not. However, that does not detract from the fact that careful consideration of the need for privacy, the need for interaction with other people, and the daily routine of the local environment were considered extensively in the case of the former. In many privately developed units, there seems to have been little consideration of the impact of the environment on possible levels of integration and hence reduction of loneliness.

Housing. Housing is of crucial importance because (1) the housing needs of the elderly change along with their levels of personal competence, and (2) it is the most fundamental symbol of independence. In addition to cost, location, and safety features of the housing environment, already referred to in this chapter, there are also a number of design features that must be incorporated to allow people to operate within their homes even though they are disabled. These design features include, for example, ramps or elevators rather than stairs, cupboards placed at a reachable level, sinks that can be used in a sitting position, bathrooms with plenty of handles, and heating or cooling systems that can be self-regulated.

Transportation. In many studies concerning the needs of the elderly, the quality of the transportation environment is considered of central importance.[17] In the urban environment where a majority of facilities and services appear to be located on the assumption of universal automobile use, a large proportion of the elderly are disadvantaged either because they cannot afford or cannot physically operate an automobile. Bell and Olsen provide some useful estimates of the extent of the problem with survey data from Florida.[18] Whereas 89% of the eligible population of driving age in Florida are licensed to drive, only 52% of those between the ages of 65 and 75 and 39% over the age of 75 were licensed to drive an automobile. Consequently, some form of public or private transit is required and rightfully must be regarded as part of the social delivery system if people are to be linked effectively to essential destinations. It follows, therefore, that a transit system must be client oriented rather than designed to provide maximum coverage regardless of whether certain areas really need the system. The transportation environment and the location of the elderly vis-a-vis a variety of transport modes are, therefore, vital areas of inquiry (see Chapters 9 and 10).

CONCLUSION

There is a distinct need for research that investigates and for planning that takes into account the interaction between the physical environment and the older population. We have referred to a number of different environmental scales, such as personal space, buildings, neighborhoods, cities, and rural areas, their locational and physical attributes, and their relationship to the roles and needs of older people.

The physical environment can be arrayed along a continuum according to geographic scale, and it can be assumed that certain roles and needs of the elderly can be addressed most appropriately at certain of these levels. These are indicated in Figure 7 by shaded cells. For example, it is postulated that research and planning involving housing and self-care are most appropriately addressed at the scale of personal space. The other shaded cells in the housing column indicate that the location of residential units within neighborhoods and cities is also an area for concern. The paucity of shaded cells in the "finances" column is not meant to imply that the issue is unimportant, because the opposite is true. However, there are few cases in which interest in the physical environment

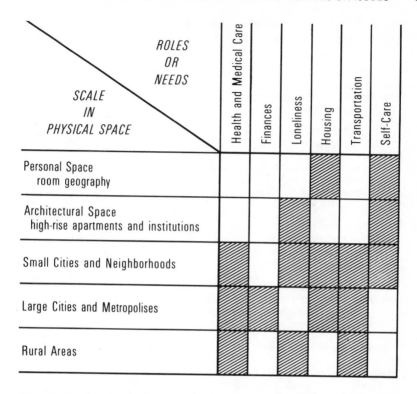

Fig. 7. Areas requiring research and planning analyses for better understanding of the interaction of the elderly population with its physical environment.

intersects with this general problem, the only obvious case concerning the previous example of the inner-city poor.

For those interested in the interaction between the physical environment and the elderly, Figure 7 should suggest several of the areas that should be addressed by researchers and planners in the hope of improving the older population's quality of life.

NOTES AND REFERENCES

[1] T. O. Byerts, "Symposium: The City—A Viable Environment for the Elderly, Phase 1, Background," *The Gerontologist*, Vol. 16 (1975), pp. 13–14.

[2] M. P. Lawton, "Planning Environments for the Elderly," *Journal of the American Institute of Planners*, Vol. 36 (1970), pp. 124–129.

[3] G. Rowles, *Prisoners of Space? Exploring the Geographical Experience of Older People* (Boulder, Co.: Westview Press, 1978).

[4]S. Newman, *Housing Adjustments of Older People: A Report of Findings From the Second Phase* (Ann Arbor, Mich.: Institute for Social Research, University of Michigan, 1976).

[5]R. Newcomer, "Environmental Influences on the Older Person," in R. H. Davis, ed., *Aging: Prospects and Issues*, (Los Angeles: E. P. Andrus Gerontology Center, University of Southern California, 1976).

[6]Lawton, op. cit., note 2, p. 124.

[7]B. Neugarten, "The Future and the Young-Old," *The Gerontologist*, Vol. 15 (1975), pp. 4–9.

[8]D. Gray, "This Alien Thing Called Leisure," in V. L. Boyack, ed., *Time on Our Hands: The Problem of Leisure* (Los Angeles: E. P. Andrus Gerontology Center, University of Southern California, 1973).

[9]B. Strehler, "Ten Myths About Aging," *The Center Magazine*, Vol. 3 (1970), pp. 41–48.

[10]R. F. Wiseman and M. Virden, "Spatial and Social Dimensions of Intraurban Elderly Migration," *Economic Geography*, Vol. 53 (1977), pp. 1–13.

[11]T. F. Saarinen, *Environmental Planning: Perception and Behavior* (Boston: Houghton Mifflin, 1976).

[12]A. Williams, "Measuring the Quality of Life of the Elderly," in L. Wingo and A. Evans, *Public Economics and the Quality of Life* (Washington, D.C.: Research for the Future, 1977), pp. 282–297.

[13]D. H. Fischer, *Growing Old in America* (New York: Oxford University Press, 1978).

[14]M. J. Lowenthal, "Psychosocial Variations Across the Adult Life Course: Frontiers for Research and Policy," *The Gerontologist*, Vol. 15 (1975), pp. 6–12.

[15]J. D. Porteous, *Environment and Behavior* (Don Mills, Ontario: Addison-Wesley, 1977).

[16]I. Rosow, *Social Integration of the Aged* (New York: Free Press, 1967). For a detailed discussion of the positive and negative functions of age-segregated places, see S. Golant, "Locational-Environmental Perspectives on Old-Age Segregated Residential Areas in the United States," in R. J. Johnston and D. T. Herbert, eds., *Geography and the Urban Environment*, Vol. 3 (London: John Wiley & Sons, 1979).

[17]S. Golant, "Intraurban Transportation Needs and Problems of the Elderly," in M. P. Lawton et al., eds., *Community Planning for an Aging Society* (Stroudsburg, Pa.: Dowden, Hutchinson & Ross, 1976).

[18]W. G. Bell and W. T. Olsen, "An Overview of Public Transportation and the Elderly: New Directions for Social Policy," *The Gerontologist*, Vol. 14 (1974), pp. 324–330.

Chapter 6

THE LAST NEW HOME: FACILITATING THE OLDER PERSON'S ADJUSTMENT TO INSTITUTIONAL SPACE

Graham D. Rowles[1]

In spite of a recent wave of concern with providing alternatives to institutional care, a large number of older people must live in long-term care facilities.[2] Although less than 5% of the elderly population (older than 65) presently resides in institutions, almost 20% live in such a setting at some time during their lifetime.[3] Many residents of long-term care facilities are very old, and many spend their final days in this environment.[4] For most, the move to such a setting symbolizes removal from the community into a kind of limbo preceding death. Dread of entering this last new home is not unwarranted. Numerous studies have documented increased mortality and morbidity rates, particularly during the first 3 months after institutionalization.[5] In addition, a substantial portion of the literature identifies experiential correlates of the process: severance from familiar social roles and personal relationships; the trauma of adapting to an "institutional" milieu characterized by loss of personal identity; and the forfeiture of control over one's life.[6]

Concern with social and psychological issues sometimes obscures the fact that institutionalization is also a geographical problem. It represents a *spatial relocation*. More important, it is a life event requiring an environmentally vulnerable individual to develop a totally *new mode of being* within space. Adjustment from a macro "outside" environment to a micro "inside" space (sometimes no more than a single room) implies a radical reorientation of geographical experience, defined here as "the individual's involvement within the spaces and places of his life."[7] Gerontologists are increasingly aware of the role of geographical considerations in facilitating institutional adjustment. Indeed,

Gubrium's study of "Murray Manor" nursing home commences with a "topophiliac's" discussion of "The Meaning of Place."[8]

This chapter provides a context for geographical inquiry by isolating major dimensions of the older person's changing geographical experience as he accommodates to his last new home. A conceptual framework developed from research on elderly in the community facilitates an interpretation of the experiential environment of a 99-bed, long-term care facility in West Virginia.

TRANSFORMATION IN THE QUALITY OF GEOGRAPHICAL EXPERIENCE

I have argued elsewhere that the older person's geographical experience in the community involves a complex of modalities—action, orientation, feeling, and fantasy—that together provide a holistic expression of the individual's "being" within a dynamic transactional person-lifespace system (Fig. 8).[9] The precise manifestation of this "being" in each case expresses an adjustment consonant

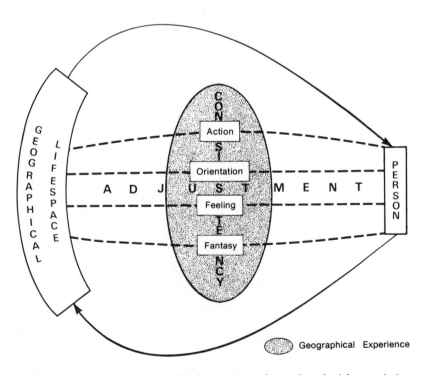

Fig. 8. A model of geographical experience (reproduced with permission of Westview Press).

with the individual's physical and psychological capabilities and unique life history. The move to an institution, frequently following a stressful period of hospitalization, usually entails disruption of this generally accepted pattern and substitution of an alien micro-scale environment for a familiar neighborhood context. What does this mean in terms of the older person's geographical experience?

On the most basic level, adjustments must be made in the individual's pattern of *action*. In the community, sequences of movement at scales ranging from locomotion within the proximate environment (moving around a room) through patterns of everyday activity (the journey to the store), to the occasional long-distance vacation trip, provide a regular time/space rhythm of characteristic paths. The older person is able to accommodate to changing personal capability through a variety of incremental adjustments extending from a gradual reduction of the distance traveled during a daily stroll to increasing reliance on family and friends to make "surrogate" trips.

Such gradual adaptation is not feasible during the move to an institution. A new imposed routine of movement (breakfast is at 7 A.M., the beds are made at 9 A.M.) must be immediately adopted in a setting where the arrangement of furniture and other physical obstacles are not intimately known. Adjustment must also be made to the reduced scale of the potential action space.

Over time, a pattern of *action in microcosm* may develop comparable to that formerly sustained within the community. As Gubrium observes: "For many patients leaving their rooms and going 'outside' (the equivalent of the everyday trip) means walking or wheeling down the hallway and sitting in the dining room or lounges."[10] In the facility studied, going to church down the hall or to the activities room is referred to by one resident as a journey "down the street." The process is extended in the transformation of the occasional vacation trip into the no less eagerly anticipated "stepping out" of the institution to spend Christmas or a weekend with family or friends.

Actions are framed in relation to the individual's spatial orientation—a cognitive differentiation of space involving mental schemata. In the community, schemata provide both an intimate awareness of familiar routes (specific schemata) and a cognitive differentiation of space into an aureole of experientially distinct and generally less defined zones away from home (a general schema) (Fig. 9).[11] Advancing age and reduced perceptual competence result in increasing emphasis on habitual response and selective attention to particular environmental cues in negotiating familiar routes.[12] As more time is spent at home, nearby zones of space, particularly the surveillance zone (the area that may be seen from the window), gradually assume greater significance in the older person's perception of the known environment.[13]

Relocation to an institution requires developing a new sense of orientation. In journeying down the corridor, a new set of orienting cues must be identified, a process often made difficult by the uniformity of the architectural and interior design of institutions. Zonal differentiation of space around the home is replaced by the differentiation of institutional space into a number of fragmented cognitive realms that focus on the individual's room.[14] Some areas are known to

SPECIFIC SCHEMATA

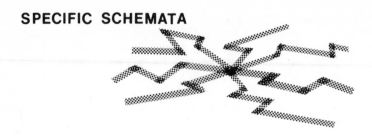

GENERAL SCHEMA

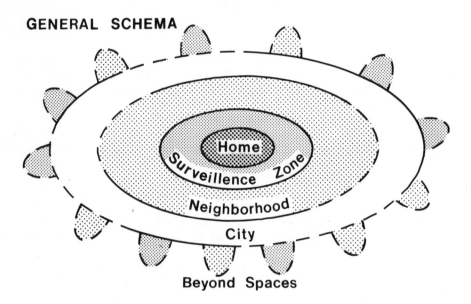

Fig. 9. Dimensions of orientation (reproduced with permission of Westview Press).

be the domain of institutional staff, some are the preserve of the opposite sex, and other places are construed as public spaces. A temporal variability pervades many of these cognitive designations because of the multiple use of spaces. Thus, the television room is also known as the locus of meetings and parties and several times a week its use as a chapel transforms it into sacred space.

The perceived landscape is further complicated by the development of multiple surveillance zones (Fig. 10). On one level, the surveillance zone comprises the area outside the institution that may be monitored from the lobby or entrance hall or from the older person's window. However, consonant with

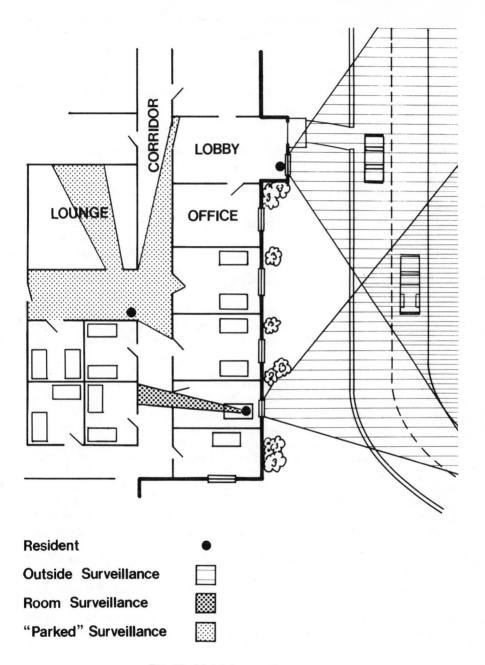

Fig. 10. Multiple surveillance zones.

the notion of action in microcosm, similar zones of visual control may develop internally. The area of the corridor and perhaps the nurses station that can be viewed from the older person's room, and the space around the area where he is "parked" during the day, assume considerable significance as cognitive spaces.

A third modality of geographical experience is *feeling*, the affective meaning with which place is imbued. In the community, feelings for place reflect the accumulation of layer upon layer of experience. The essence of such affective identification lies in the selective integration of the memory of key events that transpired within the space. Over time, place becomes imbued with a reservoir of affective meanings reflecting an experiential biography. Developing an equivalent depth of feeling—both temporal and emotional—within the semipublic space of the institution may be one of the most difficult experiential tasks in adjusting to life within a long-term care facility. Yet, people in institutional spaces do make them meaningful.

On the level of uniquely personal feeling, the ambulatory resident often develops affinity for certain frequently used locations. A chair by the window, a favorite alcove in the lobby from which activities outside may be observed, or a corner of the activity room may come to be known as "Bertha's" place.

In the community, acknowledgement of feeling for "possessed" space is implicit in both legal rights and societal norms prescribing places (for example, one's home) to which the individual may legitimately retreat without expectation of invasion. In the long-term care facility, the notion of "home" and associated expectations of privacy are much more ambiguously defined. Extending the experience in microcosm theme, can the inner sanctum of the person's room, often already violated by enforced coresidence and constantly vulnerable to encroachment by staff, ever become his or her home?

In the community, shared feelings for place evolve through the ongoing interaction of individuals who share residence in a neighborhood and hence infuse it with an array of socially defined meanings that reflect the social order.[15] In the institution, a comparable social order develops in microcosm that is also translated into feeling for place. Cliques often emerge among mobile residents who commandeer a lounge, an activity area, or the lobby during segments of the day and through their presence instill in it a distinct "aura."

A final extremely important modality of geographical experience is *fantasy*—vicarious immersion in displaced environments. The older community resident, even if subject to progressive locational limitation, may range far afield in the realms of imagination. The older person may venture back through time; through reminiscence he can participate in the events of his past.[16] As remembrance of event implies remembrance of place, this process encourages involvement in the locations of his past.[17] He can also vicariously traverse space and become immersed in the spatially displaced contemporary worlds of his children living one or several thousand miles away.[18] This propensity to live through the lives of children who become the embodiment of cherished values and traditions enhances a sense of generational continuity and ongoing participation in life.

Relocation to an institution cannot, in itself, reduce the potential for geographical fantasy. Indeed, one might hypothesize an increased propensity for vicarious involvement in space beyond the institution as a coping or adaptive strategy. However, because of separation from familiar physical and social cues that seem to be important stimuli to fantasy, such activity may be unwittingly discouraged. Lack of opportunity to transport important cues, such as family photographs and important personal artifacts to the institution,[19] progressive isolation from contact with family and friends who constitute living cues,[20] and institutional policies, including some "reality therapy" programs that effectively discourage fantasy, all serve to accentuate the severance of the individual from the spaces and places of his life.

Considered independently, the four modalities of geographical experience indicate a diverse array of necessary accommodations in adjusting to the last new home. In concert, they suggest the magnitude of a total transformation in the experience of space. Stresses result from the process of adapting a mode of being within community space, in which the modalities are integrated within a coherent whole, to a new environment where *physical relocation is abrupt but psychological relocation is much slower.* Indeed, the sharpness of physical displacement is deceptive. It suggests that the process of institutionalization involves the exchange of one spatial world for another. Instead, the evidence from my field observation indicates that the older person develops a more ambiguous *dualistic form of being in space* in which vestiges of involvement within a physically abandoned outside milieu are juxtaposed with a new spatial world in microcosm established within the institution. Simultaneous habitation of two worlds creates a composite form of geographical experience in which elements of both find expression.

During years of institutional residence, as formal separation from the physical context of "outside" becomes more irrevocable, emphasis may gradually shift to almost total involvement within the spatial world of the institution.[21] However, the transition is made grudgingly,[22] as evidenced by strenuous efforts to maintain both direct and indirect linkage with the outside. For instance, a number of residents of the institution steadfastly maintained ownership of their previous houses even when the property was left vacant and deteriorating and long after it had become apparent that physical return to this residence was impossible. They were eager to talk about their previous lives, the neighborhood they had left, and the activities of their children, relatives and friends. A visitor, a letter, a telephone call all seemed to provide crucial reassurance of a continuing link with physically abandoned spaces.

FACILITATION

What are the implications of these observations on geographical experience with regard to easing the traumas of institutionalization and improving the quality of institutional life? In the absence of detailed empirical substantiation of the observed themes, suggestions are necessarily speculative. However, it would appear that an approach to intervention focusing upon two general themes expressing complementary poles of a continuum would greatly facilitate adjustment to institutional space. On one end of the continuum are efforts oriented toward facilitating the older person's *construction* of a comfortable mode of being or spatial identity within institutional space. Such strategies may be particularly important during the traumatic initial months of residence. At the other extreme are approaches emphasizing a theme of *continuity* in which the importance of continuing links to the places of the past and the contemporary world outside the institution is acknowledged. A fundamental assumption of such strategies is that older people are neither able nor willing to separate themselves from their history. Inasmuch as the last new home can provide a context in which the continuity of the individual's geographical experience is maintained, it can become a supportive environment. Three sets of specific strategies may be summarized within the rubric of the proposed continuum: support through design, provision of a supportive social context, and emphasis upon institutional permeability.

Facilitation Through Environment Design

Supportive environmental design has long been acknowledged both in the gerontological literature and in practice as an important aid in adjusting to institutional space.[23] Table 10 lists some aspects of design that facilitate the construction of a comfortable pattern of geographical experience.

Action can be encouraged by a design that minimizes distances between important nodes within the institution and by the strategic placement of alcoves that provide a place to step out of the main flow of bustling corridor activity—to sit down and rest. Clear labeling of corridors, especially cul de sacs, can aid in conserving energy. Nonslip floors, handrails, and ramps rather than stairs (which may appear as slopes to an individual with failing eyesight) can also be important aids to movement. However, it is important to acknowledge an inevitable tension between providing a supportive prosthetic environment and one that further reduces the functional capabilities of older people by "infantilizing" them and increasing their environmental dependency.[24]

Developing a sense of spatial orientation can also be facilitated through design. Prudent placement of lighting, color differentiation of walls and floors, and the deliberate positioning of orienting cues (a vase of flowers or statuette to differentiate otherwise similar visual spaces) are options. In addition, the tactile differentiation of surface helps in the negotiation of institutional space. Careful placement of beds and chairs facilitates the development of surveillance zones by maximizing visual access to active scenes both within and outside the institution. There are other design implications. How often has a window ledge 6 inches too high prevented a person from seeing outside?

Design-related strategies can also foster feeling for place. Personalized nameplates on doors provide a sense of identification with "home" territory. Such identification is further enhanced by allowing residents to decide on the decoration of their rooms and by encouraging them to use their own furniture. Provision of personal lockers can provide the older person with at least a symbol

Table 10. Facilitating the Construction of Geographical Experience
Through Design

Action

1. Distance minimizing spatial design
2. Provision of nonslip floors
3. Ramps rather than stairs
4. Handrails
5. Resting alcoves

Orientation

1. Visual clarity
   a. Prudent location of lighting
   b. Color differentiation of surfaces
   c. Provision of visual landmarks
2. Tactile cues
3. Bed and chair location for:
   a. Surveillance of internal space
   b. Surveillance of external space

Feeling

1. Providing identity
   a. Nameplates on doors
   b. Encouraging own furniture and artifacts
   c. Encouraging own design
2. Providing privacy
   a. Private lockers
   b. Space for privacy (still allows observation)
   c. Screens
3. Sociopetal placement of furniture

Fantasy

1. Shelves and wall space for memorabilia providing important physical cues for vicarious participation in displaced environments.

of inviolable space, allowing him an expression of privacy. On the level of shared feelings for space, a sense of privacy and hence identification can also be encouraged by a design that provides open space where residents can converse without the possibility of being overheard. The physical frailty of institutionalized elderly populations generally precludes providing private space to which staff is denied physical access. Using space as a mechanism for allowing privacy overcomes this problem because the possibilities for visual monitoring by staff ensure that help can be quickly on hand in the event that an individual collapses. Finally, it is now widely acknowledged that sociopetal arrangement of furniture in lounges and hallways encourages conversation and the development of socially defined areas of meaningful space for various subpopulations within the institution.[25]

With regard to the fourth modality of geographical experience, fantasy, the potential for supportive intervention through design seems limited to the provision of sufficient shelf and wall space for the display of photographs and other memorabilia that provide such important cues for this activity. In this domain, however, a second set of strategies become far more important.

Facilitation Through a Supportive Social Context

Accommodation to the physical setting of an institution may be fairly rapid once the initial trauma of movement is overcome. However, adjustment to the space of the last new home is as much a function of the social milieu as of the physical setting. For the older person, the task involves both the construction of a social world in microcosm through integration within the existing social/spatial order of the institution and the maintenance of viable involvement within a former community social space. The challenge is to provide support that will sustain such dualistic involvement. Three possibilities are worth noting.

The first pertains to staff conduct. Educating the staff as to the novel aspects of the older person's geographical experience—ranging from differing conceptions of interpersonal distance to the role of geographical fantasy[26]—would heighten sensitivity to the specific accommodations the new resident is making in adjusting to institutional space. Such efforts could be extended to providing new staff members with information on the specific social spatial order of the setting, a process that at present seems to evolve on an informal trial and error basis. Options here range from reminders to honor obvious human courtesies of not violating "possessed" spaces (in the long-term facility studied there is a large sign in the main hallway urging staff and visitors to "Please Knock before Entering Rooms—Residents Need Privacy Too") to explicit consideration of established social/spatial cliques in the day-to-day operation of the institution and in intrainstitutional relocation decisions.[27]

A second possibility involves preparing the older person for the transition from one mode of being in space to another more ambivalent one. Recent research indicates that much of the stress of institutionalization lies in the trauma of "anticipation" once the decision to enter a long-term care facility has been made.[28] Many people display the negative symptoms of institutionalization prior to the actual relocation. Programs to lessen both the actual and perceived abruptness of severance from existing social and physical worlds and immersion within alien ones might include a series of introductory visits, together with educational and counseling services preparing the older person for the inevitable spatial adjustments.[29] Overall, such strategies emphasize an ethos of continuity rather than exchange.

A final facet of social support is largely implicit and pertains to the location of the institution. Older people favor movement to an institution close to their community residence. Community location makes it easier for family and friends to visit and increases the options for continued participation either directly through trips outside or indirectly through surveillance of a familiar street. In addition, a community location and clientele may allow the reconvening of elderly populations who have lived within a common neighborhood within the walls of the institution. I have observed this phenomenon in a long-term care facility located in a small town in Massachusetts. Some relationships within this institution reflected a continuation of patterns established in the community. Moreover, the strong community ties of the institution and the "cultural continuity" provided by its local staff ensured a lengthy waiting list and an informal "booking" of places within the home among community members anticipating their own future institutionalization.[30] Support during the process of institutionalization emanated from a sense of continuing involvement within a familiar outside space, of which the institution was but an extension.

Facilitation Through Institutional Permeability

Acknowledging that the process of institutionalization involves more than the exchange of one spatial world for another suggests the value of strategies that maintain a sense of continuity by fostering institutional permeability. Excursions ranging from "stepping out" for a weekend with relatives, or a trip to a local fair, to the weekly visit that Eleanor (a 12-year resident of the institution I visited) took to her church can be complemented by visits from relatives and friends. Such visits provide cues that stimulate a continuing sense of involvement with a community. Exchange of letters and telephone calls provide a less direct form of continuing involvement with physically abandoned space, but it is one that is highly valued, as any visitor who has been assailed by an excited resident eager to share the latest news from outside will attest. Increasing such permeability may require no more than an informal program to encourage the exchange of letters and telephone calls between volunteers from the older person's former neighborhood and the institutionalized individual—a kind of institutional pen pal system.

Increasing institutional permeability may assume more subtle forms. Indulgence in geographical fantasy is extremely frequent among the institutionalized individuals with whom I have conversed. Talking of the world outside, whether it be the distant environments of children or the neighborhood left behind, facilitates a continuing sense of involvement within these spaces; it seems to provide a form of compensation for physical separation. The significance of this activity should be recognized. Staff and visitors, not necessarily professionals, can be particularly important cues in legitimizing such reverie insofar as they can become sensitive and open to the importance of vicarious immersion in displaced worlds as an adaptive strategy. Some might argue that such a policy increases moroseness through harping on space left behind. However, though the spaces of the past may be physically abandoned, the accumulated ~baggage of one's personal history is never erased. Residents indulge in geographical fantasy anyway; surely this propensity can be acknowledged and utilized as a source of life enrichment.

CONCLUSION

This chapter has argued that movement from the community to a long-term care facility entails a transformation of the older person's geographical experience having important implications for facilitating institutional adjustment. However, the discussion has been developed solely from the client's perspective. It has been strongly oriented toward consideration of more "competent" individuals during the early phases of their residence. Many long-term care facility residents are not mobile (even on a micro scale). Indeed, they are often very sick and oblivious to subtleties of environmental design and the social/spatial order of the milieu. The grim reality of institutional existence is that often little more than the provision of competent and sanitary custodial care is involved in maintaining a quality of life realizing these persons' maximum potential. Moreover, it is necessary to reconcile residents' needs with the legitimate requirements and limitations of the staff and with constraints of institutional management. However, there is a danger that acknowledgement of these operational constraints may lapse into lack of concern with less obvious experiential issues affecting the quality of institutional life. Insensitivity to the older person's changing geographical experience provides an important example. Yet, given the magnitude of our own ignorance in this area, we can hardly blame institutions for their failure to recognize the spatial needs of their clients and the problems they face in accommodating to institutional space.

NOTES AND REFERENCES

[1] Thanks are due to John Lozier and Nancy Lohmann for their comments on a draft of this essay.

[2] There is some confusion within the literature over the appropriate definition of a "long-term care facility." In this essay, a "long-term care facility" is defined as an institutional facility under voluntary, governmental, or proprietary auspices, including sectarian homes for the aged, county homes, and proprietary nursing homes, that provides either a permanent or a temporary place of residence for individuals whose functional capabilities are chronically impaired. Cf. E. M. Brody, *Long Term Care of Older People* (New York: Human Sciences Press, 1977), p. 14.

[3] R. Kastenbaum and S. Candy, "The Four Percent Fallacy: A Methodological and Empirical Critique of Extended Care Facility Program Statistics," *Aging and Human Development*, Vol. 4 (1973), pp. 15–21.

[4] There is a great variation in statistics on this subject, ranging from studies indicating an 87% death rate to more conservative figures suggesting a 50% mortality rate. Cf. U.S. Senate, Subcommittee on Long Term Care, *Nursing Home Care in the United States: Failure in Public Policy* (Washington, D.C.: Government Printing Office, 1974), pp. 16–17.

[5] A plethora of studies have investigated mortality and morbidity rates after institutionalization. Although most of these studies record increasing death and morbidity rates, there is a growing ambivalence concerning this issue as a result of inquiries that have failed to substantiate the relationship. A continuing controversy exists within the field of gerontology on this subject. For comprehensive reviews, see M. P. Lawton and L. Nahemow, "Ecology and the Aging Process," in C. Eisdorfer and M. P. Lawton, eds., *Psychology of Adult Development and Aging* (Washington, D.C.: American Psychological Association, 1973); S. S. Tobin and M. A. Lieberman, *Last Home for the Aged* (San Francisco: Jossey-Bass, 1976), pp. 1–24.

[6] E. Goffman, *Asylums* (New York: Anchor, 1961), pp. 3–124; M. A. Lieberman, "Institutionalization of the Aged: Effects on Behavior," *Journal of Gerontology*, Vol. 24 (1969), pp. 330–340.

[7] G. D. Rowles, *Prisoners of Space? Exploring the Geographical Experience of Older People*, (Boulder, Co.: Westview, 1978), p. xviii.

[8] J. F. Gubrium, *Living and Dying at Murray Manor* (New York: St. Martins, 1975).

[9] Rowles, op. cit., note 7.

[10] Gubrium, op. cit., note 8, p. 29.

[11] The individual also possesses what may be called a personal schema that furnishes psychobiological orientation allowing him to maintain his balance and to distinguish horizontal from vertical, back from front, left from right, and up from down. As such orientation appears to be largely independent of the particular environmental context, it is not considered in this essay.

[12] Rowles, op. cit., note 7, p. 197; Lawton and Nahemow, op. cit., note 5, pp. 630–635.

[13] J. Jacobs, *The Death and Life of Great American Cities* (New York: Vintage, 1961); Rowles, op. cit., note 7, pp. 167–169.

[14] Although I have been unable to gain any strong supportive evidence as yet, it seems reasonable to hypothesize that, as length of residence within the institution increases, awareness of space beyond the walls of the facility becomes the cognition of a progressively less differentiated "outside." Buildings and environments that may no longer exist may be fused within a historically defined schema. For discussion of this "after image" phenomenon, cf. J. D. Porteous, "Design with People: The Quality of the Urban Environment," *Environment and Behavior*, Vol. 3 (1971), pp. 155–78.

[15] G. D. Suttles, *The Social Order of the Slum* (Chicago: University of Chicago Press, 1968); A Buttimer, "Social Space in Interdisciplinary Perspective," *Geographical Review*, Vol. 59 (1969), pp. 417–26.

[16] R. N. Butler, "The Life Review: An Interpretation of Reminiscence in the Aged," *Psychiatry*, Vol. 26 (1963), pp. 65–76; A. W. McMahon and P. J. Rhudick, "Reminiscing in the Aged: An Adaptational Response," in S. Levin and R. J. Kahana, eds., *Psychodynamic Studies on Aging: Creativity, Reminiscence and Dying* (New York: International Universities Press, 1967).

[17] Rowles, op. cit., note 7, pp. 181–183.

[18] A. R. Hochschild, *The Unexpected Community* (Englewood Cliffs, N.J.: Prentice-Hall, 1973), pp. 88–111; Rowles, op. cit., note 7, p. 183; Tobin and Lieberman, op. cit., note 5, p. 145.

[19] E. Sherman and E. S. Newman, *The Meaning of Cherished Personal Possessions for the Elderly* (Albany, N.Y.: Institute of Gerontology, School of Social Welfare, State University of New York, 1976).

[20] D. B. Miller and S. Beer, "Patterns of Friendship Among Patients in a Nursing Home Setting," *The Gerontologist*, Vol. 17 (1977), pp. 269–75.

[21] This changing emphasis seems to parallel the changing health status of the individual. It may be reflected in a social differentiation within the institution between "residents" who are often relatively mobile, maintain their faculties, and sustain continuing participation in the world beyond the institution and "patients" who are far more sickly and generally have fewer and weaker ties to the world beyond the facility. The distinction is often reflected in physical separation of institutional subpopulations according to the levels of care they require. Cf. Gubrium, op. cit., note 8, pp. 5–6.

[22] The grudging abandonment of one milieu for another is, of course, consonant with observations of researchers who have noted the reluctance of individuals to physically, socially, or psychologically abandon familiar spaces after relocation due to urban renewal. Cf. A. Buttimer, "Social Space and the Planning of Residential Areas," *Environment and Behavior*, Vol. 4 (1972), pp. 279–318; M. Fried, "Grieving for a Lost Home," in L. J. Duhl, ed., *The Urban Condition* (New York: Basic, 1963).

[23] A. J. Koncelik, *Designing the Open Nursing Home* (Stroudsburg, Pa.: Dowden, Hutchinson & Ross, 1976); R. J. Maxwell, J. E. Bader and W. H. Watson, "Territory and Self in Geriatric Setting," *The Gerontologist*, Vol. 12 (1972), pp. 413–417; D. K. Trites, F.

D. Galbraith, M. Sturdavant, and J. F. Leckwart, "Influence of Nursing Unit Design on Activities and Subjective Feelings of Nursing Personnel," *Environment and Behavior*, Vol. 2 (1970), pp. 303–334; and A. N. Schwartz, "Planning Micro-Environments for the Aged," in D. S. Woodruff and J. E. Birren, eds., *Aging: Scientific Perspectives and Social Issues* (New York: Van Nostrand, 1975).

[24] Schwartz, ibid., p. 291.

[25] R. Sommer, "Personal Space: The Behavioral Basis of Design," (Englewood Cliffs, N.J.: Prentice-Hall, 1969); A. Lipman and R. Slater, "Status and Spatial Appropriation in Eight Homes for Old People," *The Gerontologist*, Vol. 27 (1977), pp. 250–255.

[26] A. J. DeLong, "The Micro-spatial Structure of the Older Person: Some Implications of Planning and Social and Spatial Environment," in L. A. Pastalan and D. H. Carson, eds., *Spatial Behavior of Older People* (Ann Arbor: Institute of Gerontology. University of Michigan-Wayne State University, 1970).

[27] E. P. Friedman, "Spatial Proximity and Social Interaction in a Home for the Aged," *Journal of Gerontology*, Vol. 21 (1966), pp. 566–70; R. Y. Pablo, "Intra-Institutional Relocation: Its Impact on Long Term Care Patients," *The Gerontologist*, Vol. 27 (1977), pp. 426–34.

[28] Tobin and Lieberman, op. cit., note 5.

[29] K. F. Jasnau, "Individualized Versus Mass Transfer of Nonpsychotic Geriatric Patients from Mental Hospitals to Nursing Homes, with Special Reference to the Death Rate," *Journal of the American Geriatric Society* Vol. 15 (1967), pp. 280–284; R. Locker and A. Rublin, "Clinical Aspects of Facilitating Relocation," *The Gerontologist*, Vol. 14 (1974), pp. 295–299; N. C. Bourestom and L. Pastalan, *Death and Survival*, (Ann Arbor: Institute of Gerontology. University of Michigan, Relocation Report No. 2, undated).

[30] E. Kahana, "The Humane Treatment of Old People in Institutions," *The Gerontologist*, Vol. 13 (1973), pp. 282–89.

Chapter 7

SOURCES OF RESIDENTIAL SATISFACTION AMONGST THE ELDERLY:

AN AGE COMPARATIVE ANALYSIS

James R. Bohland and Lexa Davis

Most studies considering how the quality of the urban environment contributes to an individual's well-being or satisfaction, have not carefully considered the significance of age differences. Often the elderly population is singled out and their environmental dispositions analyzed separately from those of other age groups. However, findings from these analyses leave unclear whether the neighborhood factors significantly sustaining or diminishing the well-being of older persons would have the same effects on other population age groups. To address this issue, in this chapter we have two objectives. The first is to assess the contribution of four neighborhood dimensions—safety, neighborliness, physical condition, and convenience—to overall neighborhood satisfaction of residents in an urban environment; the second is to determine how these relationships varied among different age groups.

To achieve these objectives, a causal model was constructed linking reported neighborhood satisfaction to a resident's feelings about the four dimensions of his neighborhood. These evaluations were then correlated with specific neighborhood attributes. Coefficients describing the relationship between the exogenous and endogenous variables were estimated for six different models—all of the same structure, but one for each of six age groups. In this way, a set of causal inferences can be drawn between objective elements of the neighborhood environment and the subjective evaluation of those attributes by residents of different ages.

DIMENSIONS OF NEIGHBORHOOD SATISFACTION

Literature reviews by Fischer, Rossi, and by Kasl and empirical analyses by Smith, Angrist, and by Knox and MacLaren have concluded that the residential environment has some influence on various aspects of life satisfaction.[1] Unfortunately, most of this literature has ignored effects of age on the relationships. An exception, however, is the recent work by Campbell, Converse, and Rodgers, in which differences in the relationships between overall life satisfaction and other life domains, including the neighborhood environment, are described for different age groups.[2] Although their analysis indicated that some important changes existed between age groups, the authors did not attempt to identify any causal sequence between the environment and avowed satisfaction, which incorporated the influence of age, nor did they consider how distinct components of the neighborhood environment were evaluated differently by persons of various ages.

Several studies of neighborhoods, including those focusing specifically on the elderly, have considered the relative importance of different dimensions of the neighborhood environment to individual satisfaction. Bennett, Lawton and Kleban, and Schooler, for example, stressed the effects of the physical appearance of the neighborhood on the morale of the elderly.[3] Concern with personal safety has been identified by Sundeen and Mathieu and by Goldsmith and Tomas as being of particular concern to the elderly.[4]

The sociability and helpfulness of neighbors, herein referred to as neighborliness, appears to be particularly important to the elderly, in part because constraints on personal mobility require the elderly to redefine the spatial extent of their social environment.[5] Greater reliance on neighbors as friends was one reason given by Rosow in support of age-homogeneous neighborhoods for the aged.[6] Although disagreement exists over the issue of age homogeneous environments, it is true that neighborliness is particularly important to the elderly.

Accessibility to essential retail and service establishments can be inhibited by restrictions on personal mobility. For example, some inner city elderly may be confined to the immediate vicinity almost to the point of becoming "block bound." Reduced personal mobility means that for some elderly the convenience of the neighborhood to goods and services may influence the way in which the neighborhood is evaluated.[7]

Other attributes of the neighborhood may be important to the elderly in any given situation; however, on the basis of prior studies, safety, convenience, physical appearance, and neighborliness appear to be the most important. Moreover, the significance of the four is not confined to the elderly, because Marans and Rodgers have shown that these four aspects were important to persons of all ages living in planned communities.[8]

MODEL OF NEIGHBORHOOD SATISFACTION

In the model, level of satisfaction is seen as a response to stress-producing attributes of the neighborhood environment. This view is consistent with developmental theories emphasizing the dynamic process of environmental adaptation and adjustment that accompanies aging.[9] The social, economic, and psychic changes associated with aging alter an individual's physiological and psychological needs; consequently, the elderly must continually cope with stress that is created by person-environment discontinuities. As one ages, environmental attributes that were once supportive, either physically or psychologically, may become sources of irritation and stress. For example, neighborhood children who were once sources of joy and amusement may become sources of fear and anxiety with increased age. The old adage that "one man's heaven is another man's hell" certainly is true when considering the environmental needs of the young and the old.

Figure 11 illustrates the interactions that lead to an evaluation of one's neighborhood. In this schema, adapted from a model of life satisfaction suggested by Campbell, Converse and Rodgers, neighborhood satisfaction is an evaluative expression that results from an ongoing process of perception, cognition, and behavior.[10] Neighborhood attributes are perceived by residents and evaluated on the basis of personal standards of comparison. From these evaluations, an overall expression of neighborhood satisfaction is derived, which, in turn, influences one's behavior toward the local environment. Although an individual's standards of comparison are a function of his background, needs, and expectations, and are thus somewhat idiosyncratic, similarities between individuals do exist because of shared experiences (i.e., cohort effects) or similarities in personal characteristics (such as income, life cycle, or age).

In the schema presented in Fig. 11, stress occurs when the environment as perceived by the individual does not fulfill the expectations he has for that particular environmental situation. Avowed satisfaction or dissatisfaction, which are verbal expressions of stress, are in response to the discrepancies existing between what is expected in the way of gratification and what is actually obtained, a view consistent with that developed by Curtis and Jackson in their analysis of role inequities and satisfaction.[11]

As diagrammed in the model, neighborhood satisfaction is a summary response. Neighborhood attributes are evaluated separately and then combined to achieve an overall assessment of the neighborhood. The manner in which the summation process occurs is yet to be determined; however, we have assumed it to be additive rather than interactive.

In the model, age influences neighborhood satisfaction in two ways. First, both the physiological and psychological changes that occur with aging influences how one perceives the local environment in terms of residential needs.[12] Thus, differences can be anticipated in the way that persons of different ages perceive the same environmental conditions. Second, expectations and aspirations, and the standards against which reality is judged, are affected by age. Angrist, for example, explained the higher levels of satisfaction expressed by the elderly by their lower aspiration levels.[13]

Because age can influence neighborhood satisfaction in several ways, determining the reasons for age differences is difficult. Not only must evaluative and perceptual effects be separated, but so must cohort and aging influences. The

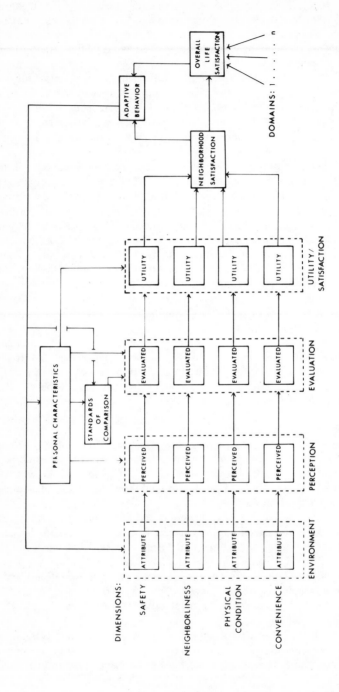

Fig. 11. Neighborhood satisfaction conceptual model (adapted with permission from A. Campbell, P. Converse, and W. Rodgers, *The Quality of American Life* (New York: Russell Sage Foundation, 1976).

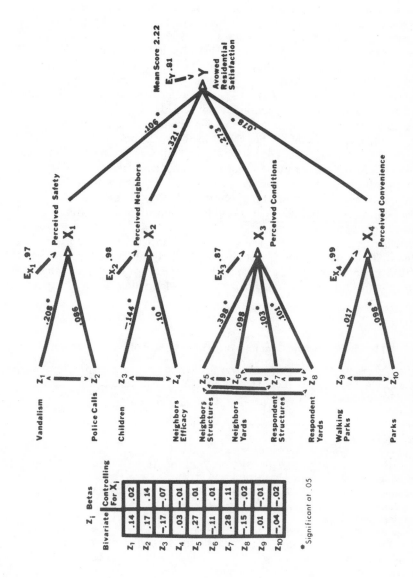

Fig. 12. Model of neighborhood satisfaction: total population.

lower aspirations of the elderly may be due in large part to cohort rather than aging effects. Longitudinal surveys would be required to separate out aging from cohort effects, but, unfortunately, the data requirements for such analyses limit their use. However, a comparative design will at least begin to establish whether differences exist in how people of different ages evaluate their neighborhoods.

We have operationalized the relationships in Figure 11 with the causal structure shown in Figure 12. In the causal model, avowed neighborhood satisfaction (Y_i) is a function of the evaluation of four neighborhood dimensions ($X_1 \ldots X_4$). These evaluations are, in turn, causally related to a set of neighborhood attributes ($Z_i \ldots Z_n$). No direct effects between environmental attributes and neighborhood satisfaction are postulated.

It was assumed that the four neighborhood dimensions were not correlated with one another and therefore no causal paths were postulated. Zero-order correlations for the four dimensions substantiated the assumption because none exceeded 0.17. Also, it was assumed that environmental attributes correlated to specific dimensions were not correlated with the remaining three, which is consistent with the assumption of the orthogonality of dimensions. Again, zero-order correlations between all possible combinations of attributes and dimensions confirmed this assumption.

Coefficients were estimated for the six models associated with the age groups described in Table 11. Although defining an "elderly" subpopulation is beset with difficulties, 65 seemed an acceptable chronological age boundary. Other age groups were defined to correspond, albeit roughly, with major life-cycle stages.

Table 11. Socioeconomic Characteristics of Members of Each Age Group

Characteristic	Age group					
	Under 25	25–34	35–44	45–54	55–64	Over 65
Percentage living in residence less than 2 years	23.7	31.5	16.7	15.0	5.7	7.4
Percentage owning automobiles	89.2	82.4	91.9	91.9	81.1	63.5
Percentage with family incomes						
Below $5,000	15.8	6.7	11.2	8.6	15.9	45.9
Over $10,000	38.0	64.0	55.0	62.2	55.7	11.4
Percentage widowed	3.7	1.4	3.6	10.7	18.6	31.5
Percentage single household	56.1	27.3	29.3	19.7	29.3	40.8
Percentage nonwhite	28.4	18.5	18.1	18.6	18.9	20.8
Percentage in labor force	36.1	53.7	57.7	52.1	48.5	6.8

DATA

Data for the study were collected in conjunction with a state-wide survey conducted in Oklahoma.[14] Analysis was limited to residents in either Oklahoma City or Tulsa who had not moved within the previous year. The sample consisted of just over 900 respondents. A check of the data showed that respondents came from a cross-section of neighborhoods in the two cities, that no spatial concentrations of age groups in particular neighborhoods were evident, and that a wide range of socioeconomic characteristics existed in each age group (Table 11). As anticipated, however, the elderly were different from the others in several ways: Their incomes were lower; most were not in the labor force; almost a third were widowed; approximately 40% lived alone; and a smaller percentage owned automobiles.

As part of the survey, respondents were asked several questions about their current level of satisfaction with their neighborhood and about four of its specific attributes—safety, neighborliness, convenience, and physical appearance. Satisfaction was measured on a 7-point scale, which ranged from a response of "completely satisfied" to one of "completely dissatisfied."

Data on various neighborhood attributes were collected in conjunction with the interview. Unfortunately, because of cost and time limitations a comprehensive set of attributes could not be obtained, and as a result the number of objective neighborhood conditions used in the analysis was limited (see Table 12 for description of variables).

DATA ANALYSIS

Causal modeling is a method for setting forth the logical consequences of an assumed causal order to a set of variables. A test of any causal structure does not prove that a particular order is the only correct interpretation; rather it only demonstrates that a particular model should correctly specify the relationship set forth by the set of assumptions.[15] Consequently, the first priority in the analysis was to determine whether the causal structure diagrammed in Figure 12 was a valid representation of the relationships between environmental attributes and neighborhood satisfaction. Having established the validity of the model, we wanted to determine whether the structure was consistent for different age groups.

To test the validity of our model, coefficients were first estimated for all paths, using the entire sample. The coefficients and the values for all latent or residual variables ($E_y \ldots E_n$) are shown in Figure 12. The values for the latent variables, particularly that for the neighborhood satisfaction variable, indicated a reasonably high level of explanation.

Whether the model correctly specifies the causal order of the relationships between the exogenous environmental attributes and the endogenous variables can be judged by considering the changes that occur in the bivariate coefficients when the variables are placed in the causal sequence.

Table 12. Path Coefficients for Age Specific Neighborhood Satisfaction Models

Endogenous or exogenous variable	Age group					
	Under 25	25–34	35–44	45–54	55–64	Over 65
Dependent variable–neighborhood satisfaction (Y)[a]						
Safety	.077	.085*	.152*	.200*	.282*	.065
Neighborliness	.347*	.417*	.378*	.203*	-.059	.358*
Appearance	.305*	.238*	.285*	.179*	.180*	.301*
Convenience	.010	.093*	.187*	.105*	.165*	-.035
Residual variable	.75	.78	.65	.70	.82	.76
Dependent variable–personal safety (X_1)[b]						
Vandalism	.151*	.151*	.279*	.286*	.174*	.400*
Police calls	.177*	.137*	.160*	-.005	-.223*	.140*
Residual variable	.97	.97	.94	.95	.97	.84
Dependent variable–neighborliness (X_2)[b]						
Number of children	-.134*	-.128*	-.129*	-.264*	.320*	-.132*
Efficacy of neighbors[c]	.070	.155*	.152*	.108	.044	.080
Residual variable	.98	.97	.98	.95	.94	.98
Dependent variable–physical appearance (X_3)[b, d]						
Neighboring houses	.001	.067	.284*	.441*	-.042	-.068
Neighboring yards	.650*	.518*	.134	.110	.382*	.479*
Houses–relative	.340*	.027	.112	-.160*	.068	-.270*
Yards–relative	-.200*	.006	-.284*	.210*	-.382*	.171
Residual variable	.88	.88	.82	.83	.80	.86
Dependent variable–convenience (X_4)[b]						
Number of parks	.080	.075	.213*	-.270*	-.028	.061
Distance to parks	-.081	.124*	-.136*	.006	.214*	.010
Residual variable	.99	.99	.95	.96	.97	.99

*Standardized coefficients that are significant at the .05 level.

[a]Endogenous.

[b]Exogenous.

[c]This variable was a measure of how effective a respondent believed it was to ask neighbors to organize for the purpose of changing local policies.

[d]Physical appearance variables were measured by the interviewer using scales developed for both structures and yards. Four measures were obtained. Two were developed using only scores for neighboring structures and yards. The remaining two were computed as the differential between neighboring structures or yards and the score for the respondent's home or yard (relative measure = score on respondent's structure–score on neighboring structures).

As we postulated the relationships, the environmental attributes influenced neighborhood satisfaction only indirectly through the four endogenous variables, i.e., no ecological effects were assumed. If this causal structure is correct, the bivariate relationships between the Z_i's and Y should be reduced to zero when the effects of the intermediary variables (X_i's) are introduced. The stipulation that $b_{yz_i \cdot x_i}$ must equal zero is somewhat unrealistic, however, because of measurement errors. A more realistic test is that $b_{yz_i \cdot x_i} < b_{yz_i}$ and that the coefficient should begin to approach zero.

The table in Figure 12 shows that the coefficients were, in fact, reduced with the introduction of the evaluative variables, and most of the coefficients did approach zero. When the data were disaggregated by age, some of the bivariate coefficients were not reduced with the addition of the endogenous variables. However, these cases were limited and normally involved relationships that were weak even in the bivariate situation.

FINDINGS

The relationships in the elderly model (Fig. 13) were similar in most respects to those for other age groups (Table 12). For example, neighborliness was the dimension contributing most to overall neighborhood satisfaction for the elderly and for all other groups except for the age 55–64 group where neighborliness was not significant.

Of the two exogenous variables thought to influence neighborliness, only prevalence of children showed any consistent association with neighborliness. For most ages, the presence of children in the neighborhood actually decreased their satisfaction with the quality of the neighbors.

The physical conditions of the neighborhood also contributed significantly to overall neighborhood satisfaction, particularly for the elderly. An age trend of sorts was evident because the significance of the dimension declined with age, reaching a low for the age 55–64 group before rising again in importance for the elderly (Fig. 14). The exogenous variables used in the model were relatively good predictors of a resident's evaluation of the physical appearance of his neighborhood. Both neighboring houses and yards were associated with the evaluation of the physical appearance of the area for most groups (Table 12).

Perhaps the most surprising result of the analysis was the relatively minor association between safety and neighborhood satisfaction for the elderly. On the basis of the accounts in the literature, it was thought that personal safety would correlate highly with neighborhood satisfaction of the elderly, yet the path coefficient for safety was lowest in the elderly group and was not significant (Fig. 14).

The two environmental attributes making up the safety dimension—vandalism and number of police calls—were significant at the .05 level in all but one case (Table 12). However, other aspects of the neighborhood environment influencing safety should also be added to increase the level of explanation.

Of the four dimensions in the model, convenience proved to be of least

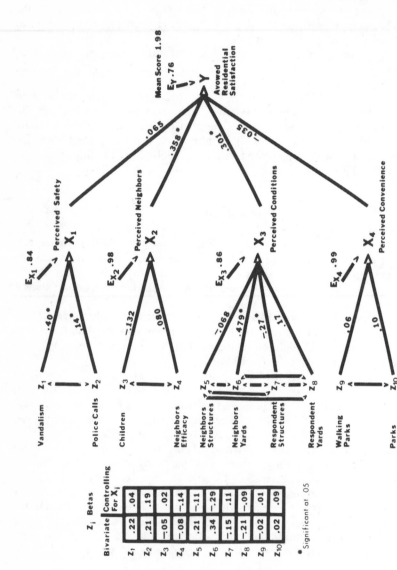

Fig. 13. Model of neighborhood satisfaction: elderly.

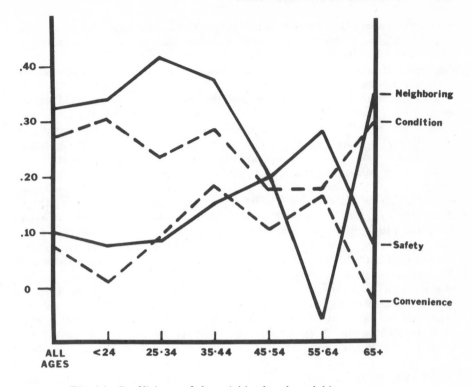

Fig. 14. Coefficients of the neighborhood model by age groups.

importance for all ages. A tendency for convenience to become more important was evident in the middle-aged groups, but even here the path coefficients were not very large (Fig. 14). Because of data limitations, only accessibility to parks was measured, and it did not prove to be very important in predicting satisfaction with the convenience dimension of neighborhoods.

INTERPRETATION

Although the literature on the elderly had emphasized the unique living requirements of this group, our analysis demonstrated that there were numerous similarities between the elderly and younger age groups in terms of how they evaluated their neighborhood environment. In fact, as the graph in Figure 14 illustrates, the similarities between the elderly and the youngest group were quite high.

Although the extent of the similarities between groups was considerable, some important differences were also evident. One of the most striking age differentials was between the elderly and the age 55–64 group; the two groups differed in most every respect. For example, whereas the elderly emphasized the importance of neighborliness to overall satisfaction, this dimension was of least importance to the age 55–64 group. Although safety concerns contributed most to overall neighborhood satisfaction among the age 55–64 group, safety surprisingly was of minor significance to the elderly.

The degree to which the elderly and the age 55–64 group differed would appear to support the contention of some gerontologists that the age immediately prior to retirement is a period requiring considerable adjustment and adaptation. It was apparent from our analysis that this preretirement age group represented a distinct transitional period between middle age and retirement.

The earlier work that stressed the importance of neighbors to the elderly was supported by the results of our analysis; neighborliness had the strongest association to neighborhood satisfaction. As the models indicated, however, the close association was not unique to the elderly. In fact, it was more strongly associated with neighborhood satisfaction in the child rearing age groups. During these ages, having "good neighbors" appeared to have added meaning, perhaps because neighborhood children are an important part of a child's social network. As families reached a stage in which children were less reliant on the neighborhood for their social interactions, the significance of neighborliness to neighborhood satisfaction diminished. At the age when most children had left home and the adult social life revolved around social contacts associated with work or other nonlocal institutions, neighborliness was of less importance in predicting overall neighborhood satisfaction; however, upon retirement, neighborliness again became an important predictor of overall satisfaction.

The relationship between the physical appearance of the neighborhood and overall satisfaction was almost as great as that for neighborliness with the elderly. Again, however, the association was not unique to the elderly, because physical condition was closely related to neighborhood satisfaction in most of the other age groups. For families with young children, for example, the concern may stem from worries about the safety of their children. For others it may be related to property values or visual aesthetics. For the elderly, the effects may be more psychological. As noted earlier, physical deterioration is thought to breed a climate of despair and low self-esteem among the elderly that reinforces their belief that life is becoming less purposeful or declining in quality. Although our analysis could not confirm this link between morale and the physical appearance of the neighborhood, it did show that the elderly placed a higher value on the physical condition of their surroundings when they were evaluating their neighborhood as a place to live than did most other age groups.

Our results appeared to contradict previous studies emphasizing the importance of personal safety to the elderly; however, several reasons can be given for the discrepancy. First, most of the elderly in our sample did not live in high crime areas within the inner city; therefore, concern for personal safety may have been reduced because the elderly did not perceive their area as one of high risk. Concern with personal safety among the elderly normally declines outside the inner city.[16] However, the fact that all groups in the sample were located in neighborhoods of similar characteristics does not help explain group differences.

It may be, as Gubrium has suggested, that concern with safety diminished when strong neighborhood ties exist.[17] Some support for this interpretation could be found by the inverse manner in which the safety and neighborliness dimensions contributed to neighborhood satisfaction. For ages for which neighborliness contributed to overall satisfaction, the safety dimension was of lesser importance. Conversely, when neighborliness did not contribute to overall satisfaction, safety became more important. If this interdependence between safety and neighborliness is valid, then the original assumption about the independence of the evaluative dimensions of neighborhood satisfaction must be reexamined and nonlinear relations considered.

CONCLUSION

In this chapter we considered the relative importance of four neighborhood dimensions to overall neighborhood satisfaction in order to assess whether there were important differences in the way elderly residents structured neighborhood satisfaction in contrast to younger persons.

Although the literature on the elderly emphasized their unique environmental needs, this analysis demonstrated that the elderly structured neighborhood satisfaction similarly to younger persons. For most ages, neighborliness, safety, and a pleasing neighborhood appearance contributed significantly to overall neighborhood satisfaction. However, some differences between age groups did exist in the relative significance attached to each dimension. Interestingly, the major discrepancy between groups was not between the elderly and the younger age groups, but rather between the elderly and the age 55-64 preretirement group. The results suggested that after retirement the manner in which individuals evaluated their neighborhood changed significantly.

The results demonstrated that similarities existed between groups, but the reasons for these commonalities were not resolved. It appears, for example, that although neighborliness was important to both the elderly and nonelderly people, the explanations may be quite different. One cannot assume that a neighborhood social structure that accommodates the young will necessarily be beneficial to the elderly.

Some insights as to why particular age groups emphasized particular neighborhood dimensions can be obtained by examining the manner in which the different environmental attributes influenced the evaluation of particular dimensions. For example, the number of children in the neighborhood had a positive relationship to neighborliness for the age 55-64 group but was negatively associated with neighborliness with the elderly, suggesting very different standards by which neighborliness was evaluated by the two groups.

The inability of our analysis to identify more clearly the underlying reasons for the similarities and differences between groups was in large part due to the lack of a more comprehensive set of environmental attributes. The structure of the model appeared to be valid.

The analysis focused on differences between groups and ignored variance within groups. Differences within an age group stemming from variations in income, education, or occupation, for example, were not considered; however, the model as currently constituted could be modified to include the effects of such factors on the evaluation of neighborhood dimensions. Expansion of the model in this way would enhance its ability to differentiate primarily stage-in-life effects from other social and economic influences.

NOTES AND REFERENCES

[1] C. Fischer, "Urban Malaise," *Social Forces*, Vol. 52 (Dec., 1973), pp. 221–235; P. Rossi, "Community Social Indicators," in A. Campbell and P. Converse, eds., *The Human Meaning of Social Change* (New York: Russell Sage Foundation, 1972), pp. 87–126; S. Kasl, "Effects of Housing on Mental and Physical Health," *Man-Environment Systems*, Vol. 4 (1974), pp. 207–226; C. Smith, "Residential Neighborhoods as Humane Environments," *Environment and Planning A*, Vol. 8 (1976), pp. 311–326; S. Angrist, "Dimensions of Well-Being in Public Housing Families," *Environment and Behavior*, Vol. 6 (1974), pp. 495–516; P. Knox and A. MacLaren, "Values and Perceptions in Descriptive Approaches to Urban Social Geography," in D. Herbert and R. J. Johnston, eds., *Geography and the Urban Environment*, Vol. 1 (New York: John Wiley & Sons, 1978), pp. 197–246.
[2] A. Campbell, P. Converse and W. Rodgers, *The Quality of American Life* (New York: Russell Sage Foundation, 1976).
[3] R. Bennett, "Living Conditions and Everyday Needs of the Elderly with Particular Reference to Social Isolation," *Aging and Human Behavior*, Vol. 4 (1973), pp. 179–198; M. Lawton and M. Kleban, "The Aged Resident of the Inner City," *Gerontologist*, Vol. 2 (1971), pp. 277–283; K. Schooler, "The Relationship between Social Interaction and Morale of the Elderly as a Function of Environment Characteristics," *Gerontologist*, Vol. 9 (1970), pp. 25–29.
[4] R. Sundeen and J. Mathieu, "The Fear of Crime and Its Consequences among the Elderly in Three Urban Communities," *Gerontologist*, Vol. 16 (1976), pp. 211–219; J. Goldsmith and N. Tomas, "Crimes against the Elderly: A Continuing National Crisis," *Aging* (June–July, 1974), pp. 10–13.
[5] G. Rowles, *Prisoners of Space? Exploring the Geographical Experience of Older People* (Boulder, Co.: Westview Press, 1978); Angrist, op. cit., note 1.
[6] I. Rosow, *Social Integration of the Aged* (New York: The Free Press, 1967).
[7] F. Carp, "Housing and Living Environments of Older People," in R. Binstock and E. Shanas, eds., *Handbook of Aging and the Social Sciences* (New York: Van Nostrand Reinhold, 1977), pp. 244–271; P. Niebank and I. Pope, *The Elderly in Older Urban Areas* (Philadelphia: Institute for Environmental Studies, University of Pennsylvania, 1965).
[8] R. Marans and W. Rodgers, "Evaluating Resident Satisfaction in Established and New Communities," in R. W. Burchell, ed., *Frontiers of Planned Unit Development: A Synthesis of Expert Opinion* (New Brunswick, N.J.: Center for Urban Policy Research, Rutgers University, 1973), pp. 197–227.
[9] S Golant, *The Residential Location and Spatial Behavior of the Elderly*, (Chicago: Department of Geography, University of Chicago, Research Paper No. 143, 1972); see also P. Windley, T. Byerts and F. Ernst, eds., *Theory Development in Environment and Aging* (Washington, D.C.: Gerontological Society, 1975).
[10] Campbell, Converse and Rodgers, op. cit., note 2.
[11] R. Curtis and E. Jackson, *Inequality in American Communities* (New York: Academic Press, 1977).
[12] A. Lawton and G. Azar, "Sensory and Perceptual Changes that may Influence the Housing Needs of the Aging," in F. M. Carp, ed., *Patterns of Living and Housing of Middle Aged and Older People* (Washington, D.C.: Government Printing Office, 1965), pp. 11–15.

[13] Angrist, op. cit., note 1.

[14] The survey was conducted by the Center for Economic and Management Research at the University of Oklahoma. The authors wish to thank the Bureau for permitting use of the data.

[15] H. Asher, *Causal Modeling* (Beverly Hill, Ca.: Sage University Press, 1976); H. Blalock, *Causal Models in the Social Sciences* (Chicago: Aldine, 1970).

[16] Sundeen and Mathieu, op. cit., note 4.

[17] J. Gubrium, "Victimization in Old Age: Available Evidence and Three Hypotheses," *Crime and Delinquency*, Vol. 20 (1974), pp. 245–250.

Chapter 8

LOCATIONAL CONSEQUENCES OF HOUSING POLICIES FOR THE LOW-INCOME ELDERLY:

A CASE STUDY[1]

John Mercer

Public intervention in the housing market is now commonplace in many advanced capitalist societies. Depending on the nature of the intervention, this has implications for the urban spatial structure, the distribution of the real income of residents and the urban economy, the urban landscape, and the life chances of those directly affected. This chapter considers the efforts of the state to house a particular segment of society—the low-income elderly. In Canada during the last 35 years, federal and provincial governments have combined to assist the elderly poor in various ways in their "struggle for shelter." The focus here is on British Columbia and, in particular, on its principal metropolitan center, Vancouver (1.1 million, 1971).

British Columbia is generally perceived to be *the* retirement province of Canada, with its mild climate attractive to the aging Canadian contemplating retirement; however, there are as yet no specialized retirement communities to rival those of Arizona or California. The population of the province will age appreciably during the next 50 years, as well as that of Canada as a whole,[2] and the aging will be compounded by both interprovincial and international migrations that bring the elderly and near-elderly to British Columbia.[3] The elderly are an urban population; 82% in British Columbia (76% in Canada) live in urban places. They are highly concentrated in spatial terms: 70% reside in the two demographically distinctive Census Metropolitan Areas of Vancouver and Victoria. The demographic character of a place can be indicated via a life-cycle index.[4] Only two metropolitan areas in Canada are in the "most aged" class—Vancouver and Victoria—as are a number of smaller centers in the interior of the province.

Until recently, the public response to the housing needs of the growing elderly population has been to construct new housing projects in which low-income seniors could rent decent, affordable housing. The utilization of supply-oriented programs authorized under the federal National Housing Act has created a distinct geography of senior citizen housing, particularly in the Vancouver metropolitan area where a little more than half of the provincial elderly reside (1971). The first objective of this chapter is to describe the locational consequences of this approach to housing the elderly and to outline a more rational and locationally balanced procedure whereby new projects are allocated to municipalities in the Vancouver area. A second objective is to discuss the likely locational consequences of new and different directions in provincial housing policy emphasizing financial and other forms of assistance to individual households. This trend affirms the role of the private sector as the primary supplier of shelter for older people. Finally, an attempt is made to place the knowledge gained from the British Columbia case in a wider policy framework.

HOUSING POLICIES FOR THE LOW-INCOME ELDERLY

In advanced capitalist societies, consumption of housing services is principally determined by one's income. It is well known that low-income households allocate substantial portions of their limited income for housing to a disproportionate degree.[5] Typically, in such countries, the elderly are poor. In 1971, 82% of all Canadians over 65 had incomes of less than $4,000.[6] More recently (1975), a similarly disturbing situation existed. Inflation has driven upwards the measures of poverty, and $7,000 per annum is now used as a poverty indicator.[7] Two thirds of elderly households had incomes below this threshold.[8] During the same period (1971–75), the cost of living rose substantially: the Consumer Price Index for shelter from 100 to 144, and all items from 100 to 139.[9]

It is not surprising, therefore, that the elderly are commonly viewed as "the deserving poor, obviously needing help."[10] Yet public funds have not flowed generously into the supply of new housing for this group. The history of Canadian public-sector housing policy is exemplified by the attitude that housing is best left to operations of the marketplace and that the role of government is largely a residual capacity; both federal and provincial governments were slow to develop any real program delivery capability until after 1970.[11]

HOUSING PROGRAMS

As in the United States, there has been a historic emphasis in Canadian housing policy upon the construction of new housing. Although ineffective demand was recognized early as a fundamental problem in the housing market, the raising of this demand through specific income transfers, such as shelter allowances, was not considered.[12] The approach adopted was to build new units and, through a variety of grants and subsidies, to establish rents that related to a reasonable proportion of the tenants' income.[13]

In British Columbia, three such supply-oriented programs have been used to deliver new housing to the low-income elderly: (1) public housing, (2) nonprofit housing, and (3) entrepreneurial full recovery housing. The nonprofit housing program has been most heavily utilized to serve the elderly, whereby a variety of groups, such as service clubs, church groups, ethnic organizations, and others, can form nonprofit corporations and receive assistance from both the federal and the provincial governments to enable them to construct and manage senior citizen housing projects.[14] This program was initiated under the federal National Housing Act (NHA) in 1944, and by 1949 the first such units had been built in the Vancouver area. The provincial government increased its participation in the program when, in 1957, it introduced legislation enabling it to make a grant of one-third the capital cost, thereby reducing cost to the nonprofit group and, hence, reducing rents.

The stock of new self-contained and hostel units has risen substantially in recent years. As in other Canadian and U.S. jurisdictions, it has proven easier for authorities to construct housing for seniors then for low-income family households whose introduction into an area via publicly provided housing is often vigorously resisted.[15] However, the growth in the senior citizen stock is also a function of the increased expenditures on social housing at both national and provincial levels. For example, federal funds authorized for the principal social housing programs have averaged about $570 million per annum in the 1970s. This contrasts sharply with the $270 million per annum in the late 1960s and the previous minimal expenditures.[16] A number of factors contributed to the increase in federal appropriations, including a housing program review that called for an expanded federal presence, the development of a stronger federal role in urban affairs in the context of federal-provincial constitutional relationships, the demands of provincial housing authorities, and the emergence of housing pressure groups. The acquisition of these increased authorizations by aggressive provinces resulted in an upsurge in construction, as is evident for the Vancouver area (Fig. 15).

The critical role of provincial administrations is well illustrated by the case of British Columbia. The election of a socialist government in 1972 led to the creation of a provincial *Department of Housing* with its own budget line. From 1974 to 1976, $10 million was allocated each year for capital grants toward the construction of new self-contained and hostel accommodations for seniors, allocations that were double the previous highest allocation.[17] By 1976, a nonsocialist government was in power and program changes followed. The budget allocation for grants toward the construction of new housing for seniors in the last fiscal year (1977) was reduced to $4 million.[18] No new projects were authorized in the Vancouver area in fiscal 1977, although they were authorized in other parts of the province, often in communities with fewer than 20,000 population. The most innovative step taken by the new government is the Shelter

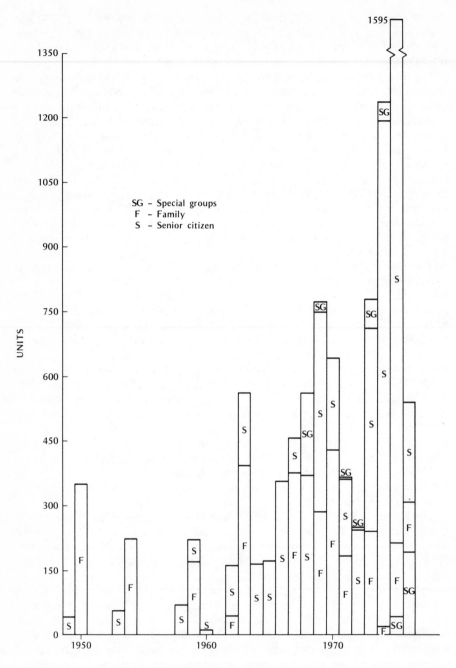

Fig. 15. Social housing in Vancouver, by year: 1949–1976.

Aid for Elderly Renters (SAFER) program; this will be discussed subsequently. Thus, the flow of senior citizen housing is considerably influenced by the political philosophy and funding decisions of provincial governments. The period of expansion of construction in British Columbia is over and the existing spatial pattern of projects should remain relatively stable in the short run.

THE LOCATION OF SENIOR CITIZEN PROJECTS IN VANCOUVER

At the metropolitan scale, the spatial pattern of senior citizen housing follows from the locational decisions of those responsible for initiating project development and those public officials who approve sites. The outcome of these decisions is shown in Figures 16 and 17 (1976 data).

In the central city pattern (Fig. 17), there are four significant features: (1) a cluster of large projects in the high-density apartment district west of the commercial core; (2) a second central cluster immediately east of the central business district (CBD); (3) a scattering of projects throughout the inner city areas ringing the commercial core; and (4) a concentration of medium and small projects in the southeast quadrant of the city. There are a number of locational factors at work; but the most powerful determinent for choosing a project site has been the availability of relatively cheap land, which in many instances was already owned by the municipality.[19] Such a factor explains the concentration of projects in the southeast quadrant, where undeveloped land was available at a cost below that of core areas and elsewhere. Public redevelopment activities have also created "new" land for housing agencies and nonprofit sponsors; the units to the east of the CBD are located in a major urban renewal area of the 1960s, and new units for seniors have been built (1977) in the False Creek redevelopment, where an obsolescent inner city industrial area is being transformed into a high-density "urban village," with a mixture of market and directly assisted housing for families, the elderly, the other nonfamily households. Initial press reports indicate a high level of satisfaction with the development.

The existence of suitable zoning is an important factor, and districts zoned for multiple housing occur throughout the inner city. The cluster of large projects west of the CBD is in a high-amenity apartment district with good access to downtown, beaches, and the 1,000-acre Stanley Park. The size of these projects is a function of the intensive use of high-cost land. In other areas zoned for apartment use, considerable private redevelopment and some gentrification have occurred. This has resulted in the displacement of those living in low- and medium-rental housing, including seniors. Such conditions will be reflected in the "need and demand" survey now required by the federal housing agency as a prerequisite to project development and may result in project proposals.[20] The construction of new units for the elderly in Kitsilano (1975–76), where redevelopment pressures are severe, has permitted low-income seniors to continue to live in this area, something that was increasingly difficult to achieve given the scale and nature of the private redevelopment.

In the suburban municipalities, units for seniors are found in every

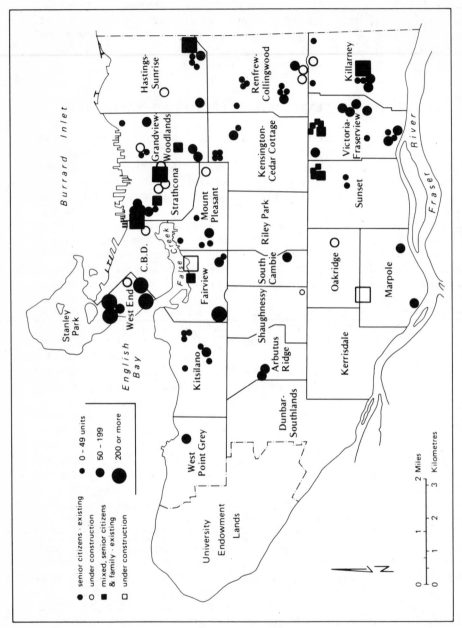

Fig. 16. The location of senior citizen housing in Vancouver, by local planning areas, 1976.

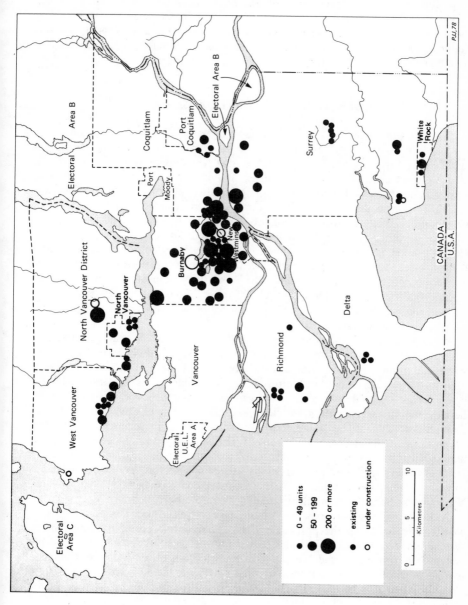

Fig. 17. The location of senior citizen housing in the greater Vancouver regional district, by municipalities, 1976.

Legend:
- 0 – 49 units
- 50 – 199
- 200 or more
- existing
- under construction

municipality except one. Clearly, one concentration is dominant at the regional scale (Fig. 17). This concentration in the South Burnaby area is historic, being the location of the first units in the suburbs built in the early 1950s, largely at the instigation of the socialist member who represented this area. Various nonprofit groups, government agencies, and a receptive municipal administration have combined to produce the present marked clustering.

CONSEQUENCES OF THE CONSTRUCTION APPROACH

One question must be posed: How well does the distribution of units serve the needs of the "client" population? In the mid-1970s, it was apparent that applications for funding of nonprofit housing for the elderly in the Vancouver area were exceeding available resources, and considerable uncertainty existed among municipal officials and nonprofit groups as to project approval. No clear guidelines existed that could assist in the allocation of projects at the regional or neighborhood scale. In this situation, some municipalities may well be overbuilt, whereas in others the eligible market is not well served. For example, if the eligible market is defined as all low-income elderly households in a municipality, then in places such as Burnaby and Port Coquitlam the proportion of the eligible market housed in state-assisted units is 81% and 108%, respectively. In Vancouver, with 23,000 low-income elderly households, only 32% of the market is so served, whereas the proportion for the metropolitan region is 36%.

Such illustrative data must be interpreted cautiously. Certainly a significant proportion of the low-income elderly will wish to remain in private-sector housing. They prefer to live in their own homes or in their rented apartment suites and rooms, or to move in with friends or family. If this fraction were known, one would be better able to define the eligible market and how well it is being served. Should a locationally sensitive housing policy discourage further development in areas with more than, say, 75% of the eligible market served? Should development be encouraged and directed to municipalities with low proportions of the eligible market served? The central city of Vancouver contains almost half the existing senior citizen housing units in the region, but there is a large eligible population not served by the public sector. Yet, Vancouver has substantial numbers of elderly in the lowest income category.[21] What should Vancouver's allocation of available funding therefore be?

A locationally sensitive policy should take into account the preferences of elderly households. In the postwar era, an elaborate and costly housing delivery system has evolved based on only partial knowledge of the wants of those the system is designed to serve. This lack of knowledge is offset in British Columbia by the reliance on the nonprofit approach because the nonprofit sponsors are closer to their clients and, in general, more sensitive to their needs than public agencies. Research is also adding to this experiential knowledge. Analysis of applications to the British Columbia Housing Management Commission confirms that many senior citizens wish to remain in their present residential areas. For example, 80% of the applicants living in Vancouver wish to remain in the city, and almost half of these want to stay in their present areas, suggesting that those areas containing sizable numbers of applicants should be primary areas for new development. Most applicants, however, come from inner city areas, and, given the operations of a private land market, these are very costly areas in which to build new projects. If units are built on a least-cost, land-available principle, elderly households may be forced to relocate from their familiar neighborhoods in order to accept a low-rent government-assisted unit, with possibly adverse sociopsychological consequences.

Government housing officials often face a difficult decision in the site approval process. Assuming, for the moment, that the critical factor of project economies is acceptable to the funding agency and that the location is neither totally unacceptable nor clearly excellent, they confront the bureaucratic dilemma—should projects in marginal locations be approved? Generally, the answer is yes, because a prevalent attitude of approval agencies is that the supply of units for the elderly can rarely meet the demand, especially in large urban areas with an aging population.

A FAIR-SHARE STRATEGY

In the case of British Columbia, a fair-share approach is not an attempt to counter exclusionary zoning and resistance to publicly assisted housing as in the United States; rather it is a procedure for allocating limited resources in the face of competing demands. The objective is to distribute housing for the low-income elderly throughout the Vancouver metropolitan area in a manner that is more equitable and representative of the spatial pattern of eligible elderly households. The central premise of this approach is that most seniors wish to remain in their present neighborhoods, although this assumption may be less tenable in suburban areas.[22] The allocation criterion employed is "unmet need," which is calculated by subtracting the total number of government-assisted housing units built in a municipality from the total estimated number of low-income elderly renters and owners in that municipality. To determine a community's fair share or portion of total regional production for seniors, the unmet needs for all municipalities are totalled and the need for each municipality is expressed as a percentage of the total for the region. Although this method does not represent the actual need, it does take into account both potential demand (i.e., those households that are eligible for government programs) and supply (i.e., those units already built in each municipality).

Applying this procedure to data for Vancouver area municipalities yields the distributional shares for each place (Table 13). This table indicates that of the units that can be produced with the available funds for any given period, say 2 years, projects located in Vancouver should represent 56% of the total; this is substantially greater than Vancouver's share of 48% to date. This approach implies that the direction of resources is away from communities like Burnaby and toward communities such as Delta. Despite the fact that only 8.6% of the region's low-income elderly live in Burnaby, 19.7% of the government-assisted

Table 13. Assisted Housing, Low-Income Elderly Households, and
Unmet Needs Within the Vancouver Metropolitan Area

Municipality	Percent of seniors housing stock in each municipality to end of 1975	Percent of low-income elderly (1974)	Percentage distribution based on unmet need approach
Vancouver	48.0	53.2	56.0
Burnaby	19.7	8.6	2.5
West Vancouver	2.2	3.9	4.8
North Vancouver[a]	4.9	5.4	5.7
White Rock	1.2	3.5	4.8
Delta	0.5	2.0	2.9
Coquitlam	2.3	1.9	1.6
Port Coquitlam	2.7	0.9	0.0
Port Moody	0.6	0.4	0.3
Surrey	7.6	8.0	8.2
Richmond	4.4	2.8	1.9
New Westminster	2.0	3.8	4.8
Langley[a]	3.7	5.5	6.5
Total	100.0	100.0	100.0

[a]Includes city and district.

Source: Bairstow, D. and J. Mercer. " 'Fair-share' approaches to the location of senior citizen housing." Unpublished paper presented to Canadian Association of Gerontology Meetings, Vancouver, B.C., Nov., 1976.

seniors' housing has been built in that municipality. Thus, when Burnaby's fair share is calculated for future allocation of units, it is only 2.5% of the total. Yet officials in Burnaby believe that if nonprofit groups in their jurisdiction wish to construct more units and have a proven record of successful delivery and management, they should not be denied this opportunity—if the demand is there, build. But this could well divert funds away from underserved areas where less well-established nonprofit groups are trying to develop projects (e.g., White Rock) or from Vancouver where there is a large absolute unmet need.

The principle of fair-share procedures for the allocation of senior citizen housing has been adopted by the City of Vancouver and by the Greater Vancouver Regional District, the metropolitan level of government (1976). The procedures have been modified, and it is recognized that other locational criteria will be important in the decision-making process. For example, in the central city, the suitability of existing social, health, and retail services and the pattern of requests suggest an emphasis in any future construction in inner-city neighborhoods. Although the city would receive more than half of the new units to be constructed in the region under a fair-share principle, its internal fair-share strategy to distribute these units according to local area targets is sensitive to such matters as the disruption of certain communities with large multiple unit projects, unacceptable concentrations of public-sector housing (already close to 40% in some areas), and the realities of high land costs close to the core and lower cost, publicly owned land available in the southeastern section of the city.

A NEW INITIATIVE IN RENTAL HOUSING

The provincial government introduced a totally new program in 1977; SAFER (Shelter Aid for Elderly Renters) is Canada's first major direct housing allowance scheme. The program is restricted to tenants aged 65 and older. Further, only those paying more than 50% of their income receive an allowance, and there are limits to the amount payable monthly. With this initiative, provincial funds allocated to new construction have been reduced by more than 50%, and the majority of new projects approved in 1977 are in smaller population centers and not in the two metropolitan areas that contain the vast majority of elderly.

This new program is attractive to the government for a number of reasons. It is expected to reach approximately 27,000 households, or 30,400 individuals, throughout the province—only 15% of the elderly population (1971) but 25% of the elderly poor.[23] In contrast, the new construction programs after 25 years had provided shelter for only about 19,000 households. SAFER can reach all regions and communities in the province; elderly renters simply apply to the Ministry, which determines eligibility and the amount of the allowance. The construction programs depended on the initiative of nonprofit groups, public agencies, and, to a lesser extent, entrepreneurs. Thus, seniors would have access to shelter assistance only if these various organizations were active in the community. It is a highly visible program—a check comes monthly from the government and the political benefits seem clear. SAFER is initially no more costly to the province than the supply of capital grants for new construction; recent unpublished data suggest that it will cost $10.6 million per annum. Most important, it avoids the necessity of long-term project-operating subsidies that are shared by the senior governments. Because of the projected magnitude of these subsidy commitments (new projects currently require subsidies of between $250 and $300 per month per unit to maintain rents at 25% of tenant income and amortize the project), provincial and federal agencies are anxious to reduce commitments that are tied to new public-sector units for seniors (and for family households). An increasing number of shelter allowance schemes can safely be predicted for other Canadian provinces, with an emphasis on the use of the existing housing stock.

The principal locational implication of this innovative program is that tenants have a greater choice of residence. If they wish to remain in their present rental units or rooms, which was becoming increasingly difficult with rising rents, that choice becomes more feasible with an easing of the substantial rent burden. A government survey (1976) indicated that a high percentage of elderly renters were indeed satisfied with their present accommodation, but many were also experiencing oppressively high rent to income ratios of more than 50 to 60%.[24]

The rent aid enables individuals to move to a higher quality unit if they wish, in that the rent aid can be used to offset a higher rent; thus, expenditures remain proportionately constant. This relocation is most likely to occur within existing neighborhoods, although relocation between neighborhoods is also possible. What should be reduced is the move from the private-sector apartments and rooms into public housing and nonprofit housing; vacancies may also increase in the latter, especially if a greater proportion of income is required for rent (an increase from the current 25 to 30% has been raised in inter-governmental discussions). However, relocation to public and nonprofit housing will occur if only because some seniors will wish to move from the social isolation of their present accommodation into age-segregated projects with their particular ambience.

ASSISTANCE TO THE ELDERLY HOMEOWNER

A significant proportion of Canada's urban elderly are homeowners and they are poor. Of those elderly below the poverty line, 77% of couples and 58% of singles are owner-occupants (1972).[25] A similar situation exists in the United States.[26] Two of the most pressing problems facing elderly homeowners are maintenance and operating costs and property taxes.

Taxes

Homeowners in British Columbia are eligible for a grant from the Provincial Government to offset municipal property taxes. The annual amount payable per homeowner is $280 for heads of household younger than 65 and $430 for those household heads older than 65. Such assistance to the elderly homeowner is also available in various U.S. states. It is difficult to estimate the impact of such aid because tax bills vary by municipality and are also a function of assessed property values. Although these flat-rate grants are not related to income and hence degree of need, making them universal would assist more homeowners to remain in their homes.

Maintenance and Operating Costs

In 1973, the federal government introduced a new program, the Neighborhood Improvement Program (NIP), and a related program, the Residential Rehabilitation Assistance Program (RRAP); participating provincial and municipal governments also share in the costs of these programs. Originally intended for inner-city areas where destabilization and redevelopment were occurring apace, NIP has been extended into communities of varying sizes. Under RRAP, a combination of low-interest loans and outright grants are available to property owners in designated areas for the purpose of rehabilitating and improving their properties. This program has proven to be especially attractive to the elderly homeowner who, not usually having to carry a monthly mortgage payment, has been willing to take on the low-interest loan and is often eligible for the maximum grant, given a low income. In urban areas, 41% of the homeowners receiving RRAP assistance are older than 64 and for rural areas the corresponding proportion is 18%.[27] The amount of financial assistance is substantial and increases the probability that elderly homeowners living in designated areas will be able to remain in their present units and "avoid" institutionalization or public-sector housing. There is currently considerable pressure on Central Mortgage and Housing Corporation (an agency that finances and administers federal housing programs) to extend the spatial coverage of the RRAP. A similar trend is observable in some U.S. jurisdictions where Community Development Block Grants are being used to rehabilitate existing stock. The elderly are likely to be owners in the rehabilitation areas and hence are the major beneficiaries.

A further critical factor determining the ability of the elderly to remain in their own homes is the availability of a range of in-home services. Canada and the United States have traditionally lagged behind advanced capitalist societies in Europe in this field.[28] However, British Columbia has introduced (1978) an expanded comprehensive Long-Term Care Program. Coverage includes homemaker services with charges graduated according to income. The annual cost of this program is estimated to be $138 million, and to illustrate the degree of expansion, the appropriations for homemaker services will increase fourfold.

An easing of the property tax burden, the present and possible wider availability of low-interest loans and grants for property improvement, and the increased access to in-home services combine to make it more likely that elderly homeowners, singles or couples, can remain in their homes longer than in the past. Thus, areas in the two British Columbia metropolitan centers with significant proportions of elderly homeowners should exhibit less residential mobility. Even structural change may be delayed because the departure of the elderly homeowners provided an opportunity for development capital to move in and subsequently transform a neighborhood.

CONCLUSION

This chapter has dealt with various forms of government assistance for the supply of housing services to the elderly. Although data have been presented for British Columbia and, specifically, Vancouver, some observations can be made that may have relevance for other jurisdictions.

Without greater income support, the elderly will continue to be a disproportionately large element of the poor in our societies. A large scale redistribution of income or other forms of wealth to the working class poor does not seem likely in the short run. Therefore, this group, once old, will continue to be among the most disadvantaged with respect to housing needs. It is important to recognize that there are different kinds of needs. As with nonelderly households, senior citizens require shelter that meets safety and public health standards, at the very least. They also have particular needs as they age, and these needs are not always readily met in the design of private-sector housing. They need, more than most, affordable housing. It is intolerable that the older members of our societies must deny themselves goods and services in order to obtain shelter, too often substandard. This adequate and affordable housing must be in locations that provide benefits to the elderly resident, rather than impose costs such as fear, social and physical isolation, and a sense of loss of control over one's property.

As a response, the preoccupation with construction programs has certainly generated physically adequate shelter for a limited proportion of eligible households; some recent projects are even above minimum standards. This housing has been made affordable so that many seniors do not pay more than 25% of their income for the assisted housing. The financial arrangements required to achieve this are such, however, that governments are becoming apprehensive about the long-term costs, although this may be more of a commentary on housing priorities and the place of social housing in the budget than a fear of fiscal disaster. If new housing for the elderly is to be built, as is the case in the United States and most Canadian provinces, then greater attention to the locational needs of the elderly will be required. With greater emphasis being placed on construction through the nonprofit route in the United States, the fair-share strategy outlined here could be of short-run value until a more carefully conceived and informed locational policy is established for particular places. This will require further research, a determination of the social costs or benefits of project locations, for example, being long overdue. Are marginal locations overcome by the mobility of the elderly or do they have adverse effects? Although location is being given more attention in the planning process, the pressures to produce new units and to make projects economically feasible remain dominant.

Shelter allowance programs should be encouraged in combination with construction programs. They can likely be effective in allowing elderly renters to utilize the existing stock of housing, thereby reducing the demand for costly new housing. However, the existing units must be maintained by owner-occupants and landlords. With increasing emphasis in many countries on state assistance for rehabilitation, there is a greater potential for this to occur although the criteria for channeling funds into specific areas remain a troublesome matter.[29] Not only the physical stock but also the quality of life in the local environment must be maintained. If, for example, fear for one's safety, poor city services and high property taxes, and an absence of affordable in-home services combine to force older people out of their residences into central city locations, then the physical rehabilitation programs will benefit the newcomers and shelter allowances will be used by the elderly in the consumption of newer and probably more expensive housing services.

The geographic implications of the various approaches are different. The construction of new projects, usually multiple units at high densities, has clear landscape impacts and can produce "ghettoization," although the effects of this on the elderly are not necessarily bad. There is also a certain amount of residential relocation as persons move into the new units, but no detailed studies have been done on this aspect of intraurban movement nor is much known about the feelings of the elderly toward the specific relocations involved. The approaches that emphasize financial assistance directly to households and in-home services will have the cumulative effect of enabling the elderly to remain in their present housing and neighborhoods. Although this would be more consistent with what is known of preferences, care must be taken that the elderly do not become "locked" in units and places that no longer meet their needs.

Ideally, the provision of assistance to the household should lead to a greater expression of locational choice by the individual, and the trend will likely to toward such an approach because it is fiscally more cautious than a construction-oriented assault on the demand for shelter. It is also more in harmony with American and Canadian cultural dispositions toward an individual property-owning society than the creation of a massive portfolio of state-owned and state-managed housing.

NOTES AND REFERENCES

[1] I appreciate the comments on Ann McAfee and Tony Lloyd on an earlier version of this chapter. I am also indebted to Dale Bairstow for his assistance and inspiration, and I acknowledge the research assistance of Mrs. S. Parsons with data collection and mapping.

[2] A. Romaniuc, "Potentials for Population Growth in Canada," in *A Population Policy for Canada* (Toronto: Conservation Council of Ontario and the Family Planning Federation of Canada, 1975).

[3] In the period 1966–1976, around 2,000 persons older than 65 migrated to British Columbia annually from other parts of Canada.

[4] The life cycle index is calculated by dividing the population aged 65 and older by that younger than 15 (cf. H. I. Hill, "Age Structure and the Family Life Cycle," in M. Ray, ed., *Canadian Urban Trends: National Perspective* (Toronto: Copp Clark, 1976), pp. 207–209).

[5] M. Dennis and S. Fish, *Programs in Search of a Policy: Low Income Housing in Canada* (Toronto: Hakkert, 1972); R. J. Struyk, "The Housing Expense Burden of Households Headed by the Elderly," *Gerontologist*, Vol. 17 (Oct., 1977), pp. 447–452.

[6] D. Bairstow, *Demographic and Economic Aspects of Housing Canada's Elderly* (Ottawa: Central Mortgage and Housing Corporation, 1973).

[7] The Canadian Council on Social Development has estimated the relative poverty lines in 1977 as being $4,400 for a single person and $7,300 for a couple.

[8] K. Collins, *Women and Pensions* (Ottawa: Canadian Council on Social Development, 1977).

[9] Canadian Housing Statistics, 1976.

[10] Dennis and Fish, op. cit., note 5, p. 243.

[11] D. G. Bettison, *The Politics of Canadian Urban Development* (Edmonton: University of Alberta Press, 1975).

[12] Ibid., p. 70.

[13] A ratio of housing costs to disposable income of 25% has gained wide currency in both Canada and the United States.

[14] During the years for which published data are available by province (1973–1976), appropriations under the NHA section for nonprofit housing are greater than for any other social housing supply program in British Columbia in 3 of the 4 years (Canadian Housing Statistics, 1973–1976, inclusive).

[15] J. Mercer and J. Hultquist, "National Progress toward Housing and Urban Renewal Goals," in J. S. Adams, ed., *Urban Policymaking and Metropolitan Dynamics* (Cambridge, Mass.: Ballinger, 1976), pp. 101–162.

[16] M. Wheeler, ed., *The Right to Housing* (Montreal: Harvest House, 1969); Dennis and Fish, op. cit., note 5.

[17] British Columbia Department of Housing, *First Annual Report* (Victoria: Queen's Printer, 1975).

[18] These and other data for 1977 are unpublished data received from Mr. T. Evans, Research Coordinator, Ministry of Municipal Affairs and Housing, Victoria, B.C., March 1978.

[19] For senior citizen only housing in Vancouver, 68% of the units are on previously or currently owned municipal land; in Burnaby, the corresponding figure is 24%.

[20] The need and demand survey that is carried out by the nonprofit sponsor includes size of waiting lists, the number of units already built, and the number of elderly in the area.

[21] In 1971, 68% of Vancouver's elderly had incomes of less than $2,000 (cf. Bairstow, op. cit., note 6, p. 78). Subsequent income assistance programs have reduced this proportion, but Vancouver still has a large proportion of very poor elderly compared to other British Columbia municipalities. This is typical of many central cities.

[22] An analysis of the waiting list of the British Columbia Housing Management Commission showed that almost one-quarter of suburban applicants wished to move into the central city.

[23] British Columbia Ministry of Municipal Affairs and Housing, *SAFER Fact Sheet* (Victoria: Ministry of Municipal Affairs and Housing, 1977).

[24] Ibid.

[25] These data are from an unpublished Statistics Canada survey of urban family expenditure (1972); they were made available by Mr. S. G. Holliday, Department of Psychology, University of British Columbia.

[26] R. J. Struyk, "Housing Situation of Elderly Americans," *Gerontologist*, Vol. 17 (April, 1977), pp. 130–139.

[27] These national data are confirmed by research in Vancouver. In the first two designated areas, 40% of RRAP users were senior citizens (cf. J. Mercer and D. Phillips, "Residential Rehabilitation in Vancouver," *Housing and People*, Vol. 7, No. 4 (1977), pp. 22–27).

[28] L. Auerback and A. Gerber, *Implications of the Changing Age Structure of the Canadian Population* (Ottawa: Science Council of Canada, 1976), pp. 106–109.

[29] A recent report in the United States notes that under the Community Development Block Grant program the allocation system favors, in relative terms, the small and suburban jurisdictions and disadvantages the older and distressed central cities (cf. R. P. Nathan, *Block Grants for Community Development* (Washington, D.C.: Brookings Institution for Department of Housing and Urban Development, 1977).

Chapter 9

TRANSPORTATION AND THE URBAN ELDERLY: LOCAL PROBLEMS, AMELIORATIVE STRATEGIES, AND NATIONAL POLICIES[1]

Rolf R. Schmitt

Goods, services, jobs, education, recreational activities, and social contacts are major components of an individual's quality of life. A person's spatial accessibility to these components can be limited by economic, social, and environmental barriers. The maintenance and improvement of geographic accessibility to these components is thus a major contribution to the individual's quality of life.

This chapter briefly surveys the following themes: transportation problems of the urban elderly; alternative strategies for ameliorating those problems; and current national policies related to those strategies. Also, it outlines some recommendations and caveats concerning the development of future national transportation policy for the urban elderly.

TRANSPORTATION PROBLEMS OF THE URBAN ELDERLY

A substantial body of literature exists on the urban elderly as constituents of the transportation disadvantaged.[2] Although this literature treats many components of geographic accessibility, including vehicle and facility design, areal coverage of transit networks, and the average frequency or length of trips, these factors are rarely analyzed concurrently in order to answer two central questions. First, does the available transportation connect the urban elderly to their desired destinations? Second, do the urban elderly actually reach those destinations (and if not, why)? Some of the literature does consider the availability of transportation for the elderly to destinations used by the general population, but the possibility is often ignored that the elderly have notably different travel desires, which would reflect an individual's changing use of time with age. Most obvious are the decrease or elimination of trips to work and the increase in trips for social and medical and leisure activities. Less obvious is whether the urban elderly are traveling less frequently to higher-order retail outlets (for example, large department stores) and more frequently to lower-order retail outlets (for instance, a neighborhood grocery store) than they have in the past.

While the individual's use of time and desired travel patterns are changing, so too are his personal mobility resources. The private automobile is the only mode that can readily accommodate changing patterns of personal travel desires. However, with increased age the car becomes increasingly less available as a result of perceptual, cognitive, physiological, and financial constraints. The usual alternative of public transit is generally oriented toward work trips and often fails to provide reasonably direct connections between the elderly and nonwork destinations. Furthermore, the older individual is more easily deterred by architectural and information barriers in facilities and vehicles, walking and waiting requirements, higher fares, and an insensitive on-board environment (seating inavailability, absence of air conditioning, little police protection, etc.). The use of another public alternative, the taxicab, is restricted because it is relatively expensive for frequent use. The remaining alternatives, the dependence on friends or relatives who drive and the dependence on the facilities available within walking distance or in the immediate neighborhood, also have obvious limitations as modes of accessibility.

Trips by the elderly to grocery stores in northeast Baltimore illustrate the problem. As in most American cities, low densities of urban development, segregation of land uses, and mass marketing have placed grocery stores beyond a short walking distance for the majority of the area's population. Many of the local elderly travel to the first supermarket that can be reached on the nearest bus route to home without making a transfer. The store reached is not always the best in the area with respect to price, selection, and quality of goods, but is the only store easily accessible. Because bags of groceries are unwieldly on a bus, the added expense of a taxicab is often incurred for the return trip home. What may appear as irrational economic behavior of elderly shoppers often simply reflects their lack of opportunities to choose among destinations and modes of travel.

Many of the urban elderly are not so constrained spatially because they continue to drive or have friends or relatives with readily available cars. Other elderly persons can afford taxicabs whenever they need to travel. Unfortunately, a substantial number of the urban elderly do not have adequate mobility resources and thus may have to restrict the frequency or the locational context of their personal travel.[3] Unless they live in the few neighborhoods that can supply all needs and wants locally, the absence of transportation alternatives will result in a decline in the older person's level of activity and possibly, in turn, his quality of life.

LOCAL STRATEGIES FOR AMELIORATIVE SERVICES

There are four basic strategies by which local geographic accessibility can be maintained for groups such as the urban elderly who do not have adequate mobility resources. First, existing fixed-route public transit systems can be modified to better serve the elderly's needs. Responses may include the increasing of the number of route-miles and the frequency of service, the making of route modifications to reduce the number of transfers needed to complete trips, and the modification of stations and vehicles to remove physical barriers and to improve the display of travel information. The second strategy is to provide or subsidize a specialized transit service that is tailor-made to a specific clientele.[4] This service, sometimes referred to as "subsidiary transit," may cover areawide destinations or be tied to a specific facility, such as a health care center. Subsidiary transit usually consists of mini-buses, vans, or cars operating on flexible schedules over a variable route system. The third strategy for ameliorating transportation problems is to provide vouchers, grants, or other forms of subsidy to the elderly, which would make taxi or other existing services more affordable.[5] Last, one can reduce travel requirements by insuring that elderly people are located within walking distance of their desired destinations.

Although these ameliorative strategies are relatively simple in concept, their local implementation is fairly difficult. There is rarely a unique correspondence between the characteristics of a possible transportation innovation and the needs of the intended clientele. This is illustrated in Figure 18, in which transportation strategies are matched against a three-dimensional classification of the disadvantaged. Even given a reasonable match between needs and services, it is nearly impossible to obtain small-area enumerations of specific groups, unless they are classified only by age or as users of a specific facility. Many ameliorative actions are difficult to implement for political, financial, and operational reasons; for example, innovative forms of taxi service are often impeded by local regulatory policies.[6]

Although transportation difficulties of the urban elderly reflect the quality of local transportation systems, much of the incentive and the resources to ameliorate their problems are provided by the federal government. More importantly, the pervasive federal involvement in urban transportation has resulted in a number of national policies that affect the desirability or viability of different local strategies. These policies must be considered in the selection of transportation alternatives to improve the mobility situation of the urban elderly.

NATIONAL POLICIES AND THEIR CONSEQUENCES

The elderly are defined by Congress as a major constituent of the transportation disadvantaged for whom federal policy attempts to encourage or to force local government sensitivity and action. It has been mandated as national policy "that special efforts shall be made in the planning and design of mass transportation facilities and services so that the availability to elderly and

PRIVATE VEHICLE AVAILABLE

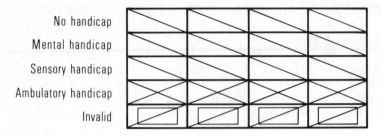

No handicap
Mental handicap
Sensory handicap
Ambulatory handicap
Invalid

PRIMARY TRANSIT AVAILABLE

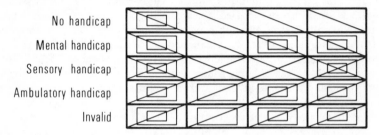

No handicap
Mental handicap
Sensory handicap
Ambulatory handicap
Invalid

NEITHER PRIVATE VEHICLE NOR TRANSIT AVAILABLE

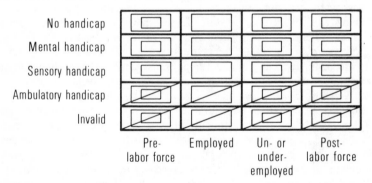

No handicap
Mental handicap
Sensory handicap
Ambulatory handicap
Invalid

Pre-labor force   Employed   Un- or under-employed   Post-labor force

RECOMMENDED SERVICE DEVELOPMENTS TO MEET MOBILITY NEEDS

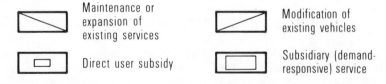

Maintenance or expansion of existing services

Modification of existing vehicles

Direct user subsidy

Subsidiary (demand-responsive) service

Fig. 18. Matching transportation services to the needs of the mobility disadvantaged.

handicapped persons of mass transportation which they can effectively utilize will be assured; and that all federal programs offering assistance in the field of mass transportation . . . should contain provisions implementing this policy."[7]

The Secretary of Transportation has attempted to implement this policy with the TRANSBUS mandate, which requires that all city buses purchased with federal assistance after September 30, 1979, must meet specific design standards for wheelchair accessibility and other factors. The intent is to make urban transit usable by all, including the elderly, by requiring local operators to implement part of the first mentioned strategy to improve existing transportation service.

Although the TRANSBUS mandate is, at present, the major explicit national transportation policy for the elderly, most current federal expenditures are supporting the development and operation of subsidiary transit, the second local strategy. A large number of small-scale, subsidiary transit services have been established under the many programs supported by the U.S. Department of Health, Education, and Welfare.[8] These services are usually provided by public or not-for-profit private organizations on a cost reimbursement basis, with capital costs occasionally funded by the Urban Mass Transportation Administration of the U.S. Department of Transportation. The resulting subsidiary transit system in a given region is often poorly coordinated, with each service tied to a specific facility, providing a very limited type and number of trips. Vehicles are often underutilized, and many travel demands (e.g., social and retail trips) remain unserved. Furthermore, the limited constituency and unstable sources of funds have tended to reduce the length of time such a service continues to be in operation.

The TRANSBUS mandate was intended to overcome these problems by integrating the elderly and other transportation disadvantaged groups into the citywide bus system, which would provide multipurpose, multidestination coverage and a wider constituency to support the service. The TRANSBUS approach, however, has three problems of its own. First, the capital and maintenance costs of TRANSBUS appear to be much greater than those for conventional designs (assuming that the design standards can be met in the first place). Second, an improved vehicle design does not guarantee adequate spatial coverage, direct connections and adequate frequency of service, which are central to maintaining geographic accessibility. Third, these factors can be reasonably guaranteed only by a demand-responsive, door-to-door service. In fact, the urban elderly may not want to be integrated with the general population that uses existing, citywide transit. For example, elderly residents of northeast Baltimore reported the potential conflicts with school-aged riders as a major reason for not using the bus.

An obvious alternative to TRANSBUS is areawide subsidiary transit. This can be accomplished either by establishing an areawide, special transit agency (as developed in Delaware) or by establishing a brokerage agency that matches service providers with potential user groups and funding mechanisms (as is being tried in Knoxville, Tennessee). The strategy of *areawide* subsidiary transit has been little used, partly because federal regulations and funding sources are not coordinated and partly because local institutions have resisted the imposition of such an organization. This strategy also raises serious questions:

—Can the clients of facilities now operating subsidiary transit receive an adequate level of service from an areawide system?
—Can the areawide service reasonably cover all of its potential users and all of their needs not otherwise served by existing transit?
—How are private providers of transportation service affected?

This last question is important if the subsidiary transit system incorporates taxicab services and thereby reduces the number of cabs and the level of service available for remaining taxicab users.

One method of avoiding this problem is to subsidize users and allow them to purchase whatever service they need. In short, use the third local strategy and make existing transportation alternatives affordable for all urban elderly. At present, this is done indirectly through social security and other transfer payments. A few demonstrations, which were inconclusive, have been attempted to test transit vouchers and other methods of user-side subsidies. The Department of Transportation prefers to subsidize the service provider and requires that transit fares be reduced by half for elderly and handicapped users.

In terms of insuring geographic accessibility, the remaining and least considered strategy is to move the origins and destinations of trips closer together. The transportation problem of the urban elderly is an exaggerated reflection of government's general failure to integrate transportation and land use planning. A large percentage of the urban population lives beyond walking distance from desired destinations and must rely completely on private automobiles both for passenger transport and for the distribution of most goods from retail outlets to the consumer. A larger percentage of the elderly population is affected because the individual's capacity to walk and carry packages is generally reduced with age. Until transportation and land use planning are thoroughly integrated and nontransportation solutions are implemented for many transportation problems, expensive and institutionally difficult strategies must be exercised to link the elderly with the locations of goods, services, and activities.

CAVEATS AND RECOMMENDATIONS

Much has been written about the transportation needs of the urban elderly. Efforts to ameliorate their problems have been fraught with pitfalls, several of which have been mentioned briefly. Much research and many policy considerations have been based on misconceptions and myopia, some of the worst of which are summarized below, with suggestions for their resolution.

Age alone is a relatively poor criterion for identifying someone as being among the transportation disadvantaged. Age is only a surrogate measure for changing employment status, income problems, and physical infirmities. Policies designed to ameliorate these conditions, such as the federally mandated fare reduction on city buses, often fail to help those in need, while aiding persons who are already served adequately (e.g., the wealthy individual who is older than 65). In fact, the urban elderly's access to automobiles is increasing as population cohorts containing higher proportions of automobile owners and drivers reach their senior years.[9] National policies should not be designed solely to address the transportation difficulties of the elderly population, but rather to help both the elderly and nonelderly with economic and physical conditions that clearly justify their being labelled as the transportation disadvantaged.

Proposed ameliorative efforts should also recognize the entire range of problems that makes someone disadvantaged with respect to transportation. Existing transit is inadequate in many ways, including vehicle design, on-board environment, service frequency, number of requisite transfers, and distance between the route and the trip's origin and ultimate destination. Solutions to one or two of these inadequacies may be rendered ineffective by the remaining deficiencies. Furthermore, solutions need not be limited to transporting people: Goods and services can be transported to people, such as in the meals-on-wheels program, or nontransportation solutions can be attempted, such as full-service retirement residences.

Finally, any ameliorative service must be evaluated very carefully. In spite of the experience and research of planners and those influencing public policy, painfully little is known about the effectiveness of most services for the transportation disadvantaged. This is due, in part, to overemphasis on the effects of architectural barriers, to a lack of careful field experimentation when service innovations are attempted, and to poorly conceived evaluation measures. Evaluation measures should emphasize the benefits and costs of providing for personal interaction rather than of system interaction. The former includes the frequency of travel and the number of destination opportunities utilized, whereas the latter includes passenger-miles traveled, number of vehicles available, etc. It does little good to provide a service that is hardly used or to provide a service for those who already enjoy an adequate level of geographic accessibility. It does even less good if a service fails on either grounds and nothing is learned from the unsuccessful experience. Only from carefully evaluated experiments and programs can appropriate and effective transportation services be developed so that no population group finds itself geographically isolated from the necessities and amenities that support its quality of life.

NOTES AND REFERENCES

[1] This chapter is based primarily on the author's doctoral dissertation (cf. R. R. Schmitt, "Accessibility, Experimentation, and the Evaluation of Transportation Developments for Disadvantaged Groups," unpublished doctoral dissertation, John Hopkins University, 1978) and on his work at the National Transportation Policy Study Commission. The findings and views expressed are the author's alone and do not necessarily reflect those of the Commission.

[2] R. Blachard, *Transportation and the Disadvantaged: A Bibliography* (Los Angeles: School of Architecture and Urban Planning, University of California, June, 1975); S. Golant, "Intraurban Transportation Needs and Problems of the Elderly," in M. Powell Lawton, R. J.

Newcomer and T. O. Byerts, eds., *Community Planning for an Aging Society* (Stroudsburg, Pa.: Dowden, Hutchinson, & Ross, 1976), pp. 282–308.

[3] U.S. Department of Transportation, Urban Transportation Advisory Council, *The Handicapped and Elderly Market for Urban Mass Transit* (Washington, D.C.: Urban Mass Transportation Administration, Oct., 1973); Abt Associates, Inc., *Transportation Needs of the Urban Disadvantaged*, Report No. DOT-FH-11-7802 (Washington, D.C.: Socioeconomic Studies Division, Federal Highway Administration, March, 1974).

[4] H. S. Perloff and K. M. Connell, "Subsidiary Transportation: Its Role in Regional Planning," *Journal of the American Institute of Planners*, Vol. 41 (May, 1975), pp. 170–183.

[5] R. F. Kirby and F. Tolson, *Improving the Mobility of the Elderly and Handicapped through User-side Subsidies*, Report No. UI 5050-4-4 (Washington, D.C.: The Urban Institute, 1977).

[6] R. F. Kirby, et al., *Para-transit: Neglected Options for Urban Mobility* (Washington, D.C.: The Urban Institute, 1974).

[7] 49 U.S.C. 1612.

[8] Institute of Public Administration, *Transportation for Older Americans* (Washington, D.C.: Institute of Public Administration, April, 1975).

[9] M. Wachs and R. D. Blachard, *Life Styles and Transportation Needs of the Future Elderly* (Los Angeles: School of Architecture and Urban Planning, University of California, May, 1975).

Chapter 10

TRANSPORTATION ISSUES AND PROBLEMS OF THE RURAL ELDERLY

Douglas J. McKelvey[1]

There is no absence of documentation of the mobility and transportation problems of people who live in rural areas. Despite the progressive efforts of local, state, and federal governments, many issues remain unresolved and problems still exist.[2] This chapter provides an overview of these rural passenger transportation issues and problems, focusing on those that affect the elderly population in particular.

BACKGROUND

The Administration on Aging and its counterparts at the state and local levels, in conjunction with the U.S. Department of Transportation and others, have attempted to meet the transportation needs of the rural elderly. The most notable programs are Title III (demonstrations) and Title VII (nutrition) of the Administration of Aging and section 16(b) 2 (capital assistance to private not-for-profit organizations) and section 147 (rural transportation demonstration programs) of the U.S. Department of Transportation. Also, some states (such as Pennsylvania, Missouri, and Ohio), provide financial assistance to systems that serve the elderly. The funds have been used primarily to initiate and subsidize specialized subsidiary systems in order to increase the mobility of the rural elderly. Often this approach is neither cost-effective nor viable in the long run, because funding itself is inadequate, unstable, and usually not flexible—in other words, cannot be used to subsidize individuals, to contract with private taxi operators or public transit systems, or as ongoing *operating* assistance. In addition, the lack of clear congressional intent, state interpretations of program guidelines, and the concern for accountability of federal funds have hindered coordination of transportation services.[3] Together, these factors have contributed to inadequate rural passenger transportation services and the inability to develop other alternatives in local areas on a continuing basis. These conditions, coupled with the low income of the elderly, their special transportation needs, and their lack of telephone service to request transportation, make rural mobility and transportation a complex problem.

THE RURAL TRANSPORTATION PROBLEM

The major problem in rural transportation is overcoming large distances between residents and their destinations. Rural residents often travel as far as 15 miles to see friends or buy groceries, and even farther for health services.[4] Therefore, most rural residents must rely on the automobile to reach desired destinations. Those without access to an automobile are isolated and must rely on friends and neighbors or pay a large portion of their income for transportation. This would suggest that giving rural residents a car and/or more money would solve the rural transportation problem. However, there are other factors that complicate the demand-supply relationship. These concern the availability and characteristics of the existing transportation system, the location of goods and services, the travel habits and needs of the elderly, the accessibility difficulties of social agencies, the cost and supply of oil and gas, and the political and institutional infrastructure.

LACK OF TRANSPORTATION ALTERNATIVES

The transportation problem of many elderly is that transportation alternatives are either nonexistent, inefficient, or ineffective, as evidenced by the following facts:

- Sixteen percent of the places with populations between 2,500 and 10,000 do not have taxi, intercity bus, subsidiary, or public transit service.
- Fifty percent or more of the places with populations less than 2,500 do not have the above services.
- Taxis do not serve 20% of the places with populations between 2,500 and 10,000 and 90% of the places less than 2,500; the average cost of a 2-mile trip is $1.50.
- Subsidiary systems do not serve 75% of the places with populations between 2,500 and 10,000 and 87% of the places less than 2,500; 90% of the subsidiary systems charge no fare and most serve the elderly.
- Intercity buses do not serve 58% of the places with populations between 2,500 and 10,000 and 88% of the places with less then 2,500.[5]

When alternatives are available, the fare is often too high for the user or the subsidy is too large for the agency or government. The cost of providing service is high owing mainly to the low density of demand, long passenger trips, and low vehicle utilization, and the inability to efficiently coordinate supply and demand. Inflation, and higher insurance rates, also contribute to increasing costs.[6] In Pennsylvania, these factors have resulted in an average cost of $1.19 per passenger trip for subsidiary rural transportation service (not including depreciation) and $3.16 per passenger trip for the section 147 Rural Highway Public Transportation Demonstration program.[7] Increasing costs are also a problem for privately operated carriers in rural areas, resulting in a decline in rural taxi and intercity bus services. The general response by federal agencies and some states has been capital grants to public and subsidiary systems, but rarely have they provided funds for operating assistance for private operators or for users (user-side subsidy). The lack of a continuing federal operating assistance program for public, private, and subsidiary transportation systems has been a major reason for inadequate and costly passenger service in rural areas. A hopeful prospect is pending legislation that would provide about $75 million annually in federal operating assistance and would make intercity bus-carriers eligible to participate.

INEFFICIENT TRANSPORTATION ALTERNATIVES

In most instances, rural transportation services are not operated as efficiently as they could be, which contributes to higher costs and less service. There are four main reasons why this occurs. (1) Neither rural systems nor user and agency travel needs are coordinated; e.g., work and nonwork trips, vehicles (such as taxi, public, school bus, specialized, and intercity bus), and agency funds. (2) Funding is usually inadequate, unstable, or inappropriate. (3) Planning, technical assistance, and marketing are often inadequate at the local and state levels. Many state departments of transportation and state social agencies do not have a person or office for rural transit, even though they fund many specialized systems in rural areas. Further, there is rarely coordinated transportation planning, and the A-95 review process is inadequate to ensure coordination. (4) Management is lacking and/or faced with program and accounting requirements from each funding source that inhibit coordination and efficiency. In addition, there is little consideration of alternatives to moving people, e.g., user-side subsidies, moving services, or communications, that may be both more efficient and more effective than current federal, state, and agency approaches (see Chapter 9).

INEFFECTIVE SYSTEMS

Many rural systems are ineffective for one or more reasons. For instance, taxi fees are often too expensive for frequent use by low-income persons. Some elderly persons may not be able to get to the intercity bus stop, or else round-trip service is not available on the same day to some rural towns.

Subsidiary systems may restrict transit to agency activities only, even though social and recreational trips may be more important to elderly persons. Also, friends and neighbors may not be available to provide continuing and timely transportation to activities and medical services. The result is that many rural elderly remain transportation disadvantaged because the level and cost of service are not appropriate, given their needs and their ability to pay. Thus, when systems are planned, they must be more sensitive to the characteristics of rural elderly and of the agencies that will use them.

INDIVIDUAL AND AGENCY CHARACTERISTICS

Many rural residents are faced with multiple disadvantages that limit their mobility, including being without a car or living in households with only one car (7.8 million), having a handicap (3.4 million), being elderly (5.2 million), or being poor (4.9 million).[8] An unduplicated count of the number of rural persons for each combination is not known. In addition, many rural residents, including the elderly, do not have a telephone, which restricts their ability to call for transportation services. In the absence of telephone communication, the demand for transportation services may increase if the life-maintenance and social needs of the elderly are to be satisfied. Usually, rural residents require door-to-door transportation service, and, if the person is nonambulatory, a lift, ramp, or a specially designed vehicle will also be necessary. However, many systems are not door-to-door and only 13% of the subsidiary systems in rural areas have specially equipped vehicles for disabled persons.[9]

Agencies, like individuals, require transportation. Because existing public and private systems have not been adequate or sensitive to agency needs (e.g., the nutrition program), agencies have initiated and operated specialized systems that serve selected persons. Consequently, the focus has been on transportation programs rather than on individuals. Thus, planning and service are frequently uncoordinated and do not solve the transportation problems of rural elderly.

The definition of what areas should be included as "rural" is not even agreed upon. The U.S. Census defines rural as places or areas with less than 2,500 population outside of urbanized areas. However, many federal programs define "rural" as places or areas with less than a 5,000, 10,000, 20,000, or even 50,000 population. The definition of "rural" is important because it determines which persons and systems are eligible for technical and financial assistance.

Even if efficient and effective transportation systems sensitive to the needs of rural persons and agencies were implemented, there would still be other factors that impact rural service and mobility.

THE LOCATION OF ACTIVITIES, ENERGY, AND THE
POLITICAL ENVIRONMENT

Many public and private services have been centralizing, which increases travel distances for rural elderly and the costs of the goods and services they consume.

Also, the price and availability of fuel have and always will significantly affect the transportation services provided by volunteers and agencies.[10] In addition, the attitudes of the federal, state, and local governments toward rural transportation are important because they fund, regulate, coordinate, or possibly operate, rural transportation services. Favorable attitudes, especially on the part of state departments of transportation, have resulted in funding and technical assistance for rural systems and have directly increased mobility in some rural areas. However, many rural residents remain transportation disadvantaged.

RURAL TRANSPORTATION ISSUES

Given the status of the transportation disadvantaged and current responses to address their needs, the following appear to be the most crucial issues:[11]

-Who are the transportation disadvantaged? What geographic areas should be defined as rural? Currently, many programs treat the elderly as one group, do not distinguish between rural and urban, and imply that all the elderly are transportation disadvantaged. This is not true.
-How much mobility is every rural resident, including the nonambulatory, entitled to? Should it be the same for all persons and rural areas? Should a standard be based on urban counterparts? Should it be the same as for those with access to a car? Should the federal or state government develop mobility standards?
-How much should transportation users pay and how much should each level of government (including agencies) pay? How should costs be calculated? Currently, most rural systems charge no fares, and the agency and government pay 90% to 100% of the costs. The major funding agency is the Department of Health, Education, and Welfare, which spends about $500 million per year on transportation, much of it in rural areas.[12]
-Who should provide and coordinate service? Potential service providers include the government (state, county, city, and others); social service agencies; private agencies; private operators (taxi and intercity bus); friends and neighbors; urban transit systems; and regional transportation authorities.
-What types or combination of services will best meet the transportation needs of the rural elderly? Potential service types include door-to-door, fixed route, feeder, public and specialized services.

Most of the issues raised here are being addressed by Congress, the General Accounting Office, the White House, the Departments of Transportation, Health, Education and Welfare, and Agriculture, as well as state and local governments and others. New funding has been proposed and working groups both within and between agencies have been established to improve coordination and efficiency. However, resolution of some of the toughest institutional and political issues will require time. These issues include mobility standards, funding to users rather than to systems, coordination of agency funds and vehicles, energy pricing, rural land use control, and maintenance and upgrading of rural roads and bridges. The responses to each will affect rural residents, especially many elderly who do not have the resources to address their transportation needs. Thus, it is important to continually ask: How will this decision, policy, or program affect rural mobility, especially that of the rural elderly?

NOTES AND REFERENCES

[1] The author is a Transportation Specialist with the National Transportation Policy Study Commission. The views expressed do not necessarily reflect those of the Commission.

[2] National Association of Area Agencies on Aging, Rural Affairs Committee, *Results of Regional Hearings*, unpublished manuscript, July, 1978; U.S. Senate, Special Committee on Aging, *The Nation's Rural Elderly; Problems and Progress*, Parts 1–6 (Washington, D.C.: Government Printing Office, 1974 and 1977).

[3] Comptroller General of the United States, *Hindrances to Coordinating Transportation of People Participating in Federally Funded Grant Programs*, Vol. 1, CED-77-119 (Washington, D.C.: Government Printing Office, Oct., 1977).

[4] U.S. Department of Agriculture, Economics Research Service, *Prelude to Legislation to Solve the Growing Crisis in Rural Transportation, Part I: Transportation in Rural America* (Washington, D.C.: Government Printing Office, Feb., 1975).

[5] A. Jackson and D. McKelvey, "Transportation Services in Places Between 2,500 and 10,000 Population," a paper presented at the meeting of the Association of American Geographers, New Orleans, April, 1978, pp. 1–3, 40–43.

[6] F. Davis, "Overview of the Social Service Insurance Dilemma," a paper presented at the Conference on Overcoming Obstacles for Improving Public Transportation, Zion, Illinois, Aug., 1978.

[7] J. Burkhardt, "Cost of Alternative Rural Transportation Services," *Transportation Research Board Record*, forthcoming.

[8] E. Hauser et al., "Use of Existing Facilities for Transporting Disadvantaged Residents of Rural Areas," a report prepared for the Federal Highway Administration, Contract DOT-FH-H-8261, Dec., 1974.

[9] Jackson and McKelvey, op. cit., note 5.

[10] U.S. Senate, op. cit., note 2, 1974.

[11] D. McKelvey, "Innovative Approaches to Rural Public Transportation," *Transportation Research Board Record*, Vol. 661 (June, 1978).

[12] S. Brooks, "Mobility for the Elderly and Handicapped, A Case of Choices," *Transit Journal*, Vol. 1, No. 2 (May, 1975), pp. 45–50.

PART III

PLANNING METHODOLOGIES AND STRATEGIES

INTRODUCTION TO PART III

If housing, transportation, and service facilities are to be spatially accessible to the elderly people who require them the most, then planning and government agencies must have good data describing where these older people are presently living and models to predict their future residential location patterns. Recognition of the need for these information systems and analytical tools provides the rationale for the first three chapters in Part III. Moore and Publicover begin by arguing that although data at the national and regional level are likely to be readily available and up-to-date, this is less likely the case at the local level—in cities, communities, neighborhoods—where census enumerations are infrequent. This is a particularly serious problem in areas that have experienced rapid population and housing changes. Communities often respond to these data needs by carrying out household surveys; however, these not only are very expensive but they also usually consist of small, purposively selected samples not representative of the total elderly population. Here, too, outdated population statistics reduce the likelihood of statistically valid sampling frames. To address this need, the authors outline a computerized data system that uses information collected in association with the property assessment application process. Two features of the data system make it particularly attractive. First, it consists of annually collected—and thus up-to-date—demographic and housing data describing the most relevant attributes of individuals and households. As the empirical example described by the authors indicates, this enables data files to be linked over time at the individual level, which, in turn, allows the planner considerable analytical flexibility in studying population and housing shifts through time.

Second, the data are recorded in computer-readable form, and the authors have developed an easily used retrieval process in which a noncomputer specialist can readily construct data cross-tabulations or obtain a visual display of his data in map form.

The advantages of an annually updated microlevel data system, such as the one outlined by Moore and Publicover, are obvious. However, for a variety of reasons, most communities have not implemented this type of system and must rely on long-term population forecasts based heavily on data collected by the U.S. Census. Data limitations aside, there are many pitfalls involved in projecting the future size of populations by age in small enumeration areas, such as census tracts. This is carefully pointed out in Chapter 12 by Lycan and Weiss, who addressed these difficulties when they developed their own methodology for projecting the future census tract location pattern of people living in the Portland, Oregon metropolitan area. The projection methodology consists of several different submodels, which are analytically combined to yield a final integrated model. A noteworthy aspect of their model is the simultaneous consideration of housing and population growth rates when projecting the size of elderly populations by census tracts. However, the authors' methodology is designed to project numbers of people in all age groups, not just the aged. They legitimately argue that competition between young and old populations for the limited supply of housing offered in different locations must be incorporated in forecasting models.

In the next contribution (Chapter 13), Birdsall contends that mere availability of data does not guarantee the planner will carry out the most effective analysis when assessing the locational efficiency of services for older people. As a simple methodological approach, he suggests the use of a population potential index as a measure of where the elderly population is located. Derived from the more familiar gravity model, a population's potential surface is calculated over a set of spatial units, such as census tracts, and it identifies the accessibility of each census tract in relation to the total city's or metropolitan area's elderly population. For illustration purposes, Birdsall compares how such population potential surfaces have changed during a 30-year period in Washington, D.C.

The common theme linking the first three chapters in Part III is the need for data and methodologies capable of monitoring and predicting the residential locations of older people and of the facilities intended to service them. In contrast, the final two chapters are concerned with developing models that are capable of assessing whether the social welfare environment of older people is adequately addressing and fulfilling their various needs. These models are increasingly necessary when some critics argue that services and benefits to older people are grossly inadequate, while other critics contend that federal and local spending must be curtailed. In the contribution by Golant and McCaslin (Chapter 14), a social indicator model is outlined in which the social and behavioral functions performed by services and benefits are simultaneously classified according to whether they address two broad welfare goals: (1) the improvement or maintenance of the individual's competence and (2) the maintenance of the individual's independent living arrangements. A methodology is developed by which to assess the supply (quantity and attributes) of services that are able to address these goals. The weaknesses of social indicator models of this type are reviewed, as well as how its findings might be used by planners and policy makers.

Using concepts similar to those found in Golant and McCaslin's contribution, Dear and Wolch describe some of the basic components of a service delivery environment (Chapter 15). The major goal of their model is to match clients with appropriate treatment settings. More generally, they are concerned with describing and explaining the extent to which the social welfare environment is congruent with the behavioral needs of a community's clients. Their model includes classifications of both clients and treatment settings (or environments); the former, along a dependence-autonomy dimension; the latter, along a dimension ranging from closed protected environments (e.g., institutions) to open unrestricted environments (e.g., community based facilities). The major goal of their model is to allocate client groups to the particular level of treatment setting that most nearly approximates their tolerable autonomy levels. The authors discuss the various constraints of their model, which emerge in connection with the behavior of clients, providers, and community groups, and the several important policy issues that are raised.

Chapter 11

THE USE OF PUBLIC MICRODATA IN LOCAL STUDIES OF THE ELDERLY

Eric G. Moore and Mark Publicover

During the last two decades, the dramatic increase in the elderly population of North America has posed particular problems for local government and for other public agencies operating at the city and neighborhood levels. Many of the services provided for the elderly are sensitive not only to the sociodemographic characteristics of this population but also to its size and concentration within the agency's jurisdiction. Yet, within the city, the shifts that are emerging strongly at the national level are often more dramatic in terms of spatial concentration and in the rapidity with which change occurs. For example, in Kingston, Ontario, Canada where part of the work discussed here is being undertaken, the population older than 55 within the city boundaries had increased from 10,000 (18.3% of total) to 12,500 (20.1% of total) between 1971 and 1974, whereas the total population of the city remained virtually unchanged. Under these circumstances, the conventional sources, such as the decennial Census, that have been used to document national and regional changes are inadequate to inform us about the nature of local concerns. This chapter focuses on the need to develop at the local level data bases capable of supporting the information needs required by public agency decision makers and their analyses of the dynamics of change in the elderly population within specific urban or community areas.

THE ELDERLY IN LOCAL JURISDICTIONS

Much of the recent writing on the elderly in North America has stressed the heterogeneity of this population. The elderly exhibit a broad range of sociodemographic attributes, attitudes, needs, interests, and political opinions, with chronological age often serving as a relatively weak common bond.[1] The need to appreciate this diversity and its implications increases as the elderly population continues to increase in size and as the social and political awareness of their interests grow.[2]

The nature of the issues arising from studies of structure, growth, and change depend, to a large degree, on the scale of analysis. For example, at the national level, the growth of the elderly population has accentuated the division between productive and dependent components of the population and has created major fiscal problems for the funding of social welfare programs. In contrast, at the regional level, major migration shifts of the more affluent elderly to high-amenity areas, particularly the southwestern United States (see Chapter 2) serve to highlight the lower population and housing status of the elderly who have chosen to remain in low-amenity regions, notably the older central cities of the northeast.[3] However, at both of these scales of analysis, conventional public data sources provide a good starting point for empirical analysis.

At the city level, however, a broad range of new concerns arise that cannot be handled so readily. Much of the behavior of the elderly, particularly with regard to the need for and consumption of social services and utilities,[4] depends on the general sociostructural attributes of local elderly populations and on territorial constraints that accompany groups with limited mobility. The sources of these latter constraints are diverse, ranging from lower rates of car ownership and a higher incidence of physical limitations on movements to strong attachments to local and familiar environments;[5] whatever the source, however, the association of limited mobility with localized and differentiated client groups renders the decisions regarding appropriate service packages highly sensitive to locational and territorial issues (see Chapters 14 and 15).

Attempts to study in detail the behavior of the urban elderly have depended almost entirely on sample surveys. These have been fruitful in that they have identified how personal well-being is related to sociodemographic attributes, personal health, attitudinal measures, the structure and quality of social interaction, and the consumption of goods and services. However, the ability to translate these into more specific policy and programmatic statements at the local level has been limited.

At least two major problems arise. First, the traditional methods of data collection and analysis tend to randomize across social institutional contexts, thus emphasizing the role of individual attributes, attitudes, and preferences rather than the plethora of formal and informal constraints acting on choice and restricting behavior. Relative access to transit systems, the location of senior citizens' projects in relation to services and amenities, and the nature of eligibility rules for local programs are often controlled by the study design and cannot be discriminated in the analysis. Second, even when we use simple relationships to estimate phenomena such as the demand for public transit using age and car-ownership rates, knowledge of the sociodemographic structure and spatial distribution of the local elderly population is often restricted. These problems are accentuated in locations experiencing more rapid population and housing changes. Census data become outmoded within 2 or 3 years (often *before* they are released with a detailed local breakdown) and data from special surveys experience similar obsolescence. The need to develop more up-to-date and disaggregate local data bases stems from the desire to relate analyses of structure and change to the specific characteristics of local populations and social institutions and from the requirements of local decision makers to identify the most needy clientele and major problem areas.

MICROLEVEL DATA SYSTEMS AT THE CITY LEVEL

The ensuing discussion is grounded in the belief that to develop effective procedures for answering questions about the detailed structure and change of local populations for planning and policy purposes, much more use must be made of existing disaggregate data in the public sector. Local, state, and federal agencies regularly collect a great deal of data that contain basic information on the sociodemographic characteristics of households, their housing consumption, and use of services. Thus the issue often is not so much the existence of relevant data but its access and use.

Although access poses problems of both a technological and a financial nature, the most formidable barrier arises from public concern over invasion of privacy.[6] Providing access to individual records is a political thistle most local officials are unwilling to grasp. To a large degree, this unwillingness to permit more general use of public data files stems from a confusion between a legitimate fear of personal dossier systems, which are designed explicitly to influence actions toward specific individuals, and statistical reporting systems, whose function is to support decision making with respect to groups, not individuals.[7] This latter activity is, in any case, the primary function of much individual data collected by specific agencies: The most important step is the construction of an appropriate institutional framework of controls and sanctions to prevent abuse rather than a blanket refusal to permit access to local data files under any circumstances.[8]

Even when access to individual data can be obtained, major technical problems of organization and integration still remain. The first, and quite a costly, step is to establish an address-based file that includes each household. Although there are numerous cities that possess individual property files, very few have associated sociodemographic data for each dwelling. The most promising situations on which to build are those in which enumeration procedures have been established in association with the property assessment process; in the United States, Kansas (especially Wichita-Sedgwick County) and in Canada, Ontario provide good examples of such data files.

THE PRISSA SYSTEM[9]

In this section we focus on a data system developed for Kingston, Ontario, Canada, which incorporates demographic data with its municipal assessment

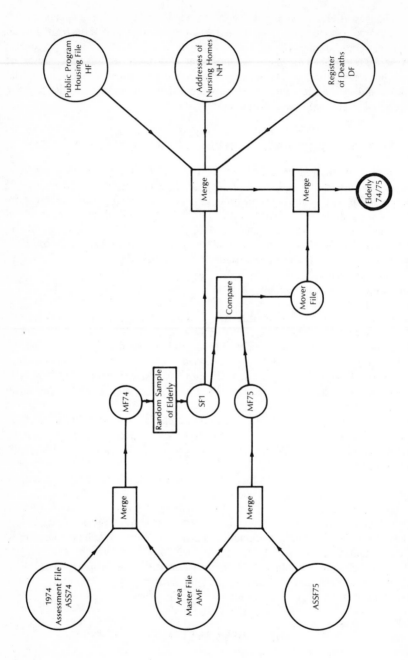

Fig. 19. The steps in the construction of "elderly 74/75."

records. Each year, the Ontario Ministry of Revenue collects demographic data on each household in the province. These data are obtained from a mailed form that contains the previous year's data for a dwelling unit and is returned to the Ministry only if changes have been made. The following data are provided: each individual's age, sex, citizenship, tenancy status, school support (public or separate), and voter eligibility; and each dwelling unit's ownership status, structure type, lot size, assessed value, and address. Groupings of individual records within dwelling units permit inferences to be made regarding the size and sociodemographic structure of households. The file containing these records for a given year is termed the Assessment File (ASSF).

A second component of the system is provided by the Area Master File (AMF) produced by Statistics Canada for each city with a population larger than 50,000. It is similar to the U.S. DIME System[10] and permits translation of any address into a geographical coordinate associated with the centroid of the relevant block-face (or street segment if the block is very long).

We then emerged the AMF and ASSF for 1974 to obtain the Master File for that year (MF74). These operations were repeated with data collected in the following year in order to create a second Master File, MF75. The two Master Files facilitated the construction of the special purpose file used in this study. A stratified random sample of 3,434 individuals aged 55 and older was selected from MF74 and this file was labelled SF1.[11] Records from federal and provincial housing sources were used to identify these dwelling units built under various housing programs, particularly for senior citizens (HF). The local agency responsible for coordinating programs for the elderly provided the addresses of nursing homes and other special residences (NH), and the local registry office provided data on those who had died in 1974–1975 (DF). Finally, SF1 was compared with MF75 to identify those who had moved within the city or had left the system during the year. Figure 19 provides a graphic representation of the steps involved in producing the composite file ELDERLY 74/75, which forms the basis of the ensuing empirical work.

It is appropriate to briefly mention the mode of access to this file because the development of interactive computer systems for planning purposes has been an integral part of the work. Part of the reason for the limited success of computer-based information systems in planning, as opposed to administration,[12] is that standard modes of access to large, sophisticated machines are not conducive to most planning uses. Therefore, the authors have developed a combined word-processing and file query language for retrieving lists, constructing complex cross-tabulations, and producing graphic displays on a dedicated minicomputer (PDP11/VO3).[13] This permits direct interaction between a noncomputer specialist (the planner or other decision maker) and complex data files, such as ELDERLY 74/75. The planner is thus able to explore his data in the light of his knowledge of the local context, without going through an intermediary, such as a systems analyst or programmer—a step that is usually both time consuming and expensive.

EMPIRICAL APPLICATIONS

Primarily the empirical work presented in this section illustrates the ways in which a microlevel data base can be used to characterize the basic elements of structure and change in the elderly population of a single community. At some point, the larger question of whether age is even a suitable variable for differentiating the population should be addressed. However, in the present discussion a more limited and pragmatic view is taken, that many programs are defined with respect to age (at least as a criterion of eligibility) and that an institutional perspective justifies a focus on the elderly as a separate group. Within this context, the main dimensions of demographic contrast, housing consumption, and spatial distribution within jurisdictional boundaries can be established. Subsequently, strategies for in-depth surveys can be developed, using this first stage as a sampling frame.

Cross-Sectional Data

Kingston is prototypical of a small, stable, aging town surrounded by youthful, growing suburban townships under separate government. Although the town's population has hovered around 60,000 for the last decade, internal demographic processes apparent in the early 1970s have resulted in a large concentration of elderly population. With a substantial bulge existing in the age pyramid between 45 and 55, this trend is likely to be sustained for some time to come.

Future pressures on the social service system depend not only on the size and composition of elderly people but also on their distribution. From the point of view of those concerned with service provision, where potential clients live is critical. The main task is to rapidly identify the location of specific population subgroups (see Chapter 13). The locational distribution of elderly people is, in turn, a function of their local housing status (see Chapter 12). Although the elderly have tended over the last three decades to be predominantly homeowners, one would expect with increased age—bringing with it, in the aggregate, both lower resources and poorer health—a decline in the propensity in ownership status. However, as Table 14 shows, the extent to which homeownership is maintained into advancing years is striking. Forty-one percent of those older than 75 still own their own homes and a sizeable proportion of this group (31%) lives alone.[14] It is in this context that the growing concerns over affordability of housing and, from a long-run perspective, maintenance of that stock, must be faced. Relatively little is known about the reasons why the elderly remain in their own homes; although it may be an attractive proposition from the point of view of keeping in touch with friends and a familiar environment, it may also reflect the fact that staying is a less expensive short-run alternative than attempting to find accommodation in the private rental market. This is a critical question in that the short-run savings to individuals may indeed turn out to be long-run costs to the community.[15] This will be the case if the substantial segment of the housing stock occupied by the elderly is subject to a more rapid rate of deterioration than are similar units elsewhere in the city.

Table 14. Living Arrangements of Elderly By Age and Tenure, 1974

Status		Age (percent distribution)		
Living arrangement	Tenure	55–64	65–74	Over 75
Living alone	Own	9.3	11.3	12.9
	Rent	4.1	4.6	5.7
Two person households	Own	48.8	40.0	21.3
	Rent	11.1	8.9	5.4
Three or more person households	Own	6.5	7.2	7.1
	Rent	18.9	25.2	28.4
Other	Nursing home	1.3	2.5	19.2
Total		100.0	100.0	100.0
N		1,582	1,091	761

Source: 1974 Assessment File, City of Kingston.

One of the main attractions of the PRISSA system is the ability to focus on specific aspects of a problem by selecting subsets of the data and displaying the associated distributions in an interactive fashion. Each map takes about 10 minutes to plot; thus, within a couple of hours, detailed examinations could be undertaken of the distribution of different age groups of those living alone, owners of units in different assessment categories, condominiums, and other subgroups of concern. Such a facility is valuable not only in gaining an appreciation for the location of different client groups but also in considering the design of surveys in which cluster samples are to be used.

Basic Dynamics

It is difficult to make judgements regarding future needs on the basis of analyses of cross-sectional data alone, although this is often done in the absence of viable alternatives. From a number of different viewpoints, it is desirable to be able to identify the nature and direction of change. Within a community, what types of locational redistributions are being produced by the housing adjustments of the elderly: Are there transfers between different segments of the housing market (e.g., owners, renters, institutionalized)? There are no sufficiently strong theories to predict these shifts as a function of changes in the market and in other institutional arrangements associated with public programs. Therefore, the problem must be tackled by a more mechanistic forecasting procedure, supported by monitoring of detailed change.[16] The foundation of such an approach lies in the development of demographic accounts for which specification of classes depends on the particular problem at hand (see Chapter 12).

Because it has been suggested that the concentration of the elderly in

Table 15. Residential Transitions of the Elderly in Kingston, 1974–1975

Residential status 1974		Residential status 1975									Left city	Died	Total
		Age 55–64			Age 65–74			Age over 75					
		Own	Rent	Inst.	Own	Rent	Inst.	Own	Rent	Inst.			
Age 55–64	Own	867 (.872)	1 (.001)	0 (.000)	70 (.070)	1 (.001)	1 (.001)	0 —	0 —	0 —	45 (.045)	10 (.010)	995 (1.000)
	Rent	13 (.023)	444 (.783)	0 (.000)	1 (.002)	53 (.094)	0 (.000)	0 —	0 —	0 —	49 (.087)	6 (.011)	566 (1.000)
	Inst.	0 (.000)	0 (.000)	16 (.762)	0 (.000)	0 (.000)	4 (.190)	0 —	0 —	0 —	1 (.048)	0 (.000)	21 (1.000)
Age 65–74	Own	0 —	0 —	0 —	545 (.857)	7 (.011)	1 (.002)	39 (.061)	1 (.002)	1 (.002)	29 (.046)	12 (.019)	635 (1.000)
	Rent	0 —	0 —	0 —	4 (.009)	350 (.818)	1 (.002)	0 (.000)	26 (.061)	0 (.000)	36 (.084)	11 (.026)	428 (1.000)
	Inst.	0 —	0 —	0 —	0 (.000)	0 (.000)	22 (.786)	0 (.000)	0 (.000)	1 (.036)	3 (.107)	2 (.071)	28 (1.000)
Age over 75	Own	0 —	0 —	0 —	0 —	0 —	0 —	265 (.855)	1 (.003)	6 (.019)	20 (.065)	18 (.058)	310 (1.000)
	Rent	0 —	0 —	0 —	0 —	0 —	0 —	1 (.003)	250 (.823)	5 (.017)	26 (.085)	22 (.072)	304 (1.000)
	Inst.	0 —	0 —	0 —	0 —	0 —	0 —	0 (.000)	0 (.000)	116 (.789)	8 (.054)	23 (.157)	147 (1.000)

Note: Dash refers to value which is zero by definition. Numbers in brackets represent proportions of row sums.

Table 16. Summary of Movement
Rates[a] By Age and Tenure,
1974–1975

Age	Tenure	
	Own	Rent
55–64	5.5	15.9
65–74	6.6	15.0
Over 75	9.7	7.7

[a]Percentage moved both within city and
out of city, 1974–1975.

owner-occupied units presents a potential problem for the local community, this issue will be used as a focus for an illustrative application of record linkage. In order to identify which transactions are taking place in the housing arena, files from successive years need to be linked at the individual level, as described in a previous section. Transactions can then be characterized in terms of transitions between predefined residential states. In this case, initial states will be defined in terms of the occupancy of owned, rented, and institutional units by persons in three age categories. The same states are used to define destinations after one time period, together with two additional states—"death" and "left the system." A table of transitions can then be constructed between these states, which could be used to estimate the likelihood of such moves (Table 15). Although these data are still somewhat crude, the table does possess some interesting properties. In particular, apart from the evidence of transfers from renting to owning for those aged 55 to 64 (mainly the purchase of condominiums), the amount of transfer between tenure categories within the city is very small. Owners have a high propensity to remain where they are, although, as Table 16 shows, this decreases with age. It would appear that this latter outcome reflects the mounting burden of running a single-family house as years advance. In contrast, the mobility rate for renters falls with age, probably as a function of the increasing difficulties of searching for someplace new. However, these data are not really suitable for detailed analyses of why mobility occurs, but could be used for characterizing the magnitude of mobility and its direct effects on predefined elderly groups.

As a final step, the consequences of maintaining this transition structure can be examined. If the pattern described in Table 15 were to be sustained during, for example, a 10-year period, one result would be the slow but steady increase of the proportion of those older than 65 living in their own homes. By 1984, this group would form almost 55% of those older than 65, compared with the present 46%.[17] At the same time, more and more of the housing owned by the elderly would have come on the market as a result of migration, institutionalization, or death. If much of the housing is relatively poor in terms of size and condition, not only will tax problems increase for the city but also the specter of potential abandonment will arise if the houses are unattractive to younger households. It is clearly a very difficult situation to forecast, but this only emphasizes the importance of being able to monitor change at a fine temporal scale. Also, there is no senior citizen housing at present in the suburban townships and in Kingston there is a residency requirement to enter this housing under public programs. Any change in this institutional environment would presumably have consequences that could only be evaluated with respect to an appropriate data base, such as the one presented here.

Microdata as a Sampling Frame

No claim is made that files like ELDERLY 74/75 can provide the sole basis for design or assessment of service programs or for analyses of the behavior of the elderly. Evaluation of the needs for health services, "meals on wheels" programs, or special transit and the characterization of the reason for differential responses to various housing situations and programs require in-depth surveys. Golant and McCaslin's[18] classification of services (see Chapter 14) emphasizes the range and depth of sociopsychological, economic, and health data required to understand the needs and responses of a highly differentiated elderly population. Yet, in bridging the gaps between analysis, program design, and implementation, such base data are extremely valuable.

At the initial stage of a study, one usually encounters a problem of providing a sampling frame such that the results of detailed surveys can be interpreted in the context of the entire elderly population of the community. If no such frame is available, the temptation is to focus on special populations[19] or to use inferior sources as a sampling base; in the latter category are lists of current users of facilities, the use of which poses major problems in linking concepts of need and demand. Even when detailed studies are available for one community, it would be undesirable on cost grounds alone to require that they be fully replicated at different times either for that community or for other communities. Simple estimating equations are required that identify those easily measured variables that could be used in a wide variety of cities—variables that should be included in each data base.

Finally, the advantages of a microlevel data base are again made evident in communicating information about the plethora of programs and in evaluating a monitoring response. In the former case, as has been successfully tried in Kingston, the individual records can be used as a basis for directed mailing to elderly households regarding the nature and availability of specific services; in the latter, the data base again provides the most effective sampling frame for surveys of reactions to public programs.

CONCLUSION

At the core of this chapter is a concern with the relation between theory and practice. Most academic discussions of phenomena relating to the needs for social services are based on in-depth surveys with limited numbers of observations. Small sample sizes reflect the substantial costs of household surveys and even these cannot be justified in each community. However, the translation of general relationships into specific policy and programmatic statements depends critically on the local context—an appreciation of the size, structure, location, and dynamics of the client population. Conventional secondary data cannot provide this context, and the samples themselves are usually inadequate for these purposes. Thus, one is forced to look for alternatives, such as those presented above.

It is clear that the argument for linked microdata files creates political difficulties. Concern for individual privacy is very strong and has severely constrained the use of such files in the past. Yet, without making use of these valuable resources, estimates of need and issues of program design at the city level become a guessing game, leading to neglected subgroups, inefficient delivery systems, and design of service packages that are already inappropriate at the time they are implemented. Because many potentially useful data are already in the public sector, the issue of privacy becomes relative rather than absolute. If the effort is spent to develop appropriate controls and sanctions with respect to misuse, the returns to design and management of social welfare programs can be substantial.

NOTES AND REFERENCES

[1] B. L. Beckham and C. S. Kart, "Heterogeneity of the Elderly in Large Metropolitan Areas," *Urban Affairs Quarterly*, Vol. 13, No. 2 (Dec., 1977).

[2] See H. J. Pratt, *The Gray Lobby* (Chicago: University of Chicago Press, 1976).

[3] Peter Morrison, "Overview of Demographic Trends Shaping the Nation's Future," *Testimony Before the Joint Economic Committee, U.S. Congress*, May 31, 1978, Rand Paper Series, P-6128 (Santa Monica, Calif.: Rand Corporation).

[4] The term "social utilities" is preferred by Stephen M. Golant and Rosemary McCaslin, "A Functional Classification of Services for Older People," *Journal of Gerontological Social Work*, Vol. 1, No. 3 (Spring, 1979).

[5] See Stephen M. Golant, *The Residential Location and Spatial Behavior of the Elderly: A Canadian Example* (Chicago: Department of Geography, University of Chicago, Research Paper No. 143, 1972); and William Michelson, *Environmental Choice: Human Behavior and Residential Satisfaction* (New York: Oxford University Press, 1977).

[6] The issue has been raised forcefully by Westin on a number of occasions, as in Alan F. Westin, *Data Banks in a Free Society* (New York: Quadrangle Books, 1972).

[7] E. S. Dunn, Jr., *Social Information Processing and Statistical Systems: Change and Reform* (New York: John Wiley & Sons, 1974).

[8] Possible approaches to the issue of controls are described in M. Dammann, "Datenschutz und Zugang zu Planungsinformationssystemen," in *Proceedings of the Fourth European Symposium on Urban Data Management* (Madrid, 1974).

[9] The Population Research and Information Systems for Small Areas (PRISSA) project was initiated in 1975 to develop a system for monitoring and projecting school enrollment changes within urban areas in Ontario; Kingston was used as a pilot study.

[10] See *The DIME Geocoding System* (Washington, D.C.: U.S. Department of Commerce, Census Use Report, 1968) for a discussion of this system.

[11] The first 1-in-7 sample taken provided insufficient observations so a second 1-in-7 sample was taken and added to the first.

[12]K. L. Kraemer, J. N. Danziger, and J. L. King, "Information Technology and Urban Management in the United States," *Public Policy Research Organization* (Irving: University of California, 1976).

[13]The details of both hardware and software are contained in E. Moore and R. Tinline, *The PRISSA System: Final Report* (Department of Geography, Queen's University, 1978).

[14]For comparable trends in the tenure adjustments of the U.S. elderly, see S. Golant, "The Housing Tenure Adjustments of the Young and the Elderly," *Urban Affairs Quarterly*, Vol. 13, No. 1 (Sept., 1977), pp. 95–108.

[15]For further discussion of this point, see ibid., note 14.

[16]This link between forecasting and monitoring is developed in E. G. Moore and G. A. van der Knaap, *Demographic Accounting Models for Enrollment Projections*, Technical Report No. 1, Population Research and Information Systems for Small Areas (Department of Geography, Queen's University, 1976).

[17]These figures were obtained by assuming that in-migration had no effect on transition structure, but that the in-migrants adopted the existing transition behavior. Further work is required to assess the degree to which this is valid. It is our belief, in any case, that the monitoring function is paramount as the transition matrix is likely to exhibit high variability in the off-diagonal elements.

[18]Golant and McCaslin, op. cit., note 4.

[19]For an example, see I. K. Malozenoff, J. G. Anderson, and L. V. Rosenbaum, *Housing for the Elderly: Evaluation of the Effectiveness of Congregate Residences* (Boulder, Col.: Westview Press, 1978).

Chapter 12

AGE COHORT PROJECTIONS OF POPULATIONS FOR METROPOLITAN AREA CENSUS TRACTS

Richard Lycan and James Weiss[1]

A model was designed to project population by age groups in census tracts located in a four-county area of the Portland metropolitan area. It was developed to assist a regional health planning agency in determining needs for new or expanded health facilities.[2] Local health facilities must obtain a "certificate of need" from the designated state agency when they want to add beds or otherwise expand. The determination of need requires a knowledge of the distribution of existing facilities, as well as a knowledge of the population in the area to be served. The age distribution of the population in the service area is one key characteristic that must be determined; for example, the need for nursing home beds will be related to the number and location of persons older than 65.

Dever has outlined the requirements for small-area projections for use in health care planning and development.[3] Because the issues identified were important in the development of the present model, they are summarized below:

1. Only one agency should be authorized to make and release forecasts.
2. Forecasts must supply adequate information to meet requirements of federal funding programs.
3. Forecasts must supply adequate information to meet the needs of the region for health planning and evaluation, including the development of new facilities.
4. Forecasts must be done in a way that permits frequent updating because of changes in patterns of fertility and migration.
5. Forecasts should be made at the most geographically detailed level possible and then aggregated.

6. Different methods of forecasting should be used as checks to minimize the uncertainty of a single method.

AVAILABLE SMALL AREA PROJECTION MODELS

Cohort-Component Method

Most demographers use the cohort-component method to project population. It considers births, deaths, and migration as distinctive components underlying population change. Highly detailed information is available on birth and death rates of different population age-sex groups, but future migration rates are more difficult to estimate. For large geographic areas, such as the United States, estimate errors are less serious than is the case for small areas, such as county census divisions, enumeration districts, and census tracts, where migration is usually a major force affecting population changes. Consequently, cohort-component models are seldom used to forecast populations of areas as small as census tracts.[4]

Other Projection Models

Most attempts to forecast populations of small geographic areas are either relatively simple extrapolations of historic trends or one part of a comprehensive land use and services planning model. Pittenger has reviewed several of these noncomponent models. He includes:[5]

1. Models that allocate subunit share of a larger population, usually through the projection of trends.
2. Density models that fill areas in to some capacity level; the rate at which they are filled in depending on observed trends and often an S-shaped function, such as a logistic curve.
3. Models that relate population to some other variable, such as housing or employment.

Difficulties in Using Existing Models

When the available models were considered, several difficulties surfaced. The large complex land use and transportation models were too costly to implement because they required data not readily available and were expensive to calibrate and test.[6] A second option was to update the type of density ceiling model described by Pittenger and used by the local regional planning organization. However, this approach was rejected because of concern about its subjectivity and the lack, at the time, of any meaningful land use plan. A method used by Greenberg, which combined desirable features, such as the use of density ceilings, systematic allocation of changes from larger aggregates to local areas, and a general approach that was subjective in only a few aspects was impressive.[7] Nonetheless, although the way the Greenberg model projected historic trends for individual areas was feasible for county census divisions (the units used by Greenberg), it had drawbacks for census tracts in rapidly changing metropolitan areas. Such an approach tends to project excessively concentrated growth in areas where growth was observed historically. Also, the use of data from the 1950s and 1960s to predict change during the 1970s, 1980s, and 1990s, as was done with the Greenberg model, was reason for concern. Recent increases in the proportions of multiple family units and the addition of mobile homes to the housing inventory, as well as some shifts in the occupancy patterns of older housing in the city, were arguments for using the most recent data available.

In reviewing attempts to model the changing population age structure of census tracts, the authors were familiar with procedures used in large-scale urban forecasting models. For example, the land use and transportation model used for the greater Detroit area by the Southeastern Michigan Council of Governments[8] projected future neighborhood types (based on age, categories, and quality of its housing) by analyzing their association with the demographic profile of the occupants.[9] However, the erratic changes in the age of the neighborhood population over time when the neighborhood was reassigned to a new classification were a troublesome aspect of the model. A somewhat similar approach was used in the EMPIRIC model implemented in the Puget Sound Governmental Conference, which used a multiple regression equation to project ages of census tract populations.[10] A regression equation was used to predict the changing proportion in an age group, e.g., persons aged 0 to 4 years, on the basis of the relationship between changes in the proportion in this age group and the proportions in all other age groups during the 1960-1970 period. The main problem with this approach is that it carries forward demographic trends that are often unique to one period of time. A specific example is the passage of the "baby boom cohort," which has had very different effects on the amount and type of housing demand in the 1950s, 1960s, and 1970s.

DESCRIPTION OF MODEL

In developing an integrated model designed to project census tract populations by age grouping, four submodels were constructed, which are referred to as demographic, housing, population, and age (see Table 17). Population and housing data for these models were based on readily available information and were used as input in a set of regression equations.[11] The model was designed to step projections forward in time without the injection of new information, such as plans for the development of new sewer systems.

Data Used

The information required to implement these submodels included the following:

1. Population by age group for each tract and for the study area. Most of this information is available in the U.S. Census Bureau tract volumes, but the

Table 17. Outline and Calibration of Submodels

Submodel	Purpose	Dependent variables	Independent variables	Observation units included	Regression model's multiple correlation
Demographic	Provides control totals by age group for overall study area	Cohort-component methodology requiring age-specific birthrates, deathrates, and migration rates		Total study area	not applicable
Housing Single family units Multiple family units Mobile homes	Project housing by type of unit for tracts as a basis for population projection	1970-1973 growth rates of housing units by dwelling unit type	−1960-1970 growth rate of housing units by dwelling unit type −1968-1970 spatially smoothed trends in housing inventory −1970 net and residential densities	All tracts except some core area and peripheral rural tracts	S.F. .76 M.F. .60 M.H. .31[a]
Population	Convert housing projections to population projections for tracts	1960-1970 population gains or losses	−1960-1970 gains or losses of housing units −number of persons in each age group in 1960	All tracts	.98
Age (groupings) 0–17 18–29 30–44 45–59 60+	Modify age structure for tracts	1960-1970 change in the proportions of populations in each of five age groups	−proportion of population in each age group, 1960 −1960 housing inventory −1960 net and residential population densities	Core tracts removed All tracts Core tracts removed All tracts All tracts	0–17 .77 18–29 .72 30–44 .86 45–59 .87 60+ .77

[a]The regression model was not used to forecast trends for mobile homes. They were projected from a simple trend model utilizing spatial smoothing of historic trends.

particular age groups chosen necessitated tabulations from the Census summary tapes. These data were needed for two points in time, 1960 and 1970, requiring some adjustments to compensate for tract boundary changes.

2. Housing units by type and age for 1960, 1970, and the most recent date available, which, in this case, was 1973. Data for 1960 and 1970 were available from Census summary tapes. Data for 1970-1973 were derived from locally published tract summaries of building and demolition permits.

3. Acreage data for residential and vacant land areas by tract. This information had been prepared in both map and tabular form by the local regional planning agency.

SUBMODELS

Demographic Submodel

The demographic submodel consisted of a cohort-component method used to project the total population and the population in 5-year age groups of the overall study area for 5-year time periods from 1970 to 2000. The model was based on the assumption that age-specific birth rates would rise slightly from the low levels of the early 1970s to a rate that approximately corresponds to the U.S. Census Bureau's series D (2.5 children per woman completed fertility). It also was assumed that the present age-specific mortality rates would continue unchanged. Net migration was assumed to be at the average rate that prevailed for the study area from 1965 to 1974. The age structure applied to in-migrants and out-migrants was comparable to that which prevailed during the 1965-1970 period for the Oregon portion of the Portland SMSA, with an adjustment made to reflect the end of the military draft. Data not tabulated in this chapter show this projection to be similar to those produced by other local agencies.

Housing Submodel

The housing submodel projects changes in the number of housing units at the census tract level for single family, multiple family, and mobile home housing. For single and multiple family units, 1970-1973 trends for location of housing development were predicted from (1) 1960-1970 growth rates for single and multiple family housing in that tract; (2) averaged 1960-1970 housing growth rates for single and multiple family units in nearby tracts; and (3) net and residential housing densities for each tract. The models developed were relatively successful in explaining 1970-1973 growth trends for single and multiple family units.[12] When they erred, it was generally through prediction of a more regular pattern in space than had actually occurred. The fit of the models, as expressed by their multiple correlation coefficients, ranged from poor to good. The smallest multiple correlation was .31 and resulted from attempting to predict the pattern of 1970-1973 mobile home sitings (see Table 17). Consequently, a simpler trend model was used to distribute mobile homes. The regression models predicting single and multiple family housing unit changes were modestly successful. $R =$

.76 and .60, respectively, but seemed adequate considering that the dependent variable represented housing data for only a 3-year period. Because residential development, especially for multiple family units, occurs in large chunks in subdivisions and apartment developments, the authors believed this level of explanation was acceptable.

Growth rates for 1970–1980 estimated by the regression model for each type of housing were applied to 1970 housing counts to obtain 1980 housing projections. A recursive approach projected 1980 housing to 1990 and 1990 to the year 2000. At the end of each decade, files on housing inventories by age and type were revised. When housing decreases were projected, units were subtracted from the oldest housing in the inventory for that tract.

One criticism commonly directed at trend projection models applied to small areas is that they tend to perpetuate unrealistically high growth rates in a few areas, resulting in the projection of highly concentrated patterns of development. Two techniques were used in this model to circumvent this problem: spatial smoothing of growth trends and application of density constraints.

In general, the regressions demonstrated that 1970–1973 census tract housing growth could be better predicted by including 1960–1970 census tract growth rates that had been "spatially smoothed"[13] over nearby tracts.[14] In particular, the analysis showed that the growth of single family units was predicted to the same degree by the earlier period "same tract" growth and the spatially smoothed tract growth (see Table 18). The results for multiple family units are

Table 18. Beta Values and Multiple Correlations for Predicting 1970–1973 Housing Unit Changes

Independent variables		Dependent variables 1970-1973 housing unit growth rates	
		Single family	Multiple family
Same tract	1960-1970 single family housing growth rate	.26	.38
	1960-1970 multiple family housing growth rate	—[a]	.11
Nearby tracts	1960-1970 single family housing growth rates	.23	—[a]
	1960-1970 multiple family housing growth rates	—[a]	.14
Net density		-.47	—[a]
Residential density		.03	-.10
	Multiple correlation	.76	.60

[a]Dropped from regression equation because values were close to zero.

somewhat surprising in that the rate of change for multiples is most dependent on previous changes in single family units in the same tract. The reason for this result probably lies in the heavy rate of apartment construction in the same suburban tracts where single family unit construction was extensive during the 1960s.

Pittenger and other authors recommend the use of population density variables in small area models to limit the growth to numbers that could be contained within area units.[15] Newling describes an abstract closed model of metropolitan population change in which density is a key variable, and Greenberg has adapted this model for his population projections of regions of New Jersey.[16]

The two aspects of density that seemed most important with regard to this study were (1) net density, the number of persons residing in a tract divided by the acres of land used for residences plus that available for development, excluding those areas dedicated to other uses, such as roadways and industry; and (2) residential density, the number of persons residing per acre of residential land. The reasoning was that the development of single family housing would be sharply limited by net density, reflecting the amount of land remaining for development and the undesirability of the high priced sites available. The growth of multiple family units was not expected to be greatly limited by net density, but it would be limited by residential density, which, in turn, is principally influenced by the mix of single and multiple family housing units located in the tract. These expectations were largely borne out by the regression analyses carried out in calibrating the model. A strong negative correlation was found between the growth of single family units and net density (see Table 18). However, the correlation between growth of multiple family units and net density is rather small, suggesting that, at the census tract level, net density does not commonly limit the growth of multiple family units.

The model employed several constraints that limit housing growth rates. For the entire study area, projection of 1970-1973 growth trends for housing to 1980 and beyond would result in an exponential growth rate that exceeds the cohort-component projections of population for the study area. Thus, overall growth rates for housing were adjusted on a decade basis to be generally consistent with the population projections for the study area. It also proved necessary to limit growth of housing in each tract to no more than a threefold increase per decade for single and multiple family units and a twofold increase per decade for mobile homes. The purpose of this constraint was to dampen trends that were largely unique to 1960-1970 housing development. These constraints were the subject of considerable experimentation. They were adjusted through trial and error until the model distributed population among the four counties of the study area in a manner consistent with locally produced county level population projections.

A number of additional variables were evaluated but discarded: (1) access to employment, (2) access to recently added employment, (3) access to shopping, (4) percentage of land with sewers, and (5) percentage of dwelling units on large tracts of land. Some of those variables made small contributions to the explanation of 1970–1973 development trends, but are not in themselves easily projected for the 1970–2000 period.

After adjustments were completed, the model succeeded in distributing housing and population at the county level in a manner generally similar to other types of county-level projections that had been made for this area. However, in all of its trials, which were based on varying parameters and limits, this model allocated more growth to the smallest and most rural county in the study area.

Population Submodel

The population submodel uses the estimates of housing gained or lost by type, which are predicted by the housing model, and converts these values into population gains or losses for each tract. Additionally, the number of persons in each of the five population age groups at the beginning of the decade were added as demographic predictor variables to the regression analysis.

In a discussion of small area models, Pittenger criticized the use of unchanging numbers of persons per household in converting numbers of dwelling units to area populations.[17] He illustrated this problem by describing the maturing suburban tract where the population increases for a time owing to the birth of children, but declines as children become adults and establish separate households.

The analysis initially related the net change in population for each tract to the net change in numbers of single and multiple family units. Regression analysis on 1960–1970 population changes produced a reasonably good multiple correlation of .92; however, examination of the residuals by tract showed that many of the central city tract predictions displayed considerable errors. Adding variables for the numbers of persons in each of the five population age groups as predictors considerably enhanced the prediction, resulting in a multiple correlation of .98. Examination of the residual values by tract showed only a few substantial errors, some of which could be explained by unique considerations.

Age Submodel

The projection of changes in population age composition is based on a larger number of variables than used in the two previously described submodels. The 1960–1970 changes in the proportions of census tract population in each of the five age groups (0–17, 18–29, 30–44, 45–59, and 60 years and older) were predicted in separate regression models from the following independent variables: (1) proportions of tract populations in each of the age groups at the beginning of the 1960 decade; (2) the age mix of the housing in the tract (housing that was 0–9, 10–19, 20–29, and 30 or more years of age for single and multiple family units); and (3) net and residential housing densities at the beginning of the decade. The relationships established were strongest for the populations aged 0–17 and 30–44, but only moderate for the populations aged 18–29 and 60 years and older (see Table 17). It was not surprising that the strength of the correlations was lower for the young adult and elderly population. These groups are found in diverse housing environments, including single family homes, both old and new apartments, and institutional housing. Also, these two groups often occupy similar housing because of similarities in space requirements and financial means, thus complicating the prediction of each group's residential location.

INTEGRATION OF THE SUBMODELS

The numbers of persons in each of the age groups for the overall study area were forced to correspond to projections produced by the demographic submodels. The numbers, by age group, in each tract were proportioned upward or downward by a constant value so that the totals for the 239 census tracts would correspond with the totals projected by the demographic submodel.

Projections were made for the 10-year periods from 1970 to 2000. Mid-period populations were interpolated on a constant growth rate basis and adjusted to demographic controls, as explained above, for 1975, 1985, and 1995.

The age-adjusted housing tract submodel, which is referred to as the integrated model, is recursive in nature in that the tract data for 1970 are used to project 1980 values, the projected 1980 values are used as a basis for projections of 1990 values, etc. At the end of each decade, the files for land use, housing, and population were revised for use in projecting change during the next decade.

ADJUSTMENTS TO THE INTEGRATED MODEL

When all the equations were determined and the errors in the projection program were eliminated, the model was tested, using the parameters obtained in the regression analyses. The integrated model tended to project the growth of total housing more rapidly than the demographic model expanded population. Although the use of exogenous population control totals kept population in bounds, the distortion of projected housing inventories biased the estimation of population age structure. This problem was solved by altering the growth rates for housing (intercept values in a logarithmic regression model) until the projected population totals of the integrated model were reasonably close to those exogenously imposed by the control totals, which were produced by the demographic submodel.

IMPLICATIONS OF PROJECTIONS BY AGE

The integrated model illustrates the value of a set of interrelated projections for all age groups rather than a projection of the future spatial patterning of a single age group. For example, one can make some assumptions regarding the housing requirements of the elderly and develop a set of projections on that basis. However, if no account is taken of the competing needs of young adults for low-cost apartment housing, one can err seriously in the projection of the future location of the elderly.

Table 19. Comparison of Age Structure Predicted by Demographic and
Integrated Models

Age group	1970 popu- lation	1990 population projected from:		Predicted population ratios	
		Demographic model	Integrated model	Integrated / Demographic	Demographic model / 1970 Population
		Thousands of persons			
0–17	296	467	437	.93	1.58
18–29	166	234	293	1.25	1.41
30–44	149	305	223	.73	2.05
45–59	156	176	216	1.23	1.13
Over 60	141	179	190	1.06	1.27
Total	908	1,360	1,360[a]	1.00	1.50
		Percent distribution			
0–17	32.6	32.1	21.4	—	—
18–29	18.3	21.6	17.2	—	—
30–44	16.4	16.4	22.4	—	—
45–59	17.2	15.9	12.9	—	—
Over 60	15.5	14.0	13.2	—	—
Total	100.0	100.0	100.0		

[a]Population figures for the integrated model were forced to the same total as that projected by the demographic submodel.

The projection of the 1990 spatial distribution of the elderly by this model
displays an interesting pattern of central city decline and suburban growth[18] (see
Chapter 3). This apparently results from the model associating this group's
housing needs in 1990 with the then aging suburban apartments constructed
during the 1960s and 1970s.

One of the most striking results of the model is the difference between the
1990 projections by age group resulting from the demographic submodel and the
projections from the integrated model (Table 19). The integrated model projects
smaller numbers of persons in the 0–17 and the 30–44 age groups. This disparity
is due to the differing nature of the passage of the postwar baby boom cohort
through the two models. During the calibration time period for the housing
submodel, most of this age cohort was in the model's 18–29 age class, implying
demand for multiple family and smaller, cheaper single family units. By 1990,
this cohort will pass on, in the model, to age 30–44 and 45–59. The fact that the
mismatch is less pronounced for the 0–17 age group than for the 30–44 age
group likely reflects the assumption in the demographic submodel of a
moderately low fertility rate.

This implies that if housing development continues at the pace of the 1970s,
with a large part of the construction being apartments, it is not likely to produce
the quantity of single family houses that may be required by the "postwar baby

boom" cohort when these persons reach their 30s and 40s, unless there are major shifts in their housing preferences. By contrast, the integrated model increases the growth of the 45-59 and the 60 and older populations at a more rapid rate (Table 19), which suggests that some of the shortfall in housing for the 0-17 and 30-44 age groups could be made up by attracting housing from the overhoused 45-59 and 60 and older age groups. Thus, if present trends continue, there may be strong competition between young families with expanding space needs and older age groups. This is by no means an original observation; Golant and others have noted this same problem on the basis of other evidence.[19] It does suggest that this model may be enacting a reasonable simulation of this phenomenon.

CONCLUSIONS

There is no simple way to determine whether the integrated model provides a good projection of the future growth of age-specific population groups located in the study area. Because no reliable tract estimates are available, the 1980 Census of Population will provide the first real opportunity to check the results of the model.

Other researchers may find it useful for their purposes to adapt only one of the described submodels rather than making use of the entire integrated model. The population submodel used to project total tract population changes over the decade, based on housing unit changes, seemed to be particularly successful (R = .98 in the calibration). This submodel could form the basis for a model used to estimate current tract populations, for which current figures on changes in the numbers of housing units by tract are available. A problem with most existing models that attempt current tract population estimates is that they use data from the most recent Census to relate household size to number of units, only compensating for changes in household size by forcing tract totals to current county or city estimates. Given the rapid decline in household size for single family units that has occurred in most metropolitan areas since the 1970 Census of Population, this can lead to errors as great as 15% to 20% for individual tract populations.[20]

Also, the series of models that were used to modify tract population age structure might be used to develop current tract estimates of population by age group. Although the authors were not completely satisfied with the level of explanation provided by these models (R = .77 to .87), it is likely that further experimentation would improve these results.

NOTES AND REFERENCES

[1] James Weiss died at the time this chapter was being written. Without his support as director of the Population Center and his professional contributions as a demographer, this study would not have been attempted. Appreciation is expressed to the Institute on Aging at Portland State University for financial assistance that facilitated its preparation and to Gloria Edwards, the research assistant, who carried out most of the bibliographic research.

[2]The projection model was developed by the Center for Population Research and Census at Portland State University for the Comprehensive Health Planning Association of Portland, Oregon, since reorganized as Northwest Oregon Regional Health Systems. The actual projections are available under the title, *Population Projections: Oregon Administrative District II* (Portland: Comprehensive Health Planning Organization, 1975).

[3]Alan Dever, "Forecasting Population of Small Areas to Facilitate State Health Care Planning and Development," in *Population Forecasting for Small Areas* (Oak Ridge, Tenn.: Oak Ridge Associated Universities, 1977), pp. 83–90. For a discussion of the needs for demographic information specifically concerning the elderly, see Harold Kendig and Robert Warren, "The Adequacy of Census Data in Planning and Advocacy for the Elderly," *The Gerontologist*, Vol. 16, No. 5 (1976), pp. 392–396.

[4]For a discussion of the applications of cohort-survival projection models to small geographic areas, normally county sized or larger, see the review by Peter Morrison, "Forecasting Population of Small Areas: An Overview," in *Population Forecasting for Small Areas* (Oak Ridge, Tenn.: Oak Ridge Associated Universities, 1977), pp. 3–13. For a more comprehensive treatise, see Donald Pittenger, *Projecting State and Local Populations* (Cambridge, Mass.: Ballinger Publishing Co., 1976); or Richard Irwin, *Guide for Local Area Population Projections* (Washington, D.C.: Government Printing Office, 1977).

[5]Pittenger, op. cit., note 4, pp. 135–143.

[6]Leslie King surveys various large scale projection models in "Models of Urban Land-Use Development," in David Sweet, ed., *Models of Urban Structure* (Lexington, Mass.: Lexington Books, 1972), pp. 3–26.

[7]Michael Greenberg, Donald Kruekeberg, and Richard Mautner, *Long-Range Population Projections for Minor Civil Divisions: Computer Programs and User's Manual* (New Brunswick, N.J.: Center for Urban Policy Research, Rutgers University, 1973).

[8]CONSAD Research Corporation, *An Urban-Regional Model of Small Area Change for Southeastern Michigan* (Pittsburgh: CONSAD Research Corporation, 1969).

[9]See Edgar Hoover and Raymond Vernon, *Anatomy of a Metropolis* (Garden City, N.Y.: Doubleday, 1962), pp. 168–172 for an early and lucid description of the dynamic interrelationships between a city's housing stock and demographic changes. The authors had also experimented previously with factorial ecology-type studies of the spatial distribution of persons by age in the Portland metropolitan area. We observed that the shifts in the mappings of the factor scores for the several age groups appeared to be closely related to housing factors. The age groupings used in this study were drawn from this analysis and group persons by age according to their tendency to occupy similar areas.

[10]Puget Sound Governmental Conference, *Development and Initial Application of the EMPIRIC Activity Allocation Model for the Central Puget Sound Region, Final Report* (Seattle: Puget Sound Governmental Conference, 1973).

[11]Most of the regression analyses were initially attempted using data for 230 census tracts comprising three of the four counties in the study area. Data for the nine enumeration districts in one county were not used in calibration because these data were incomplete. Subsequent analyses resulted in the elimination of certain tracts when they appeared to be clearly anomalous. Those eliminated included, variously, about a dozen tracts clustered around the central business district, two other tracts where commercial and industrial development have largely replaced residential uses, and a peripheral band of rural census tracts.

[12]Attempts to create a similar model explaining 1970–1973 mobile home unit sitings were not successful. Consequently, mobile home sitings were extrapolated from 1970–1973 trends in mobile home development. The extrapolation used was based on growth trends in each tract along with its adjacent and nearby tracts.

[13]Waldo Tobler discusses the use of a smoothing or "filtering" model that can be used to project population in *Display and Analysis of Spatial Data* (New York: John Wiley & Sons, 1975). In this same volume, see M. L. Hsu, "Filtering Process in Surface Generalization and Isopleth Mapping."

[14]The appropriate choice of "nearby tracts" was the subject of some experimentation. The following alternate definitions were attempted: (1) adjacent tracts; (2) adjacent tracts

plus a second surrounding band of "once removed tracts"; (3) numbers 1 and 2 above plus a constraint that only tracts closer to the city center were considered; (4) numbers 1 and 2 or numbers 1, 2, and 3 above plus weighting of tract values inversely proportional to the distance from the tract under consideration. The third option was the one used, because it showed a slightly better predictive value and because it seemed that it would have the desirable effect of tending to spread growth outward rather than diffusing it symmetrically.

[15] Pittenger, op. cit., note 4, pp. 102–105.

[16] Greenberg, op. cit., note 7, bases his projection model on a theoretical model developed by Bruce Newling in which population density and growth are intricately interrelated. See Brian J. L. Berry and John Kasarda, *Contemporary Urban Ecology* (New York: Macmillan, 1977), pp. 88, 89, for a discussion of Newling's model.

[17] Pittenger, op. cit., note 4, pp. 123–125.

[18] Stephen Golant, "Residential Concentrations of the Future Elderly," *The Gerontologist*, Vol. 15, No. 1 (Feb., 1975), Part III, pp. 16–23.

[19] Stephen Golant, "The Housing Tenure Adjustments of the Young and the Elderly: Policy Implications," *Urban Affairs Quarterly*, Vol. 12, No. 1 (1977), pp. 95–109. See also David R. Goldfield, "The Limits of Suburban Growth," *Urban Affairs Quarterly*, Vol. 12, No. 1 (1976), pp. 161–171.

[20] Changes in household size for the Portland metropolitan area have been documented through sample surveys since 1974 by the Center for Population Research and Census at Portland State University.

Chapter 13

PLANNING URBAN SERVICE LOCATIONS FOR THE ELDERLY[1]

Stephen S. Birdsall

Social and health services will not be used if the client population cannot reach the dispensing center. Nevertheless, many services for elderly persons— financial aid offices, health clinics, senior centers—are found in fixed locations, and in spite of increasing mobility problems, elderly "clients" are expected to gain access to them.[2] At the other extreme, relatively immobile institutionalized elderly persons obtain on-site services in congregate residential accommodations. Between these two extremes—the totally mobile and the immobile—exists a large percentage of the elderly population who are underserviced because they do not have full locational access to service facilities.[3] Service provision can be viewed as inefficient to the extent to which it is inaccessible to its client populations, or it requires excessive resources (e.g., high transportation costs and special bus facilities) in order to bring client and service together. Therefore, those who plan urban services for the elderly must continually confront this potentially serious problem.[4]

This chapter addresses locational inefficiencies and servicing inequities which must be considered when planning for the elderly and suggests a means to assess the locational efficiency of service plans. The methodology offered should be considered one of many techniques to be considered by the planner involved in service location decisions. For illustration purposes, the procedure is applied to the elderly population located in Washington, D.C.

ASSUMPTIONS

One of the most important elements to consider when planning service delivery for the elderly is decreasing personal mobility with increasing age. There are four major assumptions implicit in this view of service planning. First, a certain level of personal support is accepted by society as minimal; those who are physically, mentally, or financially unable to provide for themselves above this minimum will be supported at least to this level by public services.

Second, it is assumed that as an individual becomes older, his physical and mental competence generally decreases.[5] There is a good deal of individual variation in this, because many elderly people are highly competent both physically and mentally. Nevertheless, a larger share of those aged 65 or older are physically or mentally unable to maintain themselves independently than any other age group, except for the very young.

Third and fourth, it is assumed that physical limitations on personal mobility do not reduce the desire for personal independence and that service provision buttresses the individual's capability and desire to live independently. Previous studies have confirmed the positive relationship between life satisfaction and personal autonomy or independence.[6]

It is proposed here that to efficiently provide "independence fostering" services for the elderly[7] (see Chapter 14) within an appropriate public jurisdiction, the relevant service planning agencies must (1) know where the elderly are located within their service area, in other words, the geographic distribution of their client population, and (2) have that locational information in a useable form, with the proper methodology, to determine the best location for the service center. This chapter, therefore, will provide an example of a fairly simple methodology using readily available data that permits identification of an efficient service center location within an urban area. The methodology can be used in rural regions as well, and with relatively simple mathematical alterations, data scale problems and irregular rural road network structures may be taken into account. A brief caveat may be appropriate. "Efficiency" in location is used throughout the chapter as a relative, not an absolute, concept. A place is described as the "best" service center location in approximate terms subject to limitations arising from data quality and the methodology itself.

METHODOLOGY

The most usual data source for describing the residential locations of the urban elderly is the U.S. decennial census. Population counts by 5-year age categories are published by tract for each major urban area. Intercensal changes in elderly distribution may be estimated from local surveys and records (see other chapters in Part III).

Despite their availability, these data may not be used most advantageously to identify the location of elderly people relative to service facilities. A city map of the number of elderly per tract may present a sufficiently complex pattern to

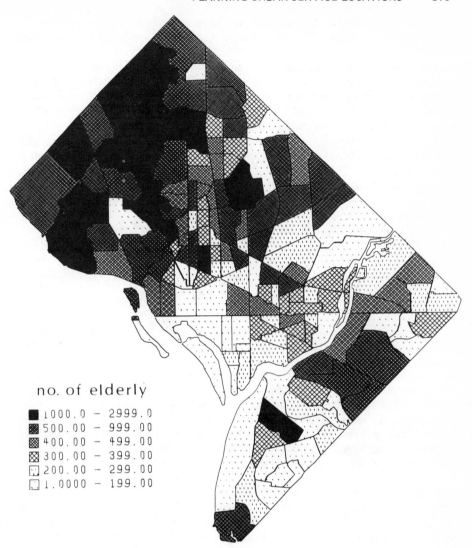

no. of elderly

◼ 1000.0 - 2999.0
▓ 500.00 - 999.00
▨ 400.00 - 499.00
▧ 300.00 - 399.00
⬚ 200.00 - 299.00
⬚ 1.0000 - 199.00

Fig. 20. Number of persons aged 65 or older, 1970, Washington, D.C.

suggest several alternative sites for the service center (Fig. 20). An intuitively sensible solution would be to locate the center in the middle of one of the larger clusters of the elderly. In St. Petersburg, Florida, for example, a door-to-door transportation service for the elderly and handicapped was begun in 1973.[8] The portion of the entire 58-square-mile area of the city that was to receive this service "was chosen because three-eighths of the 80,000 elderly residents in the city were located within this area and most of the trips would terminate there."[9] In effect, the remaining 62.5% of the city's elderly were precluded from receiving this particular service.

This dilemma can be resolved by a methodology which assigns services to locations which are "central" to the city's entire elderly population. Such a procedure should be sensitive to locationally isolated but large clusters of elderly population, thus indicating where alternative secondary support centers might be located. Finally, the preferred methodology should use readily available published data and require relatively simple mathematical calculations. These goals can be met by a measure of the *population potential* of an intraurban elderly population.

Suggested by Stewart and Warntz as a variation of the more familiar gravity model,[10] the population potential is an index of a region's relative capacity for interaction as measured by its aggregate proximity to people. For each location or place in the region (P_i), an index value is constructed as follows:

$$\text{Potential at place i} = \frac{P_i}{1/2\, d_*} + \sum_{j=1}^{n} \frac{P_j}{d_{ij}}$$

where P is the population size, d_{ij} is the distance from place i to place j (where $j = 1,\ldots,n$) and d_* is the distance from i to its nearest populated neighbor places.

The surface defined by the set of values for a region indicates the relative proximity of each place to the region's population, or more generally, the relative access each place has to the total population. Large groups of people far away from a place (or small numbers close by) will aggregate to a small index value, which is indicative of poor access. Such a place possesses a low population potential. Conversely, relatively large numbers of people near each other will yield high population potential values.

The population potential of a city's elderly, therefore, offers the basis for selecting sites most proximate to the entire elderly population in that city. Using census tracts as place units, with the elderly population of each tract assumed to be located at the tract centroid, one can calculate elderly potential values for each tract. The tract with the highest value is the most accessible (in other words, the closest) to the city's entire elderly population. The use of straight-line distances as measures of access between the tract centroids is unlikely to influence the city-wide pattern of the potential. The distribution of elderly outside the city's political limits is not relevant as long as the service to be provided is to be administered and limited to the population within the city's jurisdiction. Data are readily available; calculations are not difficult and can be programmed with relative ease for computer use. Finally, if the distribution of elderly is strongly bimodal (or, more generally, multimodal), with the major clusters significantly distant from each other, the elderly potential surface will reflect this and suggest the establishment of more than one service center.

APPLICATION

To illustrate this procedure, intraurban elderly population potential surfaces were calculated for the District of Columbia for the decade periods beginning 1940, 1950, 1960, and 1970. The number of persons aged 65 or older had increased from 41,067 to 70,143 during the period, with the percentage of the total population's elderly growing from 6.2% to 9.4%. The 30-year period was examined to identify the relative stability in the pattern of elderly potential surfaces.

The 1940 to 1970 intraurban elderly population potential patterns reflect two distinct facets of change (Fig. 21). First, each succeeding decade from 1940 to 1960 displayed more tracts of the highest category for that year, but in 1970, in contrast to 1960, there were fewer such tracts. While the highest category of potential values appeared in fewer tracts in 1970, tracts distributed in the top half of the elderly potential categories (4,000 or more) increased consistently in number and represented an increasingly higher percentage of the occupied city area over the entire 30-year period. This general increase in high tract potentials reflects the steady aging of Washington's population. As the percentage of the total population aged 65 or older increased between 1940 and 1970, the overall potential values also increased. However, because there was a reduction in area categorized in the highest potential category (6,000 or more) after 1960, a slightly more scattered distribution of those aged 65 or older was indicated for 1970 relative to 1960.

The second notable change observed over the period is related to the location of high tract potentials. High values of elderly population potential reflect relatively greater access to the entire elderly population; thus, the most accessible tracts have consistently been located in the near northwest of Washington, D.C. The tracts of high access (in other words, high potential) shifted toward the northwest between 1940 and 1950 and again between 1950 and 1960. This trend was reversed during the 1960–1970 decade with tracts of higher access tending to be located more toward the south and east.

Two demographic trends, somewhat contradictory in their effect on elderly potential distributions, appear to be involved: (1) The total population has gradually aged, and (2) the proportion of the total population that is black has increased. Because the black population of Washington has been largely concentrated in the eastern half of the city and because it is younger (4.9% and 5.6% of the black population was aged 65 or older in 1960 and 1970, respectively, whereas 14.1% and 19.3% of the white population was aged 65 or older in those years), the geographic focus of elderly population has gradually shifted toward the northwest away from the growing concentration of black population in the east. However, because the proportion of the white population dropped sharply after 1960 (45.2% white compared with 27.7% in 1970) and the proportion of the black population aged 65 or older increased, the focus of the city's elderly shifted slightly east toward the region with largely black residents.

In terms of the best location for a center dispensing services to the elderly, the dominant feature of these patterns is their locational persistence. In spite of

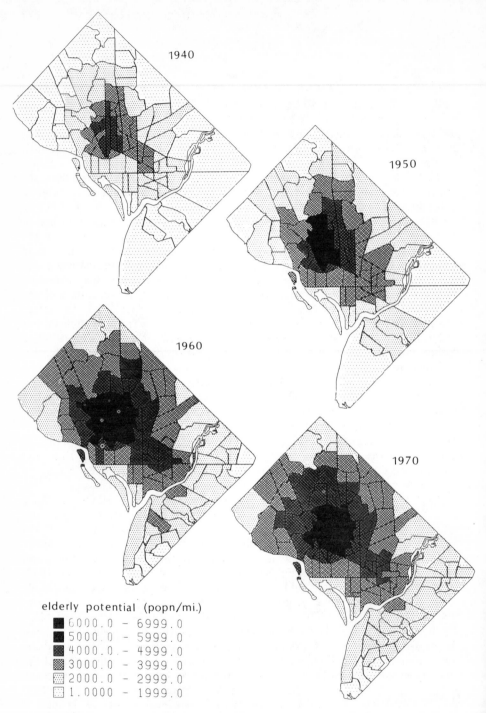

Fig. 21. Population potential of the elderly, 1940–1970, Washington, D.C.

major demographic changes in Washington, D.C., and a good deal of in-migration and out-migration since 1940, the weighted geographical center of the elderly has not changed greatly. A service center located in the tract with the highest elderly potential in 1940 would still have been in a relatively efficient location in 1970.

EXTENSIONS OF THE MODEL

Various extensions to this model can be offered which will increase its utility. Only the simplest form and application of the model have been presented in this chapter. Among the possible different applications is to consider specific subgroups of elderly population (e.g., the black, widowed, poor, or retired elderly). Each of these groups of elderly population may be recipients of distinctive social services, and therefore documentation of their distinctive patterns of location potential may be demanded. In estimating the model, a more complex distance function can be used when determining the value surface. For simplicity, an exponent of one was used for the distance variable, but when travel is shown to be especially constraining for a group, a larger exponent may be more appropriate. Also, if other local policies dictate that certain portions of the city should be treated as special cases, specific census tracts can be weighted accordingly. Lastly, the "population" variable can be weighted by such factors as personal income, information availability (e.g., newspaper circulation), education, or unemployment if these are relevant to the nature or location of the service.

CONCLUSIONS

As a methodology, determination of intraurban elderly population potential provides one indicator of the "best" location for service facilities addressing the needs of the elderly. It is easy to calculate and requires readily available data. It provides a measure of elderly location that may not be obvious from simple mapped elderly spatial distributions or concentrations. Further, its ease of computation permits periodic reevaluation of a center's locational efficiency as a city's demographic structure changes.

NOTES AND REFERENCES

[1] Preparation of this chapter was supported in part by the Carolina Population Center and by the University Research Council, University of North Carolina, Chapel Hill.
[2] Stephen M. Golant, "Intraurban Transportation Needs and Problems of the Elderly," in M. Powell Lawton, Robert J. Newcomer, and Thomas O. Byerts, eds., *Community Planning for an Aging Society* (Stroudsberg, Pa.: Dowden, Hutchinson, & Ross, 1976), pp. 282–308.
[3] Stephen M. Golant, "Housing and Transportation Problems of the Urban Elderly," in John S. Adams, ed., *Urban Policymaking and Metropolitan Dynamics, A Comparative Geographical Analysis* (Cambridge, Mass.: Ballinger, 1976), pp. 379–422.

[4]Lester A. Hoel et al., *Latent Demand for Urban Transportation* (Pittsburgh: Transportation Research Institute, Carnegie-Mellon University, 1968); Richard K. Brail, James W. Hughes, and Carol A. Arthur, *Transportation Services for the Disabled and Elderly* (New Brunswick, N.J.: Center for Urban Policy Research, Rutgers University, 1976).

[5]Leslie S. Libow, "Old People's Medical and Physiological Characteristics: Some Implications for Transportation," in Edmund Cantilli and June Smelzer, eds., *Transportation and Aging* (Washington, D.C.: Department of Health, Education, and Welfare, 1970).

[6]Frances M. Carp, "Urban Life Style and Life-Cycle Factors," in M. Powell Lawton, Robert J. Newcomer, and Thomas O. Byerts, eds., *Community Planning for an Aging Society* (Stroudsberg, Pa.: Dowden, Hutchinson, & Ross, 1976), pp. 19–40; Marjorie H. Cantor, "Effect of Ethnicity on Life Styles of the Inner-City Elderly," in M. Powell Lawton, Robert J. Newcomer, and Thomas O. Byerts, eds., *Community Planning for an Aging Society* (Stroudsberg, Pa.: Dowden, Hutchinson, & Ross, 1976), pp. 41–58; Harold M. Proshansky et al., "Freedom of Choice and Behavior in a Physical Setting," in Harold M. Proshansky et al., eds., *Environmental Psychology* (Chicago: Holt, Rinehart & Winston, 1970), pp. 173–183; Erdman Palmore and Clark Luikart, "Health and Social Factors Related to Life Satisfaction," *Journal of Health and Social Behavior*, Vol. 13 (1972), pp. 68–80.

[7]Stephen M. Golant and Rosemary McCaslin, "A Functional Classification of Services for Older People," *Journal of Gerontological Social Work*, Vol. 1 (Spring, 1979).

[8]Brail, Hughes, and Arthur, op. cit., note 4, pp. 183–187.

[9]Brail, Hughes, and Arthur, op. cit., note 4, p. 184.

[10]J. Q. Stewart and William Warntz, "Macrogeography and Social Science," *Geographical Review*, Vol. 48 (1958), pp. 167–184.

Chapter 14

A SOCIAL INDICATOR MODEL OF THE ELDERLY POPULATION'S SOCIAL WELFARE ENVIRONMENT[1]

Stephen M. Golant and Rosemary McCaslin

The need for social indicator[2] models to provide the conceptual and methodological frameworks necessary for planning, monitoring, and evaluating the goals and consequences of social programs is well established. At present an urgent need exists for the making of evaluative judgments concerning the strengths and weaknesses of programs providing social and medical services and benefits for the elderly people of the United States. The following are some of the most relevant situational factors:[3] (1) the increasingly prevalent argument that federal spending is too large and growing too rapidly; (2) the well-documented contention that older people are now receiving a disproportionately large share of society's welfare resources; (3) a projected increase in demand for these resources because of the large expected growth in the population of the elderly both in absolute numbers and in proportion to the growth of the younger populations; (4) the large, rapidly escalating and, by current estimates, relatively uncontrollable cost of age-entitlement programs of Medicare and the Old Age Survivors Insurance portion of Social Security; (5) the existence of objective indicators suggesting that the older population is better off or less disadvantaged than other minority groups; (6) increasing arguments that the family unit should bear a greater share of the burden in providing for the well-being of older people; (7) arguments that social and health problems should be handled via "broad-based universalistic social policies aimed at coping with special problems as they affect all citizens and the society at large rather than via particularistic old-age oriented policies."[4]

Together with these factors, observers such as Hudson argue that an increasingly less responsive political environment is emerging in which to maintain and increase funds for the support of the elderly population's social welfare environment. The aged, he argues, are in jeopardy of losing their favored social welfare status in the United States. He suggests the following possible outcomes:

> Major new policy initiatives or appropriations beyond those provided for under existing legislation will meet with new and perhaps overwhelming resistance.
> More critical appraisal of aging policy may also place agencies serving the elderly under new and harder scrutiny ... As the aging come to be viewed increasingly as a political problem and less as a source of political opportunity, the role and utility of these agencies will be assessed more in terms of problem resolution than problem recognition.[5]

This trend is likely to have its greatest effects on the funding of discretionary in-kind programs, such as those funded under the Older Americans Act because (1) it involves neither age-entitlement nor means-tested programs and (2) unlike Social Security and Medicare, there is no cost escalator.

Amidst threats of more restricted fiscal funding, critics from both private and public sectors argue that the existing social welfare environment of the elderly is grossly inadequate. They have made the following arguments:[6] (1) funding of the services provided under the Older Americans Act is limited and restrictive; (2) existing social and health services are poorly coordinated; (3) geographic coverage of the social welfare environment is inefficient and inequitable; (4) demand for certain functions of the social welfare environment (e.g., low-rent and congregate housing facilities) remains largely unsatisfied; (5) alternatives to nursing homes as providers of long-term care are insufficient; (6) enforcement of quality standards for long-term care benefits and programs is poor; (7) public expenditures for certain subgroups of older people such as the old-old (over age 75), the infirm, and racial minorities are insufficient; (8) mounting out-of-pocket medical expenses are assumed by the elderly; (9) inequity exists in the taxation and benefits policies of the social security system as these are applied to the poor and wealthy elderly; (10) Supplemental Security Income Programs are poorly integrated with other social welfare programs.

A SOCIAL INDICATOR MODEL–OVERVIEW AND RATIONALE

Because the future is likely to be characterized by more restricted fiscal resources, greater scrutiny of the goals and performance of existing programs and a more cautious and critical approach to new programs, the need for models of the elderly population's social welfare environment becomes pressing. In this chapter a social indicator model is constructed in which the services found in a community are conceptualized as a set of functional or output units that simultaneously address two broad welfare goals: (1) the improvement and maintenance of the individual's behavioral functioning or competence and (2) the maintenance of the individual's independent living arrangements. To operationalize the model, we develop a data base and methodology by which to measure the supply (quantity and attributes) of services and benefits that address these goals. The model's feasibility is tested in the relatively service rich middle class community of Evanston, Illinois, where several related research initiatives are taking place.[7]

The model's capabilities should first be emphasized. The model can be viewed as one analytical component—a submodel—of a larger accounting system by which the impact of the social welfare environment on the well-being of an elderly population is evaluated. Our analytical concern is restricted to the development of a language and methodology which monitors and evaluates how well the supply of services *addresses* two major welfare objectives. The model does not evaluate the latent or actual demand for these services nor the how's and why's of the congruence between service supply and demand. It also does not consider the impact these services are having on the improvement of the physical or mental well-being of an elderly population. These questions must be considered by other analytical submodels and will not be dealt with here.

The goals of our social indicator model share some similarities with those of a national economic accounting system and the model performs several of the roles attributed to such a system.[8] It enables large quantities of information on the services and benefits of the social welfare environment to be ordered in a systematically comprehensive way so that conceptual and empirical relationships can be clearly specified. This system of information can be described in a language that expresses the major objectives or performance elements of the social welfare environment, as opposed to the planning, programmatic or operational processes underlying these objectives. This language is formalized to the extent that it can be interpreted and applied in any locational or institutional context irrespective of that context's unique social, political, administrative and physical environment characteristics or programmatic structure, i.e., the structural and functional complexity of the social welfare environment itself. The model should encourage policy makers and planners to collect, interpret, and analyze data in a manner consistent with its specified objectives and systemic comprehensiveness.

CONCEPTUALIZATION OF THE SOCIAL WELFARE ENVIRONMENT

The social and health service system of a community is conceptualized as a set of outputs or products. From this perspective all programs, facilities, and benefits for the elderly are expressed in terms of the primary functions each performs. Each service output unit is classified according to its position on two theoretical dimensions, schematized as two orthogonal axes. The horizontal axis is labelled "level of competence" and the vertical axis, "level of independence." We have elsewhere described in considerable detail the rationale for selecting these dimensions and the constructs and assumptions of the classification scheme.[9] What follows below is a much abbreviated discussion.

Levels of Competence Dimension

To identify categorical positions along the competence dimension, we adopted, with minor modifications, Lawton's framework for conceptualizing the full range of behaviors which make up a normal individual's adult functioning.[10] Five levels of behavioral functioning were defined: life maintenance and health (lowest level), perception-cognition, self-maintenance, effectance, and social role performance (highest level). The position of a service output along this dimension would depend on the level of behavioral functioning or competence it addressed. If services directed to a particular level of behavioral functioning are unattainable (or lacked utility), then the individual may be exposed to a greater threat that he or she would be unable to perform successfully at this and higher levels of behavioral functioning. In this sense, levels of behavioral functioning are assumed to be hierarchically organized, whereupon the successful carrying out (according to normative standards) of higher order behavior is assumed to be dependent on the individual's successful functioning at lower levels.[11]

Levels of Independence Dimension

In order to categorically differentiate services along this dimension, we use part of the classification outlined by Tobin, Davidson, and Sack.[12] They conceive of a continuum of services for three subgroups of the elderly: the comparatively well, those who require alternatives for premature institutionalization, and those who need "institutional care or its equivalent." We adopt their three categories to specify high to low levels of independence. Level of independence refers to the extent of the individual's control over his social situation. "Social situation" refers to the individual's relationships with the people, activities, and material culture comprising his or her living arrangements.[13] "Control" refers to the extent to which the individual has mastery over the social situation and functions autonomously in it. The position of a service output along this dimension would depend on the level of independence of the living arrangements it addressed. We assume that if services directed to a particular independence level of an individual are unattainable or lack utility, then the individual is exposed to a greater threat of not being able to maintain his/her present level of independence. The lower the level of behavioral functioning that is impaired and for which services are unattainable or lack utility, the greater will be the reality of the threat.

METHODOLOGICAL FRAMEWORK

Service Output Units: Definitions and Criteria for Inclusion

The analyst confronts a philosophical and conceptual problem when deciding what services and benefits should be included within the social welfare environment. The difficult question becomes how to define or interpret the concept of "social welfare." A perusal of various social planning texts will show that the answer to this question is far from obvious.[14]

We initially set out three criteria for a service output to be included in our analytical framework: (1) it had to be formally organized and publicly identifiable as a service provider; (2) it had to be currently serving the elderly either as its primary consumer group (age-segregated clientele) or as one of several population consumer subgroups (age-integrated clientele); and (3) it had to be located in our research community of Evanston, Illinois, or identified by community leaders as a resource utilized by the community's elderly residents, if located or administered outside its boundaries. Given these criteria, both public and private nonprofit agencies, proprietary enterprises, public entitlement programs (county, state, and federal) and private professionals were included, even though substantial differences characterize their organizational, administrative, and funding structures.

We excluded from consideration an important subsystem of service providers, the informal social support system of family, relatives, friends, and neighbors. Although the informal support system constitutes an important resource component in any holistic approach to the supply of human services, our attention is restricted to the formal support system because a distinctive conceptual and methodological framework would be required for a sensitive portrayal of the informal service system.

In collecting data on these services, our primary unit of analysis, the service output unit, was defined as a quantity of service for which distinctive staff goals and functions (or staff time) and clients could be identified. Since services were conceptualized in terms of their functions rather than their structures, it was entirely possible for a single agency or organization to provide several different units of service.[15] A general hospital, for example, can be viewed as consisting of several service output units, such as in-patient department, out-patient department, mental health clinic, and speech pathology clinic. Service units were defined so that they would be mutually exclusive to facilitate the construction of aggregate measures amenable to statistical analysis.

Major Data Sources

Multiple information sources were utilized to identify service output units meeting our criteria. We examined all service inventories and assessments that had been compiled up to 5 years earlier by Evanston agencies and student trainees.[16] Other published directories, unpublished resource files, *The Evanston Review* (a weekly newspaper), and planning documents were variously consulted. Key community leaders, agency executives, and persons knowledgeable about services in Evanston were also contacted or interviewed.[17]

Classification of Services

The specification of 5 positions or categories along the competence dimension and 3 positions along the independence dimension resulted in 15 potential cells

High			
	Services for the comparatively well elderly	Consumer health education Crime prevention Health insurance Health screening Physical fitness programs Private dental care Private medical care	Accessible, informal advice & support Counseling for elderly Income management Information & referral Pre-retirement planning Tax assistance

	Services that provide alternatives for preventing premature institutionali-zation	Community-based nursing
		  practice
		Emergency food & shelter
		Emergency medical services
		Home-delivered meals
		On-site health service
		Specialized health
		  services
		Subsidized health care
			Counseling for family
			  members
			Crisis intervention
			Daily reassurance contact
			Language translation
			Outpatient mental health
			  treatment
			Supportive contact

	Services for those whose needs may demand institutional care or its equivalents	Day care
		Hospital care
		Skilled home nursing
		Skilled nursing home care
		Respite care
		Terminal care
			In-patient psychiatric
			  care
			Partial psychiatric
			  hospitalization
			Reality orientation
			Sheltered care
			Transitional residential
			  care

Low		LIFE MAINTENANCE AND HEALTH	PERCEPTION-COGNITION

LEVELS OF INDEPENDENCE

Low

LEVELS OF

Fig. 22. Community's services classified according to levels of competence and independence addressed.

186

Discounts on goods & services Employment training & referral Non-permanent living arrangements Property tax relief Residential building maintenance grants & loans Retirement insurance	Adult education Camping Cultural & spiritual enrichment Library resources & facilities Park facilities Recreational programs	Adult-child surrogate relation development Civic involvement Clubs and organizations Part-time work opportunities (paid or unpaid) Peer groups
Auxiliary instrumental transportation (para-transit) Chore services Congregate dining facilities Escort services Foster family care Groceries on wheels Homebound employment Homemaking assistance In-kind assistance Legal assistance Mutual aid Public financial assistance Sheltered workshops Specially trained housing management staff Subsidized food provision Subsidized rents	Expressive-oriented transportation services	Age-segregated living arrangements Companionship Outreach to isolated
Home personal health care Guardianship Protective services Unskilled nursing home care	Day activity programs	Carefully defined screening of residents Specially organized social functions
SELF MAINTENANCE	**EFFECTANCE**	**SOCIAL ROLE**

High →

COMPETENCE

in which the set of health and social services and benefits offered by the Evanston community to its elderly population could be classified. For this service allocation, the authors, along with several professionals in the fields of aging and social welfare, served as "expert judges." The following steps were taken to construct the service classification shown in Figure 22: (1) agency programs were divided into services for which discrete functions could be identified; (2) when a service's function was ambiguous, the determination was based on its staffing patterns or description in agency literature, funding grants, or by professionals; (3) each identified service function was defined generically without reference to its auspices, staffing, location, or mode of delivery in any particular agency program;[18] (4) as a validity check, each generically defined service was matched with coded UWASIS II definitions;[19] (5) each service defined as above was classified according to the level of individual behavioral functioning it addressed; (6) each service defined as above was classified according to the level of independence of living arrangements it addressed; (7) the services assigned to any particular matrix cell were considered functionally equivalent (and are listed in alphabetical order);[20] (8) when opinions of the judges varied, the issue was discussed and additional opinions were obtained. A final judgement reflected a majority opinion.

Variable Construction

A data quality problem is confronted in constructing a set of variables to describe the supply (quantity and attributes) of a community's service output units. Some service providers will be portrayed completely and accurately, while only limited information will be available for others. This data dilemma is resolved, unfortunately, by time and cost considerations which become the basis for deciding which variables are selected and for which service output information will be collected.

Social welfare agencies provide data which, when available, are notoriously incomplete, inaccurate, duplicative, and obscure.[21] Several factors are responsible: Agencies do not use uniform reporting intervals and procedures; competition for funding encourages inflated procedures (e.g., counting administered interviews rather than clients served); "patchwork" funding sources result in clients who are counted several times in different sets of records; the concern for confidentiality restricts access to data; proprietary agencies are often protective of details about their businesses; and many traditional social work agencies do not keep aggregate records unless required by their funders.[22]

Data collection difficulties in Evanston were manifested in two ways. First, extremely limited data were available for two groups of service providers: (a) private professionals not practicing within the context of an agency or organization and (b) churches providing service outputs for older people. Consequently, an analysis of these services was largely precluded. Second, data were sometimes either unavailable or inappropriate for certain service output units.[23] This resulted in missing data for selected variables in as many as 25% of the service output units.[24]

The major set of variables for which data were collected are described below. The first 11 variables describe attributes of the service outputs; the remaining 4 describe their quantity or amount.

1. *Category of service.* Each service output was categorized according to the level of individual behavioral functioning and the level of the independence of the living arrangements it addressed.

2. *Absolute location.* Census tract and block units as defined by the U.S. Bureau of the Census were utilized to locate the major local offices of the service output units within Evanston.[25]

3. *Relative location.* The number of walking blocks between each service unit office location (shortest route) and the nearest of three major business districts in Evanston were calculated.[26]

4. *Location of actual service delivery.* Three locational groupings were distinguished according to mode of service delivery: (a) services provided at a fixed location—those requiring that clients come to the agency office or some other permanent location in order to receive services; (b) services provided at variable locations—those available on a flexible basis at locations frequented by potential clients for other purposes (e.g., at senior centers, post offices, parks); (c) home-delivered services—those available to clients within their house or building. Services grouped in categories (b) and (c) were excluded from analyses of absolute and relative location since their mode of delivery rendered inappropriate questions of facility location.

5. *Cost of service to consumer: lowest income group served.* Services were described according to the levels of income of the older persons they were likely to serve. Three such groups were designated: (a) low-income elderly, (b) moderate-income elderly, and (c) high-income elderly. Each service unit was identified by the lowest income level of elderly persons for which it was available. By necessity, the source of funding for the service was used as the basis for determining the income groupings of its clients (see Fig. 23).[27]

6. *Cost of service to consumer: eligibility restrictions.* Services were distinguished according to whether their funding structure made them available to all elderly or restricted them to groups of elderly at certain income levels.

7. *Auspices.* Service units were described as either public, including federal, state, and local agencies, or private, including voluntary organizations, a portion of whose funding might also be from governmental sources. This variable differs from the "cost" classification in that it categorized the major funding sources of the agency or organization rather than of the specific service output unit.

8. *Age-mix of clients served.* Service units were described as either age-integrated, available to all persons (or at least to all adults) without any distinction according to age, or age-segregated, available only or predominantly to persons over the age of 60 (or some other age used to define a person as "elderly").

9. *Percentage of total clients who are elderly.* Variable 14 as a percentage of variable 13 (see below).

10. *Date service started.* The year in which the service output unit addressing the needs of older persons was started.

INCOME GROUP SERVED	FUNDING STRUCTURE						
	GOVERNMENTAL[a]			VOLUNTARY[b]		FEES[c]	
	Vendor Payments[d]	Purchase of Services & Grants[e]	Public Department[f]	Full Agency Support[g]	Sliding Scale[h,i]	Insurance[j]	Client Payments[k]
Low Income	▨	▨	▨	▨	▨		
Moderate Income		▨	▨	▨	▨	▨	
High Income			▨	▨	▨	▨	▨
ELIGIBILITY	Restricted			Unrestricted		Restricted	

[a]Service units funded by full or primary support of a government agency (federal, state, or local).

[b]Service units funded by private agencies and financed from "United Fund," independent funding drives, individual agency fund-raising, use of voluntary agency capital or investments, or foundation support.

[c]Service units financed primarily by fee-for-service payments either directly from recipients or through third-party payments from private insurance policies.

[d]Governmental payments channelled to agencies through private third-party carriers. Medicaid is included in this category.

[e]Government financing of service units provided by private agencies under contractural agreements or direct grants.

[f]Service units provided directly by a governmental department.

[g]Complete cost of service is underwritten by a private agency's budget.

[h]Fees are collected from service recipients, assessed on a sliding-scale based on the client's ability to pay. Such fees are not usually intended to provide a major portion of the agency's operating budget.

[i]It may be argued that most sliding-fee scales demand a small token payment that could be a hardship on lowest income individuals.

[j]Medicare is included in this category.

[k]Life-care contracts are included in this category.

Source: Adapted in part from Health and Welfare Council of Metropolitan St. Louis, *Guide for Community Action: The Report of the Resource-Needs Project* (St. Louis, February, 1963).

Fig. 23. Lowest income group served and eligibility restrictions according to funding structure.

11. *"Transfer" vs. "other" service outputs.* Transfer services refer to purposively developed public programs that enable persons to purchase goods and services at below market (i.e., government subsidized) prices. Examples include subsidized health care, subsidized apartment rents, food stamps, and property tax relief. All other services are in the second category.

12. *Size of service output unit: number of staff.* The number of staff persons available within each service unit in an average month (or other specified period)

were recorded in full-time equivalents (i.e., a part-time employee was counted as 1/2 staff person). Top-level administrators and clerical staff were excluded except in small agencies in which such personnel also participated in actual service delivery. (When an administrative structure included an executive assistant, the executive was excluded and the assistant included on the assumption that the latter was likely to play the active service provider role.) Housekeeping and kitchen staff were also excluded from this measurement due to the difficulty of obtaining uniform staff data in this area for all service output units. Staff personnel providing services in different units within the same agency were counted so as to reflect the proportion of their time allocated to the respective units. Where such breakdowns were not available, estimates were extrapolated.

13. *Size of service output unit: total clients served per month.* The total number of persons of all ages receiving services from the staff in an average month was recorded. For service providers such as hospitals and nursing homes, bed capacity was used for this measure on the assumption that staff must normally be maintained to support a full occupancy situation. When exact monthly figures were available, these were averaged over several representative months.

14. *Size of service output unit: number of elderly served per month.* The number of persons aged 60 and older (or as closely defined by the service provider) served in an average month was recorded in the same way as variable 13 using estimates where necessary. In some cases, the best estimate available was given as a percentage of the total client load and this was extrapolated to a monthly rate.

15. *Labor intensiveness of service output unit.* The total clients served per month was divided by the number of total staff to give a client-staff ratio.

Interpreting the Variables

The interpretation of the first set of variables is relatively clear. Service unit locations and costs to consumers measure factors which may constrain or facilitate the use of services by older persons who need them. The variable "auspices" indicates the role of the private and public sectors in providing services. If a service is age-segregated, then the older population is being addressed as a distinctive needs group. The year the service was started differentiates well-established programs from those which are newer and possibly less well-known within the community. The identification of "transfer" services distinguishes programs that improve (indirectly) the economic status of older people.

To measure the quantity or amount of services in the Evanston community, client and staff data were collected as surrogate measures (variables 12 to 14). Despite the shortcomings of these data, few methodological alternatives were available. Fiscal data can be used to measure the commitment of the private and public sectors to particular services and benefits. As a measure of "quantity" of service, however, such data suffer from comparability problems similar to those discussed below for staff and client data.[28] In this investigation, some service providers were hesitant or completely unwilling to divulge even data on staff and client loads and in several cases this information had to be obtained from public records. Agency personnel are much more likely to consider fiscal data to be highly confidential and, for services not receiving public funds, such information is usually not accessible. In study areas such as states, counties, or area aging agency planning units, fiscal data on service costs and expenditures would be more accessible. Staff data to measure the quantity of services are difficult to interpret because of the problem of equivalence. This problem involves the proverbial task of finding a common means of describing "apples" and "oranges." The amount of staff time required for the average client will vary among different types of output. For example, one can hardly equate an hour's worth of professional counselling with an hour spent at a recreation center. The radically different activities of the two services make for quite different staffing patterns and client loads. Even equating staff measures of similar service output units found in different organizations may be misleading. For example, the dissimilar physical and mental competence of residents in different nursing homes may imply that different staffing patterns are appropriate for both homes to successfully achieve the same performance levels. Thus, a service output unit with 10 staff is not necessarily five times more "available" than a service output unit with 2 staff. The former service may be more labor-intensive than the latter and require more staff to serve the same number of clients (variable 15). It is also possible that the service units are undermanned or overmanned,[29] but this is also difficult to determine. For these reasons, a proportionate increase in staff for a given service unit would not necessarily serve more elderly nor would economies of scale result from service unit expansion.

The number of clients served by a service output unit is less difficult to interpret as an "availability" measure, though problems arise when different categories of service output units are compared. We would not, for example, expect that certain categories of service units would serve as many clients as others, simply because the potential "market" of clients for particular services will be smaller. Another problem is the extent to which "clients served" figures represent unduplicated elderly persons. For example, the same elderly person might visit (for the same problem) three or four service output units in a hospital two or three times in the same month. We attempt to minimize, though obviously not eliminate, this problem by recording "client" (as well as staff) data on an "average" monthly basis.

Analytical Approach

For the purpose of data collection and variable construction, the basic unit of analysis was the service output unit. For monitoring and evaluation purposes, however, all variable measures were averaged or standardized to provide summary quantitative measures of the service supply in rows (levels of independence), columns (levels of competence), and cells (independence-competence interactions) in the classification. Thus, generalizations made about the goals or objectives of the social welfare environment will apply only to these categorical subgroupings of service outputs. Measurement error from our methodological approach will be most apparent at the "cell" level of analysis which, in contrast to the single row or column, will more likely contain a smaller number of output units.

APPLICATION OF SOCIAL INDICATOR MODEL

It is useful to identify several important issues or questions that can be evaluated by the social indicator model. (An empirical analysis of several of these questions will be reported in a future manuscript.) With appropriate quantitative measures of services found in the rows, columns, or cells of the model, it is possible to assess the levels of behavioral functioning and independence a community has chosen to support through its service structure and thereby identify the minimal level of well-being guaranteed its population. The amount of community resources addressing the different levels of competence and independence will reflect the value assumptions and constraints that have guided the decision-making process. For example, in a community holding the traditional individualistic view that each person is solely responsible for his/her own success or failure, one would expect the preponderance of services to be restricted to the support of lower levels of behavioral impairment, reflecting the belief that public support is appropriate primarily when the survival of the individual is threatened. In contrast, larger amounts of program resources allocated to the support of higher order behavioral functioning would be expected in more progressive communities which consider the older population to be entitled to a range of services and benefits that impinge on all levels of well-being.

Focusing on the attributes of these service output units, it is possible to establish how services addressing different levels of competence or independence systematically vary with respect to characteristics that may give insight into their benefits or costs. It can also be established whether services developed more recently possess attributes that differ significantly from older more traditional social services.

The model will facilitate an analysis of what "packages" of services are available in a community to address differing levels of individual impairment and dependence. A high proportion of older clients have multiple problems requiring a combination of services and treatments. Consequently, as Attkisson and Broskowski emphasize,[30] cases are rare where "a single service or treatment, in isolation of others, will be sufficient to restore a multiproblemed individual to an effective level of overall functioning." So, for example, comparatively healthy elderly persons who have experienced various cognitive disorders may have their behavioral performance threatened in several other areas, including self-maintenance, effectance, and social role functions.

Policy makers and social planners must confront many critical issues that revolve around the "correct," "acceptable," or "optimum" allocation of fiscal and staff resources to services that are distinguished by the level of independence and behavioral functioning addressed. The following questions are illustrative of what we can label as the service allocation problem:

> Should the social welfare environment be targeted at the most vulnerable subgroup of older people with more demanding service needs, or should it address the needs of all elderly, the majority of whom will have less pressing service needs?
>
> How will the demand-supply relationships for services change as a consequence of the increasingly higher proportions of elderly people predicted to be in the age group 75 and older who, on the average, will be less competent and more dependent?
>
> Will increasing the supply of neighborhood or congregate services as alternatives to long-term care facilities have an impact on the rate of institutionalization of older people and on the public costs of funding welfare services and benefits?

The answers to such questions are strongly influenced by the political and economic climate prevailing at a given place and time. While social forces may lead to major alterations in the structure of the service system, these may or may not alter the functional capacity of the system to address human needs. It is important to be able to monitor and evaluate policy changes in terms of their ultimate impact on the "mix" of services addressing the independence and competence levels of a population. To do this we must have a baseline from which to measure such changes.

Towards these ends we have presented a conceptual and methodological framework by which to monitor the extent to which the social welfare environment of the elderly population is performing two broad goals. This model represents but one of several analytical frameworks required to evaluate the impact of the social welfare environment on the well-being of the elderly population.

NOTES AND REFERENCES

[1] Preparation of chapter and the reported research supported by grant No. 5PO1 AG 00123 from the National Institute on Aging.

[2] An HEW definition of a social indicator is as follows: a statistic of direct normative interest which facilitates concise, comprehensive, and balanced judgments about the condition of major aspects of a society. It is in all cases a direct measure of welfare and is subject to the interpretation that, if it changes in the "right" direction, while other things remain equal, things have gotten better or people are "better off." See U.S. Department of Health, Education and Welfare, *Toward a Social Report* (Washington, D.C.: Government Printing Office, 1969), p. 97.

[3] For a more detailed discussion of several of the following issues see Robert C. Benedict, "Trends in the Development of Services for the Aging Under the Older American Act," in Barbara R. Herzog, ed., *Aging and Income* (N.Y.: Human Sciences Press, 1978), pp. 280–306; Sheldon S. Tobin, Stephen M. Davidson and Ann Sack, *Effective Social Services for Older Americans* (Ann Arbor: Institute of Gerontology, University of Michigan, 1976); *Aging*, No. 285–286 (July–Aug., 1978), pp. 1–4; Robert B. Hudson, "The Graying of the Federal Budget and Its Consequences for Old-Age Policy," *Gerontologist*, Vol. 18, No. 5 (Oct., 1978), pp. 475–481; Byron Gold, Elizabeth Kutza and Theodore R. Marmor, "United States Social Policy on Old Age: Present Patterns and Predictions," in Bernice L. Neugarten

and Robert J. Havighurst, eds., *Social Policy, Social Ethics and the Aging Society* (Washington, D.C.: Government Printing Office, 1976), pp. 9-21; Amital Etzioni, "Old People and Public Policy," *Social Policy*, Vol. 7, No. 3 (Nov.-Dec., 1976), pp. 21-29.

[4] Etzioni, op. cit., note 3, p. 21.

[5] Hudson, op. cit., note 3, p. 428.

[6] Op. cit., note 3.

[7] The community under investigation, Evanston, Illinois, is a municipality (with its own city government) of about 80,000 people located just north of the City of Chicago.

[8] Raymond A. Bauer, "Detection and Anticipation of Impact; The Nature of the Task," in Raymond A. Bauer, ed., *Social Indicators* (Cambridge, Mass.: M.I.T. Press, 1966), pp. 164-165.

[9] Stephen M. Golant and Rosemary McCaslin, "A Functional Classification of Services for Older People," *Journal of Gerontological Social Work*, Vol. 1, No. 3 (Spring, 1979).

[10] M. Powell Lawton, "Assessing the Competence of Older People," in D. P. Kent, R. Kastenbaum and S. Sherwood, eds., *Research Planning and Action for the Elderly* (New York: Behavioral Publishers, 1972), pp. 122-143.

[11] It bears emphasizing that higher order behaviors will be dependent *in degree*, rather than in their absolute *presence* or *absence*, on competent functioning of lower order behaviors. For instance, conditions of poor health exert a pervasive influence across all functional areas. Higher order debilities may result from or be exacerbated by restrictions imposed on lower order behaviors by illness, disability, and conditions of medical treatment.

[12] Tobin, Davidson, and Sack, op. cit., note 3.

[13] Muzafer Sherif, *Social Interaction: Process and Products* (Chicago: Aldine, 1967), pp. 120-121.

[14] See Alfred Kahn, *Theory and Practice of Social Planning* (New York: Russell Sage Foundation, 1969).

[15] Agency identification was retained for each service unit so that analyses by organizational auspices could be undertaken.

[16] The University of Chicago, School of Social Service Administration, Community Mental Health Project has used the Evanston community and its agencies as a training setting for its students since 1972.

[17] Eligible agencies were contacted personally between January and August of 1977 to obtain current data on their services.

[18] Eric Pfeiffer, "Designing Systems of Care: The Clinical Perspective," in Eric Pfeiffer, ed., *Alternatives to Institutional Care for Older Americans: Practice and Planning* (Durham, N.C.: Duke University Press, 1972), pp. 12-22.

[19] United Way of America, Services Identification System, *UWASIS II: A Taxonomy of Social Goals and Human Service Programs* (Alexandria, Va.: United Way of America, 1976). The coded UWASIS II service classification has been revised recently after fairly extensive usage by and feedback from professionals currently active in the field of social welfare. Thus, it reflects considerable consensus as to the definition of various human service functions.

[20] Thus, generalizations concerning the service matrix are applicable only at the "cell" level.

[21] James R. Seaberg and Michell A. Bell, "Evaluation of Broad-Scale Service Networks," *Social Work Research and Abstracts*, Vol. 14, No. 1 (Spring, 1978), pp. 19-24.

[22] Agencies may claim they provide several different service outputs, sometimes treating problems quite unrelated to the agency's identified function, but data to document their efforts are often unavailable.

[23] For example, agencies located in Chicago or neighboring suburbs and used by Evanston's elderly could not be described in terms of walking blocks to the Evanston business district.

[24] A total of 119 service units met the criteria for inclusion in the study and were able to be described by a relatively complete variable set.

[25] Services located outside of Evanston were coded as either "inside City of Chicago," or "in neighboring suburbs."

[26]Walking distance between each service location and transportation lines was considered but excluded as a variable because it displayed little statistical variation.

[27]Many health and social services determine fees on an individual basis, according to program-specific eligibility criteria and/or sliding payment scales. It is not possible, therefore, to specify cost to consumers in terms of actual monetary charges since these may vary widely among clients receiving the same service. It is possible, on the other hand, to obtain information on the funding-connected criteria used to determine eligibility and fees and to infer from that data the income groups to which services are made available or for whom they are financially accessible.

[28]See James A. Maxwell and J. Richard Aronson, *Financing State and Local Governments* (Washington, D.C.: The Brookings Institute, 1977).

[29]Terminology from Roger Barker, *Ecological Psychology*, (Stanford: Stanford University Press, 1968).

[30]C. Clifford Attkisson and Anthony Broskowski, "Evaluation and the Emerging Human Service Concept," in C. Clifford Atkisson et al., eds., *Evaluation of Human Service Programs* (New York: Academic Press, 1978), p. 9.

Chapter 15

THE OPTIMAL ASSIGNMENT OF HUMAN SERVICE CLIENTS TO TREATMENT SETTINGS[1]

Michael Dear and Jennifer Wolch

The similarities in providing support services to discharged mental patients, to the elderly, and to other service-dependent populations are, in many respects, quite profound. Within each group, vastly different services are needed, ranging from total life-support in a protected setting to occasional home visits from a health aide; yet each group, when compared with the general population, is relatively dependent upon institutional care-givers, and the goal of service delivery in each case is to provide a support system that is integrated into the community. The structural similarities of these goals provoke a host of research questions: How can institutional dependency be minimized, concomitant with client needs? How is community integration facilitated? To what extent is structural integration of service systems possible, given the communality of needs?

In an era of rapid expansion in community-based human services and of progressive deinstitutionalization of service-dependent populations, the importance of these questions is evident. What is not so clear, however, is how to approach the problems of need, variable dependency, and community integration simultaneously. An appropriate theoretical framework is the necessary first step in this analysis but, in our view, such a framework has yet to be provided.

In order to demonstrate the complexity and ambiguity of community-based service delivery, it is instructive to examine briefly the "career" of a typical client group (Fig. 24). As they grow older, certain segments of the elderly population lose their capacity for coping and so become dependent on the human services sector. In the first instance, service requirements may be purely

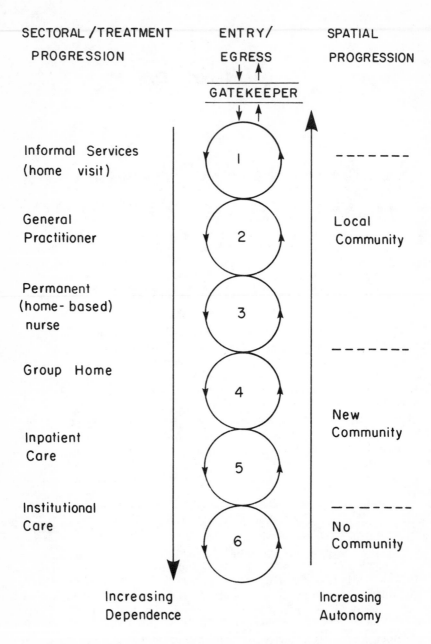

Fig. 24. Spatial/sectoral progression in the elderly client career pattern.

informal, such as the need for an occasional home visit by a nursing aide. However, if incapacity increases, clients may proceed through progressively sheltered treatment settings that reflect their degree of incapacity. Ultimately, the totally dependent person may require institutionalization. If the client's incapacity is "cured," he can regain independence by leaving the system, usually through the successive settings in reverse order. It is important to realize that a spatial progression parallels this sectoral/treatment progression (Fig. 24). As client dependency increases, the adoption of a protected treatment setting tends to imply surrender of client "community." In the initial stages, a client may receive services that are situated in the local community. However, transfer to a group home or in-patient care (for instance) assigns the client to a new community; institutionalization may even constitute a "no community" environmental setting.

At the core of our understanding of the service delivery problem is this interdependency between sectoral and spatial client assignment. Simply stated, assignment to a particular service sector (or modality) implies assignment to a particular service setting. The fundamental theoretical issue is the adequacy of this dual assignment. In practice, the assignment process may be totally inadequate due to a variety of reasons, such as problems in assessing client needs, absence of necessary resources, and community opposition to program development. We therefore require a comprehensive theoretical framework, which structures the service delivery problem in such a way that the assignment of service clients to treatment settings is optimized, subject to a set of constraints reflecting the balance of client, professional, and community goals in service delivery. More specifically, this chapter attempts (1) to provide a taxonomy of clients and treatment settings; (2) to outline the structure of a model that describes the client-setting assignment; and (3) to utilize the constraints of the model in identifying structural weaknesses in the present human service system, thereby aiding in evaluating existing assignments and in generating alternative assignment policies.

A TAXONOMY OF HUMAN SERVICE CLIENTS AND TREATMENT SETTINGS

In the analysis of human behavior or activities, two aspects of classification systems are important. First, all classifications should be purposive. Any group of individuals may be classified in several different ways according to the motives and interests of the analyst. Second, any classification is relative, being dependent upon the sociocultural setting in which it is employed as well as the characteristics of the user. The task of classification should be approached with care because:

> Categories and labels are powerful instruments for social control, and they are often employed for obscure, covert, or hurtful purposes: to degrade people, to deny their access to opportunity, to exclude "undesirables" whose presence in some way offends, disturbs familiar custom, or demands extraordinary effort.[2]

In short, abuse of the classification task may lead to "labeling" of individuals. Although there is no simple predictable consequence of attaching a specific label to an individual, the potential for damage is ever present, whether or not the individual accepts the label.[3] This process of creating categories of "difference" is important in setting social limits on what is tolerated as normal or deviant behavior.[4] It is a process of boundary marking, defining the limits of cultural identity for those within and for those outside "normal" society. Large numbers of people may be stigmatized or excluded from the normal category on the basis of absence of one or more desirable characteristics. Such stigmatism has the convenient outcome of "blaming the victim" for deviation from the sociocultural norm.[5] Boundary marking in social groups are matched by an equally important tendency for boundary marking in professions, which delimits areas of expertise, but also enhances and perpetuates a profession's existence (often at the expense of other professions). Strong professional boundary marking acts to establish and/or to reinforce boundary markings in social groups, forming a strong mechanism for social control and stigmatization of individuals coming under professional dominion.

In summary, the task of classification is far from simple; it is always purposeful and relative. Sometimes these characteristics are subordinated to the cultural values of the majority and of the professions. What, then, can guide the development of an acceptable classification system in which recognition of differences is central?

Irrespective of the specific characteristics of any service-dependent group, the principle of "normalization" has gained wide acceptance as a fundamental goal of the human system and should therefore act as the essential purpose behind classification of behavior or treatment settings.[6] The normalization principle operates on two distinct levels. For human service clients, normalization entails achieving a degree of mastery over internal drives, symptoms, and the immediate environment, and achieving a measure of social and vocational potential (however limited this may be). In addition, client normalization implies integration within a normal social network and community setting. Generally, therefore, a classification of clients ought to incorporate the extent to which normalization is achieved by individuals.

For service delivery systems, the normalization principle guides development of system strategies aimed at normalization of client behavior and life situation. Theories indicate that the most effective way to promote normalization is to alter (to the minimum extent possible) the client's everyday living situation, concomitant with treatment needs. The treatment setting itself must be normalized so as to assume as many characteristics of normal community settings as possible and to facilitate normal social activity and interaction. Hence, taxonomies of settings ought to be based on the degree to which settings fulfill the criteria of a normal physical and social environment.

A Taxonomy of Human Service Clients

A large variety of classification systems for the human services population have already been developed. These have been critically reviewed by Fincher,

Golant and McCaslin, Hobbs, and Miller, Hatry and Koss.[7] Most classifications focus on the level of client self-sufficiency and are thus obliquely related to the normalization principle. Client populations are defined according to their abilities to execute the basic activities of daily living, such as eating and walking.[8] Another common purpose is to define the degree of client employability in order to involve the client in the labor force. In this case, more specific taxonomic criteria are defined, including management of income and care of children.[9] Alternative taxonomies have been developed for specific client subgroups, reflecting their particular needs. One of the best known population-specific taxonomies is that for the mentally retarded, who are divided into mild, moderate, severe, and profound groups according to intelligence.[10] Alternatively, Golant and McCaslin outline a taxonomy for the elderly population based upon levels of competence and levels of independence.[11]

Any taxonomy here derived should be functional for clients and for those service agents involved in the task of normalization. Such a purpose suggests that the basic dimension of the client taxonomy should encompass a continuum that extends from total client dependence through to complete client autonomy. At the former end of the spectrum, the client is totally dependent on the human service system of life support; at the other extreme, the client is totally self-supporting and requires no assistance from the service sector. The objective of the service system is to move clients toward the autonomy end of the continuum, in other words, to encourage client participation in the full experience of life, including schooling, recreation, family, and community. On the other hand, the autonomy-dependence concept recognizes that certain groups will possess long-enduring handicaps that may vary in their intensity (thus providing for movement in both directions along the continuum) and that may require life-long dependence on the service system.

In principle, all members of a given client subgroup could be allocated along the autonomy-dependence continuum. (One illustrative allocation is given in Figure 25.) A comprehensive taxonomy requires the use of multiple continua, as suggested by our representation of the mental, physical, and social dimensions of service need.

A Taxonomy of Service Environments

Our treatment of the client taxonomy indicates that we require a setting taxonomy descriptive of a continuum varying from complete dependency to relative autonomy. To date, the literature appears to identify four broad categories along such a continuum: institutional settings; formal community-based settings; "invisible" community support services; and informal community-based services.

Many studies of the institutional service setting emphasize the problems of internal or within-institution integration. For instance, Braginsky, Braginsky and Ring show how adaptive patients may be to hospital settings and expectations.[12] In addition, Moos argues that the creation of an intentional environment in a mental hospital requires simultaneous manipulation of client autonomy, client

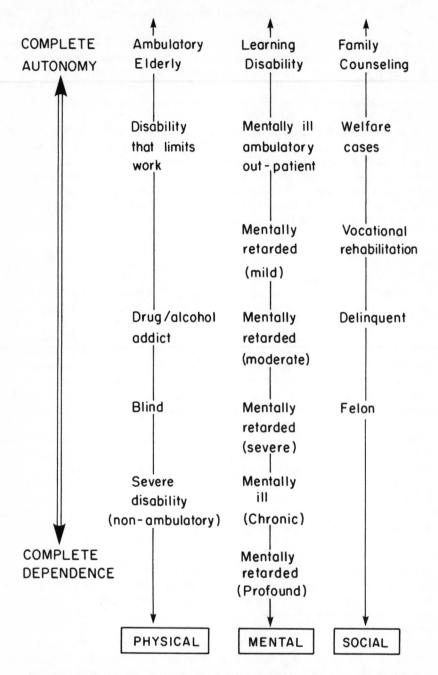

Fig. 25. An illustrative taxonomy of the service-dependent population along the autonomy-dependence continuum.

relationship to the support system, and design of the setting itself (including organization, staff control, and program clarity).[13] However, Lieberman warns that client reaction is not always predictable.[14] For example, certain elderly deinstitutionalized clients flourish in the challenge of the new "discrepant" environment, whereas for others the variety and ambiguity in such environments are highly destructive.

In a study of the integration in formal community-based care of former mental hospital patients, Segal and Aviram conclude that both internal and external integration of settings in the community are central in fostering client well-being.[15] More specifically three sets of characteristics facilitate the internal and external integration of the sheltered care population. These are:

> 1. Community characteristics, including the response of neighbors, the rural-urban location of the facility, complaints to the authorities from neighbors, and the distance of the facility from community resources.
> 2. Resident characteristics, including possession of sufficient spending money, status as a voluntary or involuntary resident, and control over one's financial arrangements.
> 3. Facility characteristics, including the extent to which the facility is an "ideal psychiatric environment," and the degree of isolation of the residents from the external community.

Smith also explored the qualities of residential neighborhoods as "humane" environments.[16] He used three descriptors of a neighborhood—its commercial/industrial character, housing unit density, and population transience—as predictors of the rate of recidivism in a cohort of discharged mental hospital patients. Using a similar approach, Trute and Segal tried to identify supportive communities for the severely mentally incapacitated.[17] Such communities appeared to be those in which neither strong social cohesion nor severe social disintegration exists; the former neighborhood tends to "close ranks" against the client, and the latter tends to be too chaotic and threatening.

In a study matching settings with the needs of the elderly, Kahana identifies three dimensions of the treatment setting: segregate, referring to the absence of other age groups; congregate, encompassing degrees of sociability and privacy; and institutional-control, summarizing the extent of staff authority and resident autonomy.[18]

Invisible community-based support services have no facility base; they depend on the informal community networks, assisting clients who live independently in the community. A classic example of such a network is the family, which serves simultaneously as a source of ideology, a haven, a reference and control group, and a contributor to emotional mastery.[19] More generally, a wide range of non-family-based social networks are important in aiding social integration and client normalization. These include the development of (1) professionally coordinated community support systems that aid the handicapped to live in the community and to gain employment;[20] (2) support systems in the voluntary sector;[21] and (3) networks consisting of ethnic, religious, or interest group affiliates who provide informal support to individuals during times of crisis.[22]

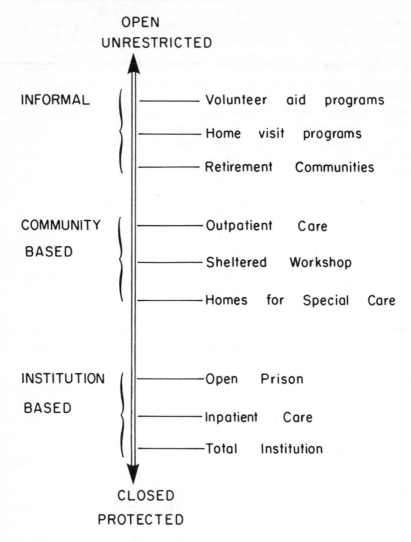

Fig. 26. A taxonomy of treatment settings for the service-dependent population.

Informal community-based services are delivered from small-scale facilities and often involve counseling or vocational rehabilitation. Such services are distinguishable from the preceding in that they tend to involve specialized services for a multitude of episodic needs; they lack a residential component, serving clients who live independently in the community or who reside elsewhere in formal settings; and they often lack formal linkages to one another, in spite of their interdependent roles in client normalization.[23] Although these informal services may be neither purposively integrated as a unified client support system nor directly influential on client residential location, they nevertheless suggest a treatment setting and hence facilitate or hinder normalization.

For our purposes, treatment settings for human service clients may be characterized along a single dimension representing a continuous progression from closed protected environments to open unrestricted environments (Fig. 26). In general, position along this axis indicates the degree of service provider control exerted over client behavior and activity. More specifically, for any given client subgroup, position on the protected-unrestricted dimension means three things: a specific facility type, a particular setting, and an associated treatment regimen.

A CLIENT-SETTING ASSIGNMENT MODEL

The two-dimensional space formed by the autonomy-dependence and the protected-unrestricted continua together contains all possible client-setting assignments. The basic task of the service delivery system is allocation of service populations to treatment settings so as to facilitate normalization. For instance, the "career" of a typical mental patient from institutionalization to independent living requires a sympathetic matching of developing client abilities to various matching types of treatment settings in order to encourage participation in the experience of life, including schooling, recreation, family, and community. The goal of normalization requires that, throughout their careers, clients undergo the least possible removal in time and space from normal activities, concomitant with treatment requirements. Translated into operational terms, the normalization goal requires that the degree of client envelopment be minimized.[24] Client treatment is therefore geared toward moving the individual down the envelopment scale toward complete autonomy.

The general structure of the assignment process can be illustrated with the use of some simple notation. Let the matrix P represent the total client population in need of service. In this $m \times n$ matrix, each column vector $(p_1, \ldots, p_m)$ represents a single service subgroup disaggregated into m specific treatment types. For example, the first column of the matrix could represent the m types of mentally disabled, varying from hospitalized chronically ill patients through to outpatient clients. We assume there are n such client groups. Now let the vector s = $(s_1, \ldots, s_m)$ represent m treatment settings available for care of the client population. Because there are m settings and n client groups, the assignment problem simply involves mapping the client population matrix, P, into the service setting vector s.

In the absence of further constraints, this assignment represents a trivial theoretical problem, because it is fully determined by the initial categorization of P and s. In practical terms, however, P and s are not fully known. Ambiguities in client classification create uncertainties in the definition of P; and absence of and capacity limits on certain treatment settings confound definition of s. As a consequence, the majority of client assignments will, to some degree, be suboptimal.

Although the theoretically optimal assignment may be uncertain, we may assume the existence of a recognizable limit to client autonomy, t_{ij}. This tolerable level of client autonomy defines the upper limit at which client group p_{ij} may function effectively. The limit may be set at a low level (e.g., for inpatients) or at a relatively high level (for outpatients). What is important is that the client cannot currently operate above the threshold, t_{ij}, on the autonomy-dependence continuum; as a corollary, the client can almost certainly operate below that level.

The assignment problem in practice is therefore translated into the need to allocate client group, p_{ij}, to that level of treatment setting, s_k, that most nearly approximates his tolerable autonomy level, t_{ij}. The objective function in this assignment is to minimize the discrepancy between the actual setting assignment and the client's tolerable (or preferred) setting assignment.

The set of constraints operating upon this model reflect the real-world conflicts of interest among client needs, professional needs, the local (impacted) community, and the wider fiscal community. Hence, the following contraints are necessary components reflecting goal structures in the real-world assignment process:

1. All clients must be allocated to some kind of treatment setting.
2. In the assignment sequence, if a particular treatment setting, s_k, is absent or its capacity is exceeded, a client will be allocated to a treatment level below the tolerable autonomy level, t_{ij}. (This requirement reflects the relatively conservative referral practices of service agencies.)
3. Because community opposition to various treatment settings may be anticipated, some manifestly fair constraint upon the geographical allocation of treatment settings must be introduced.
4. Finally, because the wider community will insist on (and is due) parsimony and cost-effectiveness in public spending on service delivery, a set of budgetary constraints based on fiscal requirements for effective service provision is also required in the model.

EVALUATING ALTERNATIVE ASSIGNMENTS

In this final section, we wish to demonstrate the utility of the client-setting assignment model in evaluating existing assignments and in generating alternative assignments for policy analysis. The model can be used to examine the sources of "slack" in the human service system. Why, for example, are there discrepancies between the intended patterns of the service system and actual service outcomes? How are system goals subverted? In what follows, the four constraints of the model are relaxed and linked to four crucial policy issues in matching service clients to appropriate settings.

Constraint 1: Coordination in Human Service Delivery

The most fundamental task of any service system—that of ensuring all clients are assigned to some service agency—is a primary source of slack or suboptimal performance in the system. There are many reasons for failure in the initial assignment process: There is no consistent, visible locus (or gatekeeper) for screening potential clients; there is no universal system for diagnosing a client's service needs; a method of monitoring the type and availability of treatment settings is usually absent; and there is no reliable method of tracking client progress in the service system.[25] Thus, slack arises because of ambiguity in the use of both client and treatment taxonomies, particularly for those clients with multiple presenting problems.[26]

The absence of reliable expertise in the induction of service clients is compounded by professional attitudes and jealousies. Very often, client mobility both within and between the various autonomy-dependence and protected-unrestricted continua is hindered by strict definitions of professional "territories" that may prevent necessary client referrals.[27] Moreover, because responsibility for clients is frequently unfixed or ambiguous, the referred client may quickly be lost to the service system. This is especially the case when the clients themselves are responsible for ensuring that the referral contact is made.[28]

The practical problems and costs of ensuring an adequate match between all clients and alternate treatment settings require innovative policy responses and delivery techniques.[29] The costs that accrue to individuals and to society when human service needs are unmet are, however, potentially greater. An effective service delivery system would seem to require a comprehensive administrative/coordinative "umbrella" agency to ensure proper care and referral in the client's interest.

Constraint 2: "Dumping" of Service System Clients

The model's second constraint reflects the relatively conservative policy of most service agencies that clients cannot be assigned to settings beyond their tolerable autonomy limit (t). However, it is not difficult to conceive of situations of excess demand that would require that clients be assigned to settings above their tolerable limit. The shock the client experiences in these "discrepant" settings has been reviewed by several authors.[30] The most outstanding contemporary example of the potentially disastrous effects of excess demand, and consequent inappropriate assignment, is that of deinstitutionalized mental hospital patients. Because of the nonavailability and inadequacy of community-based mental health services, large-scale programs of patient discharge have caused significant numbers of patients to be "dumped" onto ill-prepared community resources. This dumping has been the focus of much attention in the scholarly literature, lay journals, and the popular press.[31]

The problems faced by communities in absorbing the former hospital patients should not be underestimated.[32] However, for present purposes, the most important outcome of the deinstitutionalization policy is to assign large numbers of service clients to environmental settings far above their current autonomy level. Quite simply, many patients cannot cope with the new level of autonomy required by their settings. The high rates of readmission to mental hospitals are evidence of the coping problem faced by many patients, who frequently become involved in the criminal justice system or the "revolving door" syndrome of recurrent readmission to and discharge from hospitals.

Constraint 3: Community Saturation and Client Ghettoization

Increasing community opposition to social service facilities and agencies has been experienced as larger numbers of service-dependent people seek care in community-based public facilities. A common pattern is that of over-representation or saturation of some communities by clients and facilities, with a concomitant underrepresentation in others. In the case of the elderly service-dependent population, it has been argued that the several trends toward age segregation reflect the urbanization process.[33] However, it has also been noted that provider concerns with client access to service and housing opportunities and with minimizing the "costs" of community opposition have accentuated saturation and caused the targeting of service facilities to low-income, deteriorating neighborhoods.[34]

The tendencies toward facility saturation and client ghettoization have been observed in other sectors, most notably in mental health care. Here, ghettoization has been explained by (1) the formal assignment of patients to after-care facilities that tend to proliferate in downtown locations because of planners' actions; (2) community opposition to facilities in other residential neighbor-hoods; and (3) an informal filtering process by which some patients gravitate toward the transient areas of rental accommodation in the inner city.[35] In the absence of some manifestly fair policy for sharing the burden of providing alternative environmental treatment settings, the interdependent problems of opposition, saturation, and ghettoization are likely to persist.

Constraint 4: Shifting the Fiscal Burden

Cost-effectiveness in human service systems is a notoriously intangible concept or goal. The difficulties of definition and measurement of treatment outcomes in mental health care and drug treatment, for example, are well documented. However, more notable problems occur because cost constraints are often secondary to other considerations, such as the need for perpetuation and growth in a service profession or the need to stabilize the economic base of small communities where large-scale service facilities are major sources of local employment.[36]

CONCLUSION

We have attempted to outline a comprehensive model for assigning human service clients to treatment settings. The three components of this model are a client taxonomy, a treatment setting taxonomy, and an assignment process that minimizes the discrepancy between actual and preferred client assignments. Constraints are outlined to account for client, provider, and community interests. The model defines a theoretical framework for the analysis of the service delivery problem and thereby defines structural limits to the development of planning policies. In the final section, relaxation of the model's constraints allowed us to relate real-world policy issues to structural flaws in the service system.

This conclusion is, in effect, only a beginning of a much wider exploration of the relationship between client-setting assignment and the spatial/sectoral dimension of client treatment. Much work remains in developing an operational version of the model and in applying it in a more rigorous policy analysis. In addition, the theoretical and empirical utility of the client and setting taxonomies will require a thorough critical evaluation. Finally, the real-world complexities of client progress through service sector and spatial setting are only now being recognized; a full specification of our model requires a more complete understanding of these complexities.[37]

NOTES AND REFERENCES

[1] Research supported by Grant No. SOC77-07081 from the National Science Foundation.

[2] N. Hobbs, *The Future of Children* (San Francisco: Jossey-Bass, 1975), p. 11.

[3] Hobbs, ibid., Chap. 2.

[4] R. Fincher, "An Examination of the Notion of Difference, and its Implications for Community Survival Courses for the De-Institutionalized Mentally Ill and Mentally Retarded," unpublished paper, School of Architecture and Urban Planning, Princeton University, 1977.

[5] W. Ryan, *Blaming the Victim* (New York: Vintage Books, 1976).

[6] Although founded on appropriately humanitarian principles, the normalization concept is not without its disquieting aspects. Normalization implies strict adherence to societal norms and values on the part of the individual. The extent to which such norms and values should be imposed on clients is debatable. Nonetheless, if not abused, normalization is an intuitively appropriate goal, which, more than any other goal yet put forward, has a potentially positive influence on the delivery of human services. Cf. W. Wolfensberger, *The Principle of Normalization in Human Services* (Toronto: National Institute on Mental Retardation, 1972).

[7] Fincher, op. cit., note 4; S. M. Golant and R. McCaslin, "A Functional Classification of Services for Older People," *Journal of Gerontological Social Work*, Vol. 1, No. 3 (Spring, 1979) (see Chapter 14); Hobbs, op. cit., note 2; and A. Miller, H. Hatry and M. Koss, *Monitoring the Outcomes of Social Services*, Vol. 2 (Washington, D.C.: The Urban Institute (5039-7), 1977).

[8] Miller, Hatry and Koss, ibid., pp. 16–17.

[9] Ibid., pp. 7–9.

[10] Hobbs, op. cit., note 2, pp. 50–59.

[11] Golant and McCaslin, op. cit., note 7.

[12] B. M. Braginsky, D. D. Braginsky and K. Ring, *Methods of Madness: The Mental Hospital as a Last Resort* (New York: Holt, Rinehart & Winston, 1969).

[13] R. H. Moos, *Evaluating Treatment Environments* (New York: John Wiley & Sons, 1974).

[14] M. A. Lieberman, "Relocation Research and Social Policy," in J. F. Gurbium, ed., *Late Life: Communities and Environmental Policy* (Springfield, Ill.: Charles C Thomas, 1974).

[15] S. P. Segal and U. Aviram, *The Mentally Ill in Community-Based Sheltered Care* (New York: John Wiley & Sons, 1978), Chap. 10.

[16] C. J. Smith, "Residential Neighborhoods as Humane Environments," *Environment and Planning: A*, Vol. 8 (1976), pp. 311–326.

[17] B. Trute and P. Segal, "Census Tract Predictors and the Social Integration of Sheltered Care Residents," *Social Psychiatry*, Vol. 11 (1976), pp. 153–161.

[18] E. Kahana, "Matching Environments to Needs of the Aged," in J. F. Gubrium, ed., *Late Life: Communities and Environmental Policy* (Springfield, Ill.: Charles C Thomas, 1974).

[19] G. Caplan, *Support Systems and Community Mental Health* (New York: Behavioral Publications, 1974).

[20] A. Gonen, *Community Support System for Mentally Handicapped Adults: An Alternative to Spatially Distributed Human Service Facilities*, Regional Science Research Institute, Discussion Paper No. 96 (Philadelphia, 1977).

[21] J. Wolpert, "Social Income and the Voluntary Sector," *Papers Regional Science Association*, Vol. 39 (1977), pp. 37–59.

[22] S. Lampert, "Invisible Services in Middle Income Communities," Mimeo, Princeton (N.Y., University School of Architecture and Urban Planning, 1975).

[23] Wolpert, op. cit., note 21; J. Wolpert, M. Dear and R. Crawford, "Satellite Mental Health Facilities," *Annals of the Association of American Geographers* Vol. 65 (1975), pp. 24–35; J. Wolpert, "Service Facility Representation in Urban Communities," unpublished paper, School of Architecture and Urban Planning, Princeton University, 1976.

[24] H. R. Lamb and Associates, *Community Survival for Long-Term Patients* (San Francisco: Jossey-Bass, 1976), p. 48.

[25] M. Dear, "Psychiatric Patients and the Inner City," *Annals of the Association of American Geographers*, Vol. 67 (1977), pp. 588–594.

[26] Millar, Hatry and Koss, op. cit., note 7.

[27] Hobbs, op. cit., note 2.

[28] Although the model is intended for use with clients who go through some formal referral process, there is no a priori reason preventing its use in evaluating and designing assignment alternatives for those clients responsible for self-assignment. In this case, however, the gap between service intentions and service outcomes is much less easily predicted, because the model provides only a purely normative assignment and cannot reflect the private decisions of the self-assignment cohort.

[29] S. Sherwood, J. N. Morris and E. Barnhart, "Developing a System for Assigning Individuals into an Appropriate Residential Setting," *Journal of Gerontology*, Vol. 30 (1975), pp. 331–342.

[30] Lieberman, op. cit., note 14; and Trute and Segal, op. cit., note 17.

[31] U. Aviram, S. L. Syme and J. B. Cohen, "The Effects of Policies and Programs on Reduction of Mental Hospitalization," *Social Science and Medicine*, Vol. 10 (1976), pp. 571–577; *Scientific American* (Feb., 1978); *New York Times Magazine* (May 28, 1978); *Newsweek* (May 15, 1978).

[32] Wolpert, Dear and Crawford, op. cit., note 23.

[33] S. M. Golant, "Residential Concentrations of the Future Elderly," *The Gerontologist*, Vol. 15 (1975), pp. 16–23; J. M. Kennedy and G. F. DeJong, "Aged in Cities: Residential Segregation in Ten United States Central Cities," *Journal of Gerontology*, Vol. 32 (1977), pp. 97–102.

[34] J. Wolch, *Residential Location of Service-Dependent Households*, unpublished doctoral dissertation, Princeton University, 1978.

[35] Dear, op. cit., note 25.

[36] J. Zusman, *The Future Role of the State Mental Hospital* (New York: Heath-Lexington Book, 1975).

[37] Dear, op. cit., note 25; Wolch, op. cit., note 34.

INDEX